Accelerated Ecological Psychotherapy

Accelerated Ecological Psychotherapy

ETT Applications for Sleep Disorders, Pain, and Addiction

STEVEN R. VAZQUEZ, PHD

JASON ARONSON
Lanham • Boulder • New York • Toronto • Plymouth, UK

Published by Jason Aronson
A wholly owned subsidiary of The Rowman & Littlefield Publishing Group, Inc.
4501 Forbes Boulevard, Suite 200, Lanham, Maryland 20706
www.rowman.com

10 Thornbury Road, Plymouth PL6 7PP, United Kingdom

British Library Cataloguing in Publication Information Available

Library of Congress Cataloging-in-Publication Data Available

Vazquez, Steven R., 1947–
Accelerated ecological psychotherapy : ETT applications for sleep disorders, pain, and addiction / Steven R. Vazquez.
pages cm
Includes bibliographical references and index.
ISBN 978-0-7657-0961-5 (cloth : alk. paper)—ISBN 978-0-7657-0962-2 (electronic)
1. Emotion-focused therapy. 2. Psychotherapy. I. Title.
RC489.F62V392 2013
616.89'14—dc23 2012035402

∞™ The paper used in this publication meets the minimum requirements of American National Standard for Information Sciences—Permanence of Paper for Printed Library Materials, ANSI/NISO Z39.48-1992.

Printed in the United States of America

This book is dedicated to the memory of:

- my father, Ignacio R. Vazquez, whose enthusiasm for me and my work never stopped;
- Bart Paff, a psychologist who saw the value of ETT®, believed in me, and championed this cause;
- Linda Benson, who was willing to try my experimental techniques in its early phases, which allowed this work to evolve; and
- Sandra Valiquette, who believed in me and this approach.

Contents

Foreword

Psychotherapy, as it has been practiced in Europe and the Americas, has evolved from its earliest roots in Freud's groundbreaking work called psychoanalysis, to numerous treatments and interventions utilized today that bear little or no resemblance to the original process. It is typically a culture-bound endeavor that does not translate easily cross-culturally, if at all, which is a limitation.

Innovators appear from time to time, risking much to bring their knowledge, experience, and creativity to the therapeutic community for practice and, ultimately, scrutiny. This may include criticism and disbelief, as well as acclaim. Courage is required, in addition to brilliance, to bring forward one's theory and treatment protocol.

And so I was a skeptic when my friend and fellow therapist, Lynn Rutherford, called me from Austin, Texas, to tell me that she had discovered a therapist with an amazing innovation in treatment for notoriously stubborn physical/psychological challenges, such as chronic pain, anxiety, depression, trauma of all sorts, among other difficulties. She tried to describe the treatment that Dr. Steven R. Vazquez had developed, which consisted of some combination of a variety of colored lights that flickered at various rates. I didn't get it!

I think it is important to note here that I am a clinical and forensic psychologist, and I have been in private practice since 1980, treating a variety of presenting problems, specializing in chemical dependency and process addictions, trauma of all sorts, and psychological assessment. My state Board of Psychology requires thirty-six hours of continuing education for me to renew my license every two years, and I usually turn in more like ninety hours. I love learning that much! So I have seen and heard, as well as presented, my fair share of professional programs. My work has led me to sit on continuing education advisory committees for many mental health and chemical dependency inpatient treatment programs, as well as the California Mandatory Continuing Education for Psychologists Committee. As a result, I've experienced many presenters and their presentations.

Lynn had brought me other ideas and information in the past and these had been quite useful to me in treating my patients over the years. But I must admit that I was less than enthusiastic as she described the treatment protocol. Nevertheless, when she suggested that I host her colleague for a series of trainings in California, I reluctantly agreed. A crowd of my colleagues signed up for "Introduction to Emotional Transformation Therapy® (ETT®)." Sierra Tucson hospital graciously agreed to provide continuing education credit for those in attendance.

After listening to Dr. Vazquez explain the theory and mechanics of his treatment, he asked for volunteers to demonstrate the three tools of his trade, a set of odd-looking goggles, a chart depicting the pure spectral colors of the rainbow, and a machine, called a chromopulse, that emitted flickering colored light that could be changed and controlled by the therapist, its operator.

The audience was skeptical. I was skeptical. But, as a sufferer of chronic sciatic pain as a result of a surgical injury, I had tried everything under the sun to relieve the pain with little relief that lasted more than a few days. So I was happy to volunteer as a subject for his demonstration. Dr. Vazquez put the goggles on me and the treatment began.

Out of that initial training, twelve colleagues signed on for six weekends of training with Dr. Vazquez, spread out over two years. At each of the trainings, we trainees would practice what we were learning on each other. By the end of the third training session my back pain was gone. I couldn't believe it! Seventeen years had passed since the inception of the pain, which was, at times, excruciating and debilitating. My office mates sometimes had had to help me out of my chair at the end of a session with a patient because I wouldn't be able to stand without assistance; the pain was that severe. And the pain was gone! It has never come back in all the many years since.

I became a believer and began treating my patients with ETT®. Patients reported all sorts of good results with the process. Anxiety was reduced, sexual compulsivity declined, agoraphobia relented, and a patient on parole from a lengthy prison term for assault was relieved of his violent reactions. His mother called to say, "What have you done to my son? He's a different human being and we are so grateful." He is unlikely to return to prison, which is a boon not only to him and his loved ones, but also to us taxpayers who pay the very expensive bill for incarceration.

I observed Dr. Vazquez presenting his work to a room of seventy to eighty professionals of various therapeutic traditions. His methodology relieved an audience volunteer of his obsessive sexual thoughts, which he claimed he had had for many years, thoughts that interfered with his work as a physician and his relationship with his wife. The whole demonstration took about twenty minutes. The audience was amazed, but comments indicated they believed the results wouldn't hold up over time. But they have! The man who so courageously volunteered continues to be free of obsession. The work Dr. Vazquez did with him is chronicled in chapter 7 of this book.

And so, it is with confidence and pleasure that I encourage you, the reader, to investigate Dr. Vazquez's revolutionary treatment protocols, using the very simple tools of light, color, and vibration, configured in such marvelous healing modalities described in this long-awaited book. This book is clearly written and the sequencing of information makes it highly readable. Each concept builds on the one previously presented, which makes difficult material more easily digested. You will finish the book wanting to learn his techniques for your own particular issues as well as those of your patients.

ETT® is not only a true innovation in psychotherapy, but also one that is not culture-bound and can, therefore, be successfully used in a variety of settings with diverse patients exhibiting a multiplicity of symptoms and diagnoses.

To leave a legacy means to leave behind a contribution of some sort that will last a hundred years after one's death. There is no doubt that ETT® is Dr. Vazquez's legacy. It is an innovation that will stand the test of time and lead to relief and healing for many.

Thank you, Steve!

Sonnee D. Weedn, PhD
April 21, 2012
Novato, California

Acknowledgments

I want to thank Vicki Whitaker, who edited the entire manuscript and coached me through the writing process. Barbara Walker has been a consistent help by typing and retyping the manuscript. Dr. Jenny Wade provided extremely helpful critiques and suggestions throughout this writing process. Her excitement about the content has been encouraging. I also want to acknowledge my wife, Sue Anne Vazquez, for her patience and support through this multiyear endeavor.

Dr. Brian Breiling first introduced me to the therapeutic use of light emitting devices. He and Jennifer Breiling have been enthusiastic supporters for this work for many years. Jacob Liberman has long been helpful about encouraging my interest in therapeutic lightwork. I wish to thank Dr. Sonnee Weedn for providing her thoughtful foreword for this book. Sonnee has been a friend and colleague who saw the value of this approach for a long time. Dr. Andrea Silberman was kind enough to listen to my writing in its early phases and has always believed in me.

Several people took the time to read a chapter or two while the manuscript was in development. I thank Rick Spletter, Susan Ellis, Susan Cizmas, Lynn Rutherford, and Dave Raymond for their feedback. I especially wish to thank Marilyn Dowell for reading, critiquing, and discussing chapter 9 and for her enthusiastic support. Dr. Colin Ross was kind enough to read the entire manuscript and provide his endorsement of my work.

I thank Jerilee Merkle, Anna Sonnenburg, Connie Heaps, Lynn Rutherford, Dan Lippman, and Martha Turner, MD, for their long and continuous enthusiastic support of this approach and this book. Kristi Wetherington and Judy Boisseau have been an inspiration.

I am deeply appreciative for the insight of the staff at Jason Aronson, who saw the value of this manuscript as something that would add to the field. I especially want to thank Amy King, who has interfaced with me on behalf of the publisher. John White was kind enough to provide guidance about the publishing industry and helped me acquire an agreement with Jason Aronson.

My mother, Irene Vazquez, has supported me in everything I have done. My daughter, Amber Vazquez-Bode, gave me the original impetus for exploring the impact of light from her personal experience as a child. Her husband, Rob Rode, has always been available for my many technical questions about book production.

None of this would be possible if it were not for the thousands of clients who were open to my creative way of working. It was ultimately due to them that I could develop this miraculous method and this book. My gratitude is overwhelming.

Introduction

How could light and talk therapy change a deep-rooted crack cocaine and sexual addiction within minutes—with a long-term effect? We live in an environment of light, but this environment is seldom credited with healing us. While some people find talk therapy helpful, by itself, it is not known to alleviate a substance addiction craving within minutes. However, if we select a precise wavelength of light that targets the brain mechanisms responsible for the addictive craving, the impact can be extraordinary. This precision of wavelengths of light is extremely unlikely to occur in an everyday environment. If the type of verbal interaction used is custom-tailored to that person's unique pattern of emotional regulation, the interpersonal portion of the process acquires an impact far greater than is likely to occur in most people's daily experiences. Furthermore, the coordinated synergy of precise elements of the person's visual ecology and highly attuned interpersonal contact amplifies the effect of both components of this process. This new process is called Emotional Transformation Therapy®.

WHY WE NEED BETTER TREATMENT NOW

In 1987 when Prozac was introduced, 1 in 184 Americans were on disability for mental illness. In 2007 after a massive proliferation of psychiatric medications over twenty years, 1 in 76 Americans were on disability for mental illness. From 1990 to 2007 the number of children on disability for mental illness increased thirty-five-fold. Of course, the statistics for 2012 are even worse. These failures have motivated new trends for treating mental health conditions.

The use of new pharmaceuticals for psychological conditions has grown dramatically. Technological interventions like electroshock, transcranial magnetic stimulation, surgical deep brain stimulation, and others have arisen to compete with pharmaceuticals. Informed by new neuroscience findings, talk therapies like client-centered, cognitive, and behavioral therapies are now known to affect the brain and biochemistry. Each of these trends—drugs, technology, and new talk therapy approaches—contributes helpful ideas, but each has distinct deficits. Pharmaceuticals, which generally do not cure mental health conditions, create a dependency and have adverse side effects. Also, their effectiveness has recently been seriously called into question. While technological approaches may temporarily alleviate symptoms, their mechanistic, impersonal approach can reenact experiences of objectification and alienation in the client's past, experiences that have often created these psychological problems in the first place. Neither pharmaceuticals nor technological methods tend to produce any new learning in the clients. Without this learning, the client will likely experience dependency on the technology, dependency on pills, or a relapse. However, modern society believes in pharmaceuticals and technology and looks to these methods for help. The interpersonal neurobiology research validates that interpersonal methods not only feel good, but also promote significant brain changes. However, most talk therapies cannot efficiently access implicit somatic memory where causal factors often exist. In a society that has learned to expect a quick fix, interpersonal neurobiological approaches alone are simply too slow.

A BREAKTHROUGH IN MENTAL HEALTH TREATMENT

The overall failure of mental health treatment establishes the need for better treatment. Side effects and the inability to cure psychological conditions with pharmaceuticals, the impersonal nature of technological approaches, and the relative slowness of talk therapy all result in a demand for a better means of treatment. The phrase *Emotional Transformation Therapy®* (ETT®) literally refers to the capacity to radically transform human emotions both quickly and at a depth level. ETT® does not create artificial side effects, does not create a dependency, but does stimulate new learning in the client. ETT® typically resolves psychological disorders on a long-term basis. ETT® uses a noninvasive form of technology that precisely targets and changes brain mechanisms responsible for psychological symptoms. ETT®, a highly personable approach, usually facilitates changes of emotional distress within minutes. It is often used when all other methods have failed and often succeeds with "intractable" conditions.

Therefore, ETT® provides the speed of pharmaceuticals, the precision of technological approaches, and the inspiration of interpersonal approaches without the side-effects of drugs or technology.

ETT® possesses the capacity to relieve a wide array of conditions that would normally require entirely different methods. For example, ETT® has protocols for breakthrough treatment of sleep disorders, physical pain syndromes, couple therapy, and much more. In addition, it can be used to facilitate states of extreme wellbeing. The first book called *Emotional Transformation Therapy: An Interactive Ecological Psychotherapy* describes ETT®'s four basic techniques in great detail as well as its use for depression, anxiety disorders, and trauma resolution. This book describes its application to many more issues.

This book is organized in such a way that it is intended to be read in sequence. The first chapter explores the philosophical orientation of ETT® so that the reader can understand how its approach is different from others. The second chapter reviews the established concepts, presents research on seasonal affective disorder (SAD), and puts forth revolutionary ideas concerning the human relationship with light. Chapter 3 offers an original perspective concerning human emotions in terms of their dynamic nature and movement. Environmental light controls the brain's biological clock, which in turn controls our sleep patterns. Chapter 4 describes how emotional regulation and precise visual ecology can be used to resolve numerous types of sleep disorders. One of the greatest breakthroughs in ETT® regards its rapid alleviation of a variety of physical pain syndromes, from low back pain to migraine headaches to arthritic pain. Chapter 5 describes these new discoveries.

The second half of the book begins with the description of a revolutionary way to treat substance addictions. Then chapter 7 focuses on the current epidemic of sexual addictions fueled by internet pornography. The rapid, long-term resolution of addictions by ETT® offers a new paradigm for this rampant problem. Chapter 8 offers a new approach to couple counseling that dramatically changes relationship distress, resolves conflict, and generally speeds up the process. The ninth chapter focuses on the stunning production of outcomes of states of extreme wellbeing facilitated by ETT®. Religious and spiritual issues are carefully explored. Finally, an array of single case studies, from life-threatening illnesses to "incurable" mental health problems, demonstrates possible future directions for the use of ETT®.

Case studies are used to illustrate this method in action. Of course, the names and other identifying factors have been changed to protect each person's confidentiality. These case studies are representative of how ETT® sessions tend to transpire.

The opening case in chapter 7, referred to at the beginning of the introduction, is on tape as it occurred live at an international professional conference. The crack cocaine and sexual addiction craving continues to be extinguished for over a year now, and the subject says he cannot bring up the craving even if he tries. The combination of highly attuned talk therapy and precise visual ecological approaches offers a new level of healing at a time when it is needed most.

1

The Philosophical Orientation of ETT®

Emotional Transformation Therapy® (ETT®) is a unique approach that is based on fundamentally different philosophical orientations than psychotherapy as it has generally been known. Since its outcomes tend to be so rapid and profound, it often leaves the uninitiated observer perplexed about how and why it works. The confusion occurs, in part, because people do not possess a framework from which they can derive an understanding of it. Therefore, it is important to explain the philosophical orientation upon which ETT® is based. In addition, it may help to show its similarity to and difference from methods about which the reader may already possess some familiarity.

ETT® TECHNIQUES THAT ARE THE BASIS OF ITS PHILOSOPHICAL ORIENTATION

ETT® possesses four basic strategies or techniques of visual ecology that are coupled with attachment-based interpersonal approaches. When light enters the eyes, photoreceptors convert light into neural impulses that travel throughout the brain. However, it is not commonly known that these visually stimulated neural pathways often go to non-image forming areas of the brain that have nothing to do with our ability to see. Instead, they travel to areas of the brain that directly affect our physical and emotional experiences. ETT® uses specialized forms of visual stimulation that would rarely occur in daily life, to direct these neural impulses. This allows a facilitator to strongly impact the brain mechanisms responsible for specific psychophysical symptoms.

These techniques are more fully explained in the book *Emotional Transformation Therapy: An Interactive Ecological Psychotherapy*. However, a summary of the four ETT® techniques includes the following:

Spectral Resonance Technique

This approach uses a maximally saturated color in the form of a spectral chart that provides consistent immediate feedback in the form of specific types of visual distortion that allows the client and the therapist to know the nature and movement of affect often before or as it becomes conscious. Through this means (1) emotional escalation can quickly be stopped, (2) dissociation can be corrected, (3) relevant implicit memory can be obtained, and (4) executive attention can be acquired to regulate affect. The net effect is the acquisition of diagnostic affective patterns and enhanced affective regulation.

Multidimensional Eye Movement

This approach uses eye movement or eye fixation to replicate the eye scan-path associated with the memory of a targeted symptom. This technique uses the continuum from external visual focus to neural networks in the brain that resonate with and rapidly eliminate the symptom. The process typically eliminates distress in seconds.

Peripheral Eye Stimulation

This approach uses precise visual stimulation of specific areas of the peripheral visual field to activate awareness of affect, cognition, and physical experiences to either acquire relevant implicit memory, extinguish physical symptoms, or re-organize internal ego states. It possesses the capacity to rapidly (in seconds) reduce affective overwhelm or physical pain as well as access positive resources that were not previously conscious.

Light-Emitting Device (Chromapulse II)

This approach uses a red-green-blue system of light emission that can access any one of hundreds of precise wavelengths of colored light that is emitted into the client's eyes during verbal interaction of issues. It possesses the capacity to relieve emotional distress within seconds, or access and/or relieve somatic memory in seconds, elicit implicit memory, and produce states of extreme wellbeing. It can provide a form of amplified interpersonal attunement that rapidly repairs the consequences of dysfunctional relationships.

All four techniques use the client's visual ecology in different ways and simultaneously involve specific attachment-based interpersonal strategies.

THE VISUAL ECOLOGY PERSPECTIVE

The specialty of treating seasonal affective disorder (SAD) has promoted a massive amount of scientific research on the effects of light on humans. ETT® can often permanently eliminate SAD and several sub-syndromes within a brief series of sessions unless there are other complications. This approach is described in chapter 2. While ETT® uses light stimulation, the type of light and the means of implementation are completely different from conventional SAD treatment (Vazquez, 2004; Lam & Levitt, 1999; Rosenthal, 1993).

This radical difference is largely due to a completely different philosophical position about our relationships with our visual environment and specifically our relationship with light. ETT® is congruent with the philosophy of "externalism." Externalism is a philosophy that asserts that one's perception of one's external environment and one's internal experience are inextricably linked in such a way that a separation between the two is illusory (Putnam, 1975). ETT® also is in harmony with the perspective of ecological psychology, which holds that the continuity of the brain and its contextual environment function as a single unit (Gibson, 1979). In this case the brain's internal system operates by a continuous flow of mutually interactive feedback loops with the environment that leads to progressive changes in the unified system consisting of the person and the environment. These concepts draw support from light research in quantum physics regarding the observer effect. ETT® has harnessed this mutually regulating interactive system concept as a means to facilitate change. Specifically, by carefully selecting the most potent and precise visual stimuli to apply during the experience of interacting about distressing psychophysiological states, the visual environment can have a direct bearing on powerfully changing a person's internal psychological state.

THE NEUROBIOLOGICALLY BASED PERSPECTIVE

Significant research in the fields of cognitive science, developmental psychology, and brain science exists upon which to base modified methods of therapy. There are now several new forms of psychotherapy that base their approaches on the research and theory of attachment disorders. Work by Diane Fosha, Susan M. Johnson, and Karl Brisch are attachment-focused forms of therapy based on the new neuroscience research. (Brisch, 2002; Fosha, 2000; Johnson,

2004). These approaches focus upon the primacy of affect and interpersonal contact as a means to change brain chemistry and brain function. ETT® uses optimal interpersonal responses derived from findings in neuroscience. The ETT® use of attachment understanding allows the therapist to custom-tailor attunement according to each client's unique pattern. Attachment focused interventions are fundamental principles of ETT®. When visual brain stimulation accompanies this interpersonal approach, we achieve "amplified attunement" and rapid repair of affect dysregulation. Attachment-focused therapists would see a radical expansion of these principles in the way ETT® uses neurobiologically based principles of attachment issues and resolves deeply held attachment patterns to achieve rapid neural integration.

Most symptoms of psychological conditions concern some form of affective symptom. Therefore, most psychotherapeutic methods attempt to change the cognition, behavior, or somatic symptoms that exist in the context of an emotional experience in the hope that the emotion will change as a consequence. ETT® differs from this norm by directly targeting the affect, accessing it, and then rapidly transforming it. This capacity provides a unique methodological niche for ETT® because human emotion has been seen as an elusive aspect of the psyche. However, the fact is that when disturbing affect is relieved, the associated cognition, behavior, and somatic symptoms typically change with it.

PSYCHOANALYSIS

Sigmund Freud originated the concept of the unconscious mind in modern scientific thought. In most professional circles, this concept itself has been updated to concepts of implicit memory, subcortical activity, and somatic memory, among others. Nonetheless, the idea that a vast array of information relevant to clients exists outside of conscious awareness is an idea central to psychoanalysis. If Freud were here today and could experience the workings of ETT®, he would see previously unknown information emerge at a frequency not found in talk therapy alone. He would see the capacity of ETT® to elicit relevant memory, emotions, and awareness with a speed and precision unlike anything he ever experienced.

Freud was the first psychiatrist to describe the personality as being composed of inner parts. His system consisted of the id, the ego, and the superego. While he would see that these structures are seldom exactly as he reported them, the concept of inner parts has been resoundingly verified in ETT®. However, through ETT® we can isolate these parts within seconds. Peripheral eye stimulation technique uses controlled beams of environmental light into the periphery of the client's eyes to precisely activate separate neural networks of separate ego states as dialogue occurs. Through this ETT® approach therapy possesses the capacity to rapidly isolate, integrate, divide, and/or ultimately use these inner parts as resources to heal the client (Hall, 1954; Jones, 1963).

Freud spoke of a neuroscientific approach, but his talk therapy took him far from neurology and into psychological hypotheses. ETT® links the findings of current neuroscience with the practice of psychotherapy. Psychoanalysis proposes that when a client talks about problems, it leads to insights and ultimately relief. This assumption has not often been found to take place and even when it does, psychoanalysis typically takes several years. The talk therapy of ETT® is accelerated by precise visual ecology and provokes insight at a vastly accelerated rate.

ANALYTIC PSYCHOTHERAPY

If Carl Jung could observe a single week of ETT® sessions, he would see many of his concepts emerge in ETT®. Archetypes arise in visual symbolic forms regularly during ETT® sessions. Imagery emerges with the client's eyes open, and profound spiritual experiences are fairly common. An entire chapter (chapter 9) is devoted to spiritual phenomena using ETT®. These phenomena are less likely to emerge in talk therapy alone, but with visual brain stimulation they are common experiences.

Both Freud and Jung had an interest in dreamwork. Instead of imposing a theory about what dreams mean, ETT® procedures enhance the client's ability to become aware of his or her own dream meanings. Some of these findings support Freud and Jung's dream orientations, but new dream interpretations emerging from ETT® sessions extend far beyond these earlier dream concepts. More importantly the disturbing aspects of nightmares typically acquire substantial relief fairly rapidly with ETT®. The ETT® dream procedure can be found in chapter 4.

Among the concepts proposed by Jung was his archetype of the Self. In ETT® the authentic self is referred to in a way that is similar to the way that Jung describes the "Self" construct. During ETT® procedures, movement through emotional states and penetration of defenses often yield a new level of awareness of one's inner self. In Jung's view, while awareness of the Self is sought, actually achieving awareness is considered very difficult, let alone having the ability to access it with any degree of consistency. The unveiling of the authentic self has become a frequent revelation in ETT® sessions. ETT® possesses the capacity to activate and extend Jungian concepts (Jung, 1961; Hall & Nordby, 1973).

COGNITIVE THERAPY

More recently cognitive therapy has flourished. Its basic philosophy concerns the primacy of cognition and the use of the facilitator verbalizing cognitive rationale to change the client's emotional states, behavior, and dysfunctional thoughts themselves. By changing cognition through visual brain stimulation and interpersonal attunement, ETT® achieves enormous constructive cognitive shifts. ETT® can (1) effectively awaken the brain from amnesia, (2) spontaneously evoke insight, (3) provoke the emergence of logically coherent thoughts, and (4) change scattered thinking into clearly focused cognition. Instead of trying to correct irrational thinking through dialogue, ETT® promotes rational thinking in a very short period of time primarily through precisely stimulating the client's visual ecology during client verbalization. This type of intervention impacts the brain in such a way that new thoughts emerge. ETT® interpersonal interaction does not rule out the direct use of cognitive therapy strategies, but its use is simply an occasional adjunct to the process. However, the number of different strategies within the field of cognitive therapy is diverse. Cognitive proponents like Jeffrey Young use forms of cognitive therapy that are more compatible with ETT®. Nonetheless, consistent and substantial cognitive improvements are common during ETT® sessions (Ellis, 1958; Young, Klosko, & Weishaar, 2003).

One of the most commonly used forms of therapy today is the hybrid called cognitive behavioral therapy. Of course, this blend of philosophies is an attempt to use what is best of the two approaches. ETT® tends to facilitate changes that often bypass the client's intellect but still yields substantial cognitive and behavioral changes.

BIOCHEMICAL APPROACHES

Pharmaceuticals attempt to alter brain chemistry and ultimately improve psychological symptoms. According to neuroscientific research about interpersonal processes based on attachment theory, interpersonal processes can and do alter brain chemistry. SPECT (Single Photon Emission Computed Tomography) scans of clients who have undergone ETT® clearly show an alteration of the brain's biochemistry. An obstacle in this domain is the false cultural belief that one must take chemicals into the body in order to change brain biochemistry. Clinical observations of the relief of symptoms suggest that ETT® often improves conditions like depression faster and more permanently than psychotropic medications. These changes are consistent with the effects that occur when brain chemistry is changed.

BEHAVIORISM

B. F. Skinner devoted his career to methods that would facilitate desired changes of behavior. His principle of operant conditioning, or behavior modification, is the central tenant of behaviorism, and a massive amount of scientific research now supports it. ETT® offers a bold new process for achieving behavioral goals. In many cases ETT® is achieving behavioral change after numerous other therapies have already failed. However, it is probably the speed at which ETT® achieves behavioral change that would capture Skinner's attention. While the role of operant conditioning should certainly be recognized, the ability of ETT® to directly facilitate the portion of the brain responsible for a behavior—and change it—provides a whole new concept in behavioral management (Skinner, 1953; Mahoney, 1974).

EMDR

Eye movement desensitization and reprocessing (EMDR) is a form of therapy that has enjoyed enormous growth within the last twenty years. EMDR uses Shapiro's "adaptive information processing model" as its philosophical position. It asserts that a person stores information for future use, but when a traumatic experience occurs, the system is disrupted and memory becomes stored in a dysfunctional state that leaves the system unbalanced. This leaves the system vulnerable to be triggered, which causes excessive stress to the system. Then EMDR uses bilateral stimulation to integrate this imbalance (Shapiro, 2001). This theory is congruent with ETT®, but the means to facilitate change of this trauma is different.

Upon initial exposure, professionals who have seen ETT® demonstrated tend to categorize ETT® as more similar to EMDR than to any other method. ETT® uses an entirely different form of eye movement that is based on sound scientific concepts. There are at least twelve differences between EMDR and multidimensional eye movement (MDEM). I have been trained in EMDR. The commonality between EMDR and ETT® is that both methods use eye movement and both are designed to achieve rapid trauma recovery. ETT® provides built-in means for evoking client safety that allows for a more streamlined process than the eight-step EMDR procedure. While there is no dispute that bilateral stimulation can work, observations suggest that ETT® uses much fewer repeated trauma exposure experiences to acquire relief. This means that repeated direct confrontation of the avoidance defense can be reduced and the speed of change makes ETT® a less painful process. In addition, the repertoire of strategies in ETT® is far greater, which allows for more individualization as well as applications for each condition.

PROLONGED EXPOSURE THERAPY

Prolonged Exposure Therapy has achieved significant recognition. It has been shown to be valuable in trauma treatment. By the use of repeated exposure of the client to the disturbing stimulus, the client's responses have been shown to decrease. Due to its confrontation of a person's avoidance defense, many participants are prone to leave treatment during the early phase of therapy. The essential concern about exposure therapy is that the process can be torturous and even risks retraumatizing clients. While almost all forms of psychotherapy involve some degree of exposure, few depend exclusively upon this principle. While in some cases ETT® utilizes exposure repetition, in numerous cases the amount of disturbing exposure is so markedly reduced with ETT® that elimination of the disturbance may occur within seconds. One of the primary strengths of ETT® is the drastic reduction of long, painful, expressive sessions.

WILHELM REICH

Wilhelm Reich, Freud's first assistant in 1920, eventually split off from Freud's ideas with his own concepts. Reich's ideas deviated from Freud's in at least three main areas: (1) the role of the physical body in psychological issues, (2) the nature of biological energy, which Freud called libido and Reich described as orgone, and (3) the importance of sexuality in the overall psyche of the person. Currently, few Reichian orgonomists are left, but neo-Reichians continue to be active in bioenergetics, radix, and core energetics. ETT® addresses all of these Reichian and neo-Reichian emphases.

If Wilhelm Reich were here today and could see ETT® at work, he would see the advances of ETT® in the realm of the physical body in psychological defenses. Reich used physical manipulation, and Alexander Lowen, the founder of bioenergetics, used physical movement to assist in changing the physiological aspects of psychological issues. Through visual brain stimulation we can precisely access routes in the brain that directly impact the portion of the brain and nervous system that are responsible for a specific physical symptom. This results in the capacity to consistently and precisely change bodily symptoms in minutes. ETT® brings an entirely new level of speed and depth into changing the physical aspects of psychological issues. What used to require numerous sessions to change now may occur in minutes with ETT®. Chapter 5 includes this topic.

In terms of biological energy, Reich devoted significant attention to what he called orgone. The movement of this biological energy was at the center of all Reich's work. During ETT® sessions, most clients frequently report sensations of movement that they experience as "energy." Freud's concept of libido primarily has sexual connotations, whereas Reich used his orgone energy concept as the essential life force that appears to underlie both sexuality and the full range of life in the universe. Clients often distinctly see and feel underlying "energy" during many ETT® sessions.

During Reichian or neo-Reichian approaches the role of sexuality, catharsis, and grounding are important foci. In order to prevent emotional overwhelm and flooding, several ETT® procedures are devoted to bringing people back to a secure, well-grounded experience. ETT® accelerates emotional catharses so profoundly that numerous grueling sessions of crying, kicking, and screaming can now take place within minutes and with less intense expression.

One of the skills that body-oriented psychotherapists tend to believe can be accessed only through physical manipulation or movement is "grounding." For example, bioenergetic therapists conceive of flexion of the legs and other movements as a means for a client to feel rooted to the earth in a meaningful way. While these techniques can be helpful, embodiment is rarely maintained nor are these strategies applicable to people who may have certain physical disabilities. Through the precise use of the client's visual ecology, a sense of embodiment can often occur within seconds or minutes. Lack of perceived embodiment is only one way to be ungrounded. For example, if clients are obsessing, are they ungrounded? If they are overwhelmed with sadness, are they ungrounded? If they are intellectualizing, are they ungrounded? There are many ways to be "ungrounded" that are generally not resolved by techniques that simply seek perceived embodiment. The variety of ways of being ungrounded can also be quickly corrected with attachment-based responses and precise visual ecology.

EMBODIMENT APPROACHES

There are now a number of therapeutic approaches whose adherents believe that emotion is lodged in the body and exists below conscious awareness. These approaches include, but are not limited to Focusing, Somatic Experiencing, various forms of bodywork, applied kinesiology, and many more (Levine, 1997). Clearly, these methods have identified something of therapeutic value that appears to help relieve symptoms without significant verbal or intellectual engagement. In fact, many of these adherents attempt to avoid cognition and verbalization because these factors are seen to interfere with finding the underlying core issues which are thought to reside in somatically held emotion. ETT® is an "embodiment" or "sensory motor" oriented approach because it accesses relevant implicit affect and memory hidden in somatic symptoms. ETT® can facilitate change in somatic memory by directly accessing reptilian brain functions with extraordinary speed and precision without the use of physical touch or movement. The proficient use of ETT® for accessing and resolving somatic memory will be explored later in chapter 5. However, in many cases ETT® facilitates both conscious, verbal/intellectual expression, as well as that of the emotional and body domains.

NARRATIVE THERAPY

An opposite approach to embodiment methods is Narrative Therapy that depends on a verbal exploration of one's story. In this view the therapist is a collaborator with the client in the endeavor of revising an old dysfunctional story to a new one. Research on disclosure and confiding shows that the approach provides substantial benefits. Narrative Therapy was originated by Michael White (White, 2007). During most ETT® sessions client dialogue shows evidence of substantial change in one's autobiographical experience. While ETT® does not depend on the intellect and dialogue alone, it is a substantial part of the process.

HUMANISTIC PSYCHOLOGY

At the heart of humanistic psychology is the concept that we are born with enormous potential and that this positive psychological drive to fulfill it is inherent. Carl Rogers thought that through authentic listening and exhibiting unconditional positive regard, we enhance others to activate their potential (Rogers). ETT® utilizes this principle and substantially extends it in more precise ways. ETT® customizes interpersonal responses according to each client's attachment pattern. By attunement to clients by both verbalization and precise visual brain stimulation client-centered therapy is amplified to a new level.

Abraham Maslow is known for several of his original ideas, and among them is the concept of peak experiences. His research demonstrated a connection between peak experiences and the activation of one's fullest potential (Maslow,

1971; Maslow, 1968). ETT® sessions frequently produce peak experiences. In fact, ETT® possesses several protocols that consistently produce states of extreme wellbeing described in chapter 9.

THE EXPRESSIVE ARTS

The therapeutic use of the expressive arts has much in common with ETT®. The expressive arts include, but are not limited to psychodrama, art therapy, music therapy, journaling, and many others. Artists are the one group that tends to accept the therapeutic power of light and especially color. However, after experiencing some form of ETT®, even most artists are stunned by the speed and impact of ETT®. We share the idea that emotions should be embraced, but ETT® takes efficiency of expression to an extraordinary level. Sometimes people are driven to express their feelings through the arts, but when ETT® ends the unresolved feelings the compulsion to express ceases. For example, grief over a lost love partner is the source of numerous lyrics for music, but when the grief quickly concludes, the compulsion to express often stops. On the other hand, some people have writer's block or cannot verbalize when emotions are blocked, but after ETT® these people are suddenly able to express. Long, grueling sessions of crying, screaming, or voicing anger are often consolidated into brief moments with ETT® without losing any of the insights or ecstasy of facing fears and overcoming. The extended drama of catharsis is no longer a requirement for long-term resolution. ETT® differs from some of the therapeutic expressive arts in the concept that more and longer emotional expression is not necessarily better. ETT® can be seen as a new brief form of expressive therapy.

Apparently, there is a belief is that either one targets control of emotions for briefer outcomes with pharmaceuticals or targets emotional expression for much longer but more personable outcomes. However, there is apparently not an understanding that an in-depth, emotionally embracing method can often provide relief in less time than psychotropic medications can. This third niche is the unique position of ETT®.

HYPNOSIS

When people see ETT® demonstrated, they often conclude that it is somehow similar to hypnosis. This assumption takes place possibly because it appears to facilitate rapid changes in a "mysterious way." Although there may be some remnants of my past hypnotic skills influencing a small portion of the interaction, ETT® is not hypnosis. ETT® differs from hypnosis in that it does not use hypnotic suggestions, does not require a hypnotic trance, nor does it use hypnotic inductions. However, some of the outcomes I saw in hypnotherapy, such as the relief of physical pain, relief of phobias, and a variety of other achievements, are similar. The similarity is that ETT® also accesses certain hidden states of mind relevant to resolving a targeted symptom.

ENERGY PSYCHOLOGY

A category of methods that people often compare to ETT® involves various meridian tapping methods like Thought Field Therapy or Emotional Freedom Technique. However, the only similarities may be that both techniques tend to work quickly, involve the human energy system, and are relatively new. These meridian tapping techniques, often referred to as forms of "energy psychology," are based on the Chinese medicine model. One oriental medicine doctor who went through ETT® training described ETT® as a "hundred times faster and more precise than Chinese medicine." Meridian tapping techniques tend to require more self-work follow-up than ETT®. ETT® bears a resemblance to these techniques in that it interrupts and shifts fixated dysfunction in ways that are not solely dependent on talk. Both approaches tend to bypass the intellect to accomplish their objectives.

However, ETT® possesses a fundamental difference in philosophy from most meridian tapping proponents in that they tend to view unwanted emotions as negative, and the strategy is to neutralize emotions in order to acquire "balance." Whereas ETT® embraces all human emotions and uses processes that paradoxically bring them to a rapid conclusion. Emotional states involved in change and growth are not necessarily balanced, and certain states of extreme wellbeing facilitated by ETT® are often highly beneficial but may not be viewed as balanced. Further elaboration on how emotions occur in changes will be explored in chapter 3.

BRAIN AND HEART "RHYTHM" APPROACHES

There are methods like brainwave biofeedback (neurofeedback) and Heart Math that focus on either brainwaves or heart rate. The neurofeedback camp is based on the premise that teaching the client to learn how to develop optimal brainwaves can relieve the condition pursued. Some of the latest forms of neurofeedback incorporate colored light into their process but in an entirely different way from ETT®. One key difference is the speed at which ETT® elicits the desirable brainwaves. ETT® uses brainwave entrainment through pulsing external light that almost instantly elicits the brainwave pattern sought for a specific therapeutic task. Another difference is the interpersonal interaction during entrainment that is important in ETT®, but not necessarily an essential part of neurofeedback. Also, instead of simply relying on the idea that corrected brainwave patterns will ameliorate the problem, ETT® corrects the underlying dynamic issues from which brainwave distortions are derived. This insures a greater likelihood of long-term change of the symptoms. Professionals who use neurofeedback sometimes classify ETT® as a different form of neurofeedback that uses visual feedback.

The Heart Math clinicians base their work on the concept that the vibratory activity of the human heart is far more impactful than the rhythm of any other organ. The amplitude of the heart rhythm is sixty times greater than that of the brain. The logic is that if one can optimize the heart rhythm, its vibrating activity will resonate with all other organs and improve them as well (McCarty, 2003). While focusing on positive (emotional) heart experiences is often helpful, ETT® can arrive at emotional heart fulfillment by removing emotional blockages. By having access to the entire brain and nervous system, visual brain stimulation can precisely target the portions of the nervous system responsible for the vibrating nature of the heart. When it is appropriate, positive emotions can be extracted from hidden implicit memory by ETT®. Heart rate variability monitoring during ETT® has been conducted and yielded outcomes similar to Heart Math methods. Put simply there are different ways to access the impact of the heart rhythm, and ETT® offers an efficient means to affect it.

In addition to the focus on the brain or the heart some professionals focus upon the human intestinal system as a source for psychological distress. While ETT® may focus on the emotional or physical heart in one case and the brain in another case, far too often the organic source of many unresolved symptoms appears to be in the human gut. People often feel "a knot in their stomach" or digestive symptoms in conjunction with unresolved emotional issues. The physical location where the deepest problems are solved by ETT® is often the viscera. ETT® has a profound capacity to access and relieve psychological symptoms that are associated with the enteric nervous system of the gut (McCarty, 2003).

MINDFULNESS MEDITATION

Within the last decade numerous studies have shown mindfulness meditation to be beneficial for a wide range of psychological and medical conditions. Mindfulness offers a form of self-help that involves the development of an observer inner part to respond non-judgmentally to our issues and to promote our attention to be in the present moment. Mindfulness meditation can be done in conjunction with

ETT® or after ETT® has harnessed an improved degree of brain focus. However, certain ETT® techniques like "spectral resonance technique" (SRT) can be seen as a vastly advanced form of mindfulness meditation, because it facilitates engagement in the present moment and observations suggest that it acquires all of the benefits found in mindfulness, except that the SRT results are much faster. In many cases I have worked with people who have meditated for years but never had a direct spiritual experience until they experienced SRT. While no religious orientation is imposed on ETT® clients, states of wellbeing occur fairly frequently during ETT®. Philosophically ETT® shares many commonalities with mindfulness approaches.

DIALECTICAL BEHAVIORAL THERAPY

Certain kinds of therapeutic methods are designed for specific diagnoses. Dialectical Behavioral Therapy (DBT), for example, is designed to work with borderline personality disorder. This approach is the standard of care for borderline personality disorder. However, it is a very long process that usually takes several years to complete. Its central challenge is that of affect regulation with people who have intense emotions and intolerance for almost any emotion (Linehan, 1993). However, the first ETT® trial for borderline personality disorder—with a woman who (1) had borderline personality disorder, (2) had been in therapy for over twenty years, and (3) had made little or no progress—was completed in six months when the ETT® protocol for borderline personality was used. She is no longer showing any significant symptoms! This protocol focuses more on the interpersonal portion of ETT®.

COUPLE THERAPY

ETT® has been used in the context of marriage or couple therapy. It is an attachment-focused therapy that bears some similarity to Emotionally Focused Couple Therapy. However, ETT® visual ecology strategies used with individuals have been found to profoundly speed up the couple work. A systems concept has always been a part of ETT® and family members are taken into account during ETT®. An entire chapter (chapter 8) is devoted to couple and family therapy that incorporates ETT® methods.

BRIEF THERAPY

While there are various forms of "brief therapy" that attempt to reduce the number of sessions to meet the needs of restricted insurance reimbursement, the long-term cost of these methods may not be beneficial. These methods may relieve a narrowly focused presenting symptom or temporarily avoid many issues related to the presenting symptoms, but this approach tends to put many of these clients at a high risk for recidivism. When these clients need to return to treatment over and over after a brief series of treatments, the cost of therapy is often much more than other approaches over several years. Most forms of brief therapy are essentially strength building. This assumes that therapy focused on problematic symptoms will take longer. Strengths can also be built by overcoming obstacles. ETT® typically pursues in-depth issues, underlying sources of the symptoms, as well as relief of the presenting symptom without sacrificing a brief course of treatment. ETT® may represent the briefest brief therapy.

THE ELECTROMAGNETIC PERSPECTIVE

There are a range of treatments generally seen as electromagnetic therapies. These include electroshock therapy, transcranial magnetic therapy, deep brain stimulation, and ETT®. The Italian psychiatrists Ugo Cerletti and Lucino Bini originated electroshock therapy or electroconvulsive therapy (ECT) in 1938. It has undergone changes since its original form. Applying about 800 milliamps of electric current for up to six seconds will definitely change brain chemistry. This treatment is controversial because of the adverse effects of memory loss, amnesia, and/or disorientation. Worldwide, an estimated one million people per year receive ECT today. By inducing a seizure, ECT attempts to cure depression with an extreme measure that other electromagnetic approaches can now achieve without stifling the brain into submission.

More recently, several new forms of electromagnetic therapy with less severe side effects have appeared, but they still utilize the idea that an electromagnetic intervention can change brain chemistry and ultimately psychological symptoms. Deep brain stimulation is a procedure that involves surgically implanting electrodes into the patient's brain. Then through the use of an electronic remote, the portions of the brain related to the psychological symptoms are stimulated to provide relief. Of course, this involves the risk of brain surgery and leaves the person dependent on the technology for relief. ETT® is similar to deep brain stimulation because it also rapidly and precisely directs the electromagnetic impulses that control the portion of the brain from which symptoms occur. However, this direction of impulses is done through external visual stimulation in ETT® without invasive procedures.

Another recent development involves transcranial magnetic stimulation (TMS). This electromagnetic intervention uses magnetic stimulation around the skull of the patient in daily sessions that often require five weeks of treatment. The magnetic stimulation is thought to alter the electromagnetic activities of the brain, which in turn affect brain biochemistry to change psychological symptoms. It is an impersonal method that provides no new learning. Since loneliness is often central to depression, an impersonal method risks further alienation by the process itself. ETT® also harnesses the brain's electromagnetic impulses.

ETT® AS AN ELECTROMAGNETIC THERAPY

ETT® can be seen as an electromagnetic form of therapy due to the fact that the photoreceptor cells in the eyes convert external light into electrical impulses that course through the brain. These impulses possess tiny magnetic fields. When millions of electrical impulses are flowing through the brain, their cumulative effect can be measured as brainwave patterns. In addition to visual light stimulation, every thought or feeling we have impacts neural impulses and brainwave patterns. When a skilled facilitator guides the client's mental focus, this guidance appears to activate the targeted neural circuits, and precise, external visual stimuli appear to direct electromagnetic impulses to the portions of the brain and nervous system responsible for the targeted symptom. The results are often as follows: (1) the symptoms are relieved, (2) brain chemistry changes, and (3) brainwave patterns change. ETT® harnesses one's endogenous electromagnetic system to change the brain.

Instead of applying unnatural forces of electricity or magnetic energy, ETT® uses variations of external light that precisely activate the person's own internal electromagnetic system. By using these mechanisms, unnatural side effects are avoided, and it has been observed that in most cases ETT® may even yield faster results.

ETT® does not over-stimulate the brain to the degree that ECT does, nor does it have its severe side effects. ETT® does not require the health risk of brain surgery nor create a dependency on the treatment. ETT® does not usually require five weeks of daily sessions to resolve depression. On the other hand, similar outcomes to other electromagnetic approaches are likely, and the importance of optimal interpersonal support during treatment facilitates new learning, which sets ETT® apart from other electromagnetic approaches. This results in maximizing the outcome. Observations suggest that ETT® offers an electromagnetic form of treatment that provides most of the benefits of the other electromagnetic interventions without any of the deficiencies or side effects of these methods.

A PHILOSOPHICAL ORIENTATION OF ETT® PROCESS: CHAOS THEORY

Chaos theory matches with the philosophical orientation of the ETT® process. Chaos theory views the universe to be in continual change. However, while this change appears to be chaotic, there is in fact an organization and direction of change in that disruption of homeostatic structures eventually shifts into a new organization of a higher order of functioning. Illya Prigogine won the Nobel Prize for the verification of these principles in chemistry, but chaos theory principles can be applied to almost every field of study, especially psychology. ETT® operates in a manner that embraces the natural movement toward emotional chaos when people's lives are disrupted. This emotional turbulence has the potential to lead toward a re-organization of functioning in a higher order. Affect appears to be the central force in this movement. Visual brain stimulation amplifies the emotional process to serve as a catalyst to accelerate chaos through disorganization toward a higher order of emotional and cognitive functioning. Instead of attempting to block or stop an unpleasant symptom, ETT® accelerates movement through chaos so fast that it paradoxically reaches a higher order of functioning when it appears that the process is encouraging disruption. For example, it may be necessary to verbally express, cry, or otherwise experience distress briefly before complete healing can take place. Then new learning from the experience will tend to emerge to fortify the person so that the person can better withstand future challenges. In some cases it is necessary to activate and build strengths first, but typically the catalytic force of visual brain stimulation accelerates one's emotions through "fast forward" progression.

Mark's Case: Case Study of an ETT® Session

Mark entered the session with a willingness to try to participate but frustrated about trying to again describe his feelings because he had no feelings. He cooperated in describing his background. Mark was sixty-two and reported an alcoholic family background, emotional incest with his mother, and described both parents as emotionally absent. He left his Catholic family to be in a monastery at age sixteen. However, he was quick to say that he wasn't "grounded as his own person." Mark was in a three-year relationship. Mark described a lack of direction, lack of purpose, and lack of passion as his objective. He also said that he did not feel grounded in his body. For example, he couldn't really feel his feet.

Mark had been a psychologist for many years but was no longer in practice. Off and on, he had been through decades of psychotherapy. Mark spent at least eight years in various forms of counseling and particularly in body-oriented psychotherapy, including several years of bioenergetics. In many cases Mark's symptoms actually got worse, but in no case was he ever able to really feel his feet. His search for purpose and passion was never satisfied.

I asked Mark to sit in front of the Chromapulse II light device and view blue-green at a low saturation rate. As Mark spoke about his inability to feel, the saturation rate was elevated. Within minutes Mark began to weep. When I had Mark view the three o'clock periphery, he described feeling lonely and lost and always trying to escape when he was age five. Empathy and support were voiced while the wavelengths of light were changed to match his emotional state. Spontaneously, the emotional distress released within seconds. He reported a split feeling in his head as though he was split into two people

At nine o'clock he felt worse, so he was asked to move his viewing angle to six o'clock. Here he described feeling lonely and needing to run away to calm himself. Empathy was provided and validation for his emotions was given. The light was changed to a degree of orange, and he reported feeling better. He was then asked to verbalize the previous distress in order to assess if it was better. At the twelve o'clock position the distress was easier.

The process of verbal emotional expression, attunement to his feelings, and a change in either the wavelength of light and/or the peripheral position took place. This resulted in repeated relief. As Mark reported an inability to connect with himself, this distress quickly relinquished while viewing red-orange at two o'clock. Mark said, for the first time in his life, "I can connect with myself. It's empowering!"

Next, Mark described a splitting between his head and body, but it quickly improved at an elevated saturation of red-orange. Then he reported a need to connect to his heart and feel safe. At an elevated wavelength of red light he said, "That's good. It's invigorating!" Mark burst out laughing and said, "I can have all that energy and love!" He was validated and supported for his experience.

At the five o'clock position Mark said that for the first time he could feel safe in the world and fully present. "I think I can find direction and purpose. . . . I have more of a spiritual feeling. . . . I can feel my feet on the ground for the first time in my life!"

This case demonstrates the profound capacity of ETT® for correcting psychological dysfunction. It illustrates how amplified attunement extends client-centered principles to new levels. A few days later Mark reported continued ability to feel his feet and began to decide which activities he now felt would fulfill his purpose.

It is often a stretch for most people to recognize that facilitation of embodiment can take place by looking at a light. Subsequent to the session, Mark said that "I mirrored" his experience better than he had ever experienced and that seemed to make a big difference for him. Since he came from parents who were severely deficient in listening and validating his emotions, mirroring or attunement repaired this deficit. Mark varied from dissociation to rapid escalation of emotional intensity during the session. The perceived experience of attunement is radically maximized by selecting wavelengths of light that match a client's emotions while simultaneously responding verbally. By optimally engaging affect, the insula of the brain, responsible for perceived embodiment, is usually engaged. Therefore, Mark could re-connect with his body.

Mark's session illustrated most of the philosophical orientations described in this chapter.

- The Chromapulse II light-emitting device was used to activate appropriate brain mechanisms (visual ecological approach).
- Mark's attachment pattern was "disorganized attachment" and thus consistent, highly attuned interpersonal response took place (interpersonal neurobiology).
- Insight was provoked and ego states emerged when he said he felt "split" (psychoanalysis).
- While cognitive interventions were seldom used, his cognitive frame of reference changed substantially.
- Mark reported finding his authentic "Self" and discovered a spiritual awakening (analytic psychotherapy).
- The changes in Mark's brain activity appeared to shift drastically, which is consistent with biochemical changes (pharmaceuticals).
- While behavioral approaches were not used, his behavior shifted drastically during and after the session (Behaviorism).
- While no eye movements were used (EMDR) changes of eye position facilitated change.
- While no body movement or manipulation was used, his experience of embodiment was one of the most powerful changes (bioenergetics, embodiment approaches).
- There were minimally repeated exposures to aversive affect (Prolonged Exposure Therapy) yet traumatic affect drastically changed within a short time.
- A "peak" experience occurred (Maslow).

- Mark clearly expressed himself through the session (Expressive Arts) and his narrative changed to a new life story (Narrative Therapy).
- Evidence suggests that Mark's brainwave pattern changed (neurotherapy), but most notably his experience of love and joy were consistent with changes in heart rhythm (Heart Math).
- Since his life-long pattern changed in a single session, it could be considered an extremely "brief therapy."
- Clearly, the visual light stimulation had an impact on the brain mechanisms responsible for his symptoms (Electromagnetic Perspective).
- Overall the combined use of interpersonal interaction and visual ecology stimuli embraced his disturbing affect to catalyze his change to a new purpose (Chaos Theory), somatic experience, and passion.

While this case study showed evidence of numerous approaches and/or outcomes, they did not occur by means of those approaches. ETT® appears to offer a distinct new paradigm for treatment. In this case, as with many ETT® clients, people have already tried other approaches and failed to acquire results. While the use of other therapies may have contributed to increased awareness, his basic objectives were not achieved until ETT® was used.

SOME UNIQUE PHILOSOPHICAL ATTRIBUTES OF ETT®

One could make a case for ETT® to philosophically fit into most of the previously mentioned orientations because its outcomes match those categories. For example, ETT® could and often does yield cognitive outcomes, behavioral outcomes, somatic outcomes, insight, and more. However, its philosophical orientation in terms of mechanisms used to achieve those outcomes is actually unique. While interpersonal approaches based on the new neuroscience findings have been combined with visual brain stimulation, ETT® is original and significantly unlike any other philosophical orientation.

This long list of comparative attributes is not intended to suggest that ETT® is a panacea. There are several conditions for which ETT® has yet to be applied or protocols for treatment developed. However, what ETT® can accomplish suggests an entirely new level of treatment capacity. Hypothetically, almost anything derived from brain activity should be accessible to ETT® since it can be directed to almost any brain circuits responsible for a symptom. If appropriately guided, this change results in systemic changes of a high order.

2

Secrets of Our Relationship with Light

Marie looked serious, tired, and withdrawn. She made no eye contact as she looked downcast when she began to describe her depression. "Although I usually make it to work, I feel no motivation to do anything since the winter season started and I feel like I want to cry all the time." This has happened not just this winter but the last several winters. Marie described that once spring arrives she comes out of these depressions.

I directed Marie to the spectral chart to assess her condition. As she looked at the green band she talked about her sad experience. At first the sadness grew worse only to ease up after a couple of minutes, but her overall condition was about the same. Then I had her view red. On this color she perked up and said that she suddenly didn't feel so tired.

During the viewing of these colors Marie's sadness led to recollection of previous sadness and isolation in her life. She recalled going outside of her house often to cope when her family life made her feel alienated. Marie was adopted and never quite felt like she belonged. Darkness and aloneness was a common experience for her as a child. These feelings progressed to a release within minutes as the reflected light accelerated the process.

Then as I had her view orange everything changed. Marie said that it "feels like it should be summer outside" even though she knew it was January. Marie reported in an excited voice that she felt no more sadness and she felt awake and alert. She said, "I can't believe it but my whole body feels different!"

It took a few more sessions to stabilize this change, but the pattern appeared shifted. We knew for sure that the pattern of winter depression had been broken long-term when the next Winter came and left without depression.

SEASONAL AFFECTIVE DISORDER

Seasonal affective disorder (SAD) is the only significant psychological condition officially recognized as a disorder that involves the relationship between humans and light. When Rosenthal et al. (1984) first described SAD as a subtype of depression, this condition was immediately placed in the context of a malfunctioning "biological clock" that disturbed one's circadian rhythms. Dr. Kripke developed a bright white light source was used to correct the suprachiasmatic nucleus of the hypothalamus (biological clock) (Kripke, 1998). Appropriate light, applied on a daily basis before and during the season of symptoms and used in conjunction with antidepressants, has been accepted as the standard of care for treating SAD. Using a very bright white light source of 10,000 lux often causes the symptoms to subside as long as the treatment continues to take place. Because of this condition, hundreds of studies about the human response to light have taken place since 1984.

What Are the Diagnostic Features of SAD?

The Diagnostic and Statistical Manual's criteria for SAD include several symptoms that must be present for the condition to qualify as SAD:

- Either symptoms of major depressive disorder, recurrent, or bipolar disorder, type I or II, must be present.
- These symptoms must occur only during a certain time of year and be in remission at other consistent times of the year.
- Seasonal major depression must have occurred in at least the past two years; or a lifetime of seasonal major depression outnumbers the non-seasonal major depression episodes.

In addition, several studies on SAD have shown "reverse vegetative symptoms," referring to hypersomnia, increased appetite, carbohydrate craving, and weight gain (Oren & Rosenthal, 1992; Lam, 1998; Rosenthal et al., 1984). SAD is primarily referred to as winter depression, but technically it can occur during any specific season.

THE PSYCHODYNAMICS OF VISUAL ENVIRONMENTAL SENSITIVITY

The relationship between our psychobiological experience and the visual environment plays a larger role in the web of relationships than has been previously understood. Clinical observations of people possessing emotional and physical symptomatic responses to visual environments have revealed psychodynamic issues to be central etiological factors contributing to these conditions. Upon careful scrutiny, this relationship appears to be less like a relationship between living organic and inorganic elements and more like a relationship between two human beings. Therefore, I am proposing three new concepts:

1. a new diagnostic category regarding psychological symptoms related to visual environmental sensitivity,
2. a new theory regarding the relationship between humans and visual environments, and
3. a new treatment strategy for these symptoms that will provide rapid, long-term relief.

Diagnostic Classification of Visual Sensitivity Syndromes

Our current diagnostic standards in psychology recognize seasonal affective disorder (SAD) as the only condition related to the visual environment (American Psychiatric Association DSM IV, 1994). All other visually-evoked conditions are either classified as sub-syndromes of SAD, or these conditions are hardly recognized at all. I have observed that visually-evoked conditions are not rare, and they often cause significant emotional and/or physical symptoms. Visual environments related to significant symptoms include, but are not limited to, the following examples:

- overcast skies
- snow environments
- fog environments
- rain environments
- flashing lights
- fluorescent lighting
- sunlight
- darkness
- bright lights
- computer screens

These and other types of visual environments cause substantial distress for far more people than is typically recognized. People without this visual sensitivity often lack an experiential basis for empathy and thus fail to recognize the degree of distress that visual environments can evoke. As a result, clients with high visual sensitivity report that their claims are often discounted, minimized, or viewed as exaggerations. When this occurs repeatedly, the reactant person may experience a cognitive dissonance in which their subjective experience does not match society's general lack of recognition of these experiences. Before 1984 when seasonal affective disorder (SAD) was formally recognized as a condition, it too existed but was not recognized. It is proposed that these visual environmental responses bear substantial symptomology and should be recognized as important conditions through being given a formal psychological diagnosis.

Instead of conceiving of SAD as a subtype of depression, I am proposing that SAD would be better classified, along with other visually sensitive conditions, under the category of "visual environment sensitivity syndromes" or VESS. One reason that the current diagnostic classification is problematic is that a broad spectrum of both emotional and physical conditions may be visually evoked. These visually evoked experiences are not recognized as conditions. The acronym SAD is misleading as the only light-based condition because sadness may not be the emotional state involved. Instead, various forms of anxiety, irritability, and very specific physical symptoms may characterize these conditions. Although these symptoms have been recognized and studied in relation to phototoxic side effects to certain types of lighting, the psychological dynamics within the psyche that contributes to susceptibility to these symptoms has not been well understood. Since these conditions do not fit consistently into a category for a single existing psychological condition, it appears reasonable to identify these conditions by the attribute they have in common—their relationship to the visual environment.

Under this meta-diagnostic category of VESS, each of the variant visual environmental syndromes could be classified as subtypes of VESS. This proposal would allow us to

- classify SAD as a subtype of VESS instead of as a subtype of depression.
- identify each sub-syndrome of SAD as simply a different VESS syndrome.
- acknowledge conditions, such as the sensitivity to fluorescent lights, for example, as recognized conditions, validating the experience of millions of people.

- appropriately recognize these conditions, and then their classification may become an impetus for scientific research about them as well as treatment for them.

Most environmental visual sensitivity is commonly believed to be a minor physical problem with no relationship to a person's psychological makeup. Also, many people who have these sensitivities experience definite physical symptoms and do not want their conditions to be labeled "psychological," as if it is "all in their heads." This phrase refers to either (1) hypochondria, in which the physical symptoms are imagined; (2) malingering, in which the condition is faked for some secondary gain; or (3) conversion disorder, in which the physical symptoms are actually experienced, but are unlikely to be verified by medical testing. My new explanation for visual environmental sensitivity does not include any of these all-in-their-heads definitions. Instead, I am proposing that either trauma or attachment problems are the most significant factors that can account for the susceptibility of the vast majority of visual sensitivity syndromes.

Case Study: Michael's Visual Sensitivity

Michael reported high sensitivity to many types of visual environments such as overcast skies, sunny environments, flashing lights, bright lights, and fluorescent lights. Michael initially reported severe agitation, physical tension, and moodiness. He also reported serious relationship issues with his spouse. Both individual ETT® sessions and couple counseling sessions were used. At first, issues of conflict with his spouse were the focus of counseling. As these symptoms diminished, Michael began to see that the relationship issues with his spouse were usually projections of unresolved issues from his family of origin. Issues and emotions from his childhood were completely out of conscious awareness prior to ETT® sessions. It became clear to the therapist, and then to him, that he had dissociated most of the unresolved emotions from his family of origin. ETT® evoked recollections of this unresolved affect and the family attachment issues from which they emerged. Once these awarenesses emerged, he was able to separate his feelings toward his wife from those emerging from his family of origin. The same agitation, tension, and moodiness that he experienced in relation to the visual environment were now seen to be the exact emotions he felt in relation to this family of origin.

As these unresolved emotions were evoked one by one over several sessions through the use of ETT®, Michael underwent a fundamental change in his orientation to life. Eight different wavelengths of light were used to systematically facilitate the transformation of anger, grief, shame, sadness, and other emotional states. As each color elicited a different type of emotional bond with the light, it appeared to recreate an approximation of the traumatic bonds with each family member. Michael was the victim of physical, sexual, and verbal abuse by his parents and siblings. Through the reactivation of these bonds and the rapid processing of the associated emotions, he became individuated from pathological family bonds. Subsequent to this taking place, his sensitivity to overcast skies, sunny environments, flashing lights, and fluorescent lights markedly decreased, and his symptoms almost totally vanished. This change, in response to visual environments, continued to stabilize over several months.

SCIENTIFIC RESEARCH FOR THE ETIOLOGY AND TREATMENT OF SAD

While it is enormously helpful that the diagnosis and treatment of SAD has resulted in much needed scientific research concerning human-light effects, there are several issues regarding this research that need to be addressed. First, I am old enough to recall conducting psychotherapy with depressed clients who had SAD symptoms before 1984. While SAD did not technically exist as an identified condition until 1984, the condition and its symptoms did exist within the matrix of depression syndromes, and before 1984 psychotherapy alone was sufficient to extinguish these symptoms on a long-term basis. Therefore, it's interesting that the "new condition and treatment" has received so much scientific attention without anyone ever comparing the effectiveness of its predecessor, psychotherapy, to the currently conventional treatment methods. Producing a new treatment for any condition without first demonstrating that it is, in fact, an improvement over the previous treatment seems to be illogical. Since SAD was not officially separated from other forms of depression before 1984, we are left to use findings of outcome studies on depression, in general, in order to assess the treatment success of methods existing before the current SAD treatment. At that time, psychotherapy was the primary means of treating depression. Psychotherapy research yielded findings of success in long-term amelioration of depression within a few months (Epstein & Vlok, 1981). We can assume that a percentage of these cases were the SAD form of depression. Treatment success of depression and SAD is actually a fact, but since the diagnosis was not yet developed, it could not have been a topic of scientific research to verify what psychotherapists consistently observed.

Based on the outcome studies about the use of psychotherapy for depression before 1984, how would psychotherapy compare with the current use of bright white light and antidepressants?

- In terms of long-term relief, psychotherapy offers long-term relief; whereas, bright white light plus antidepressants usually does not. The current treatment likely continues for years and offers no real end, but psychotherapy concludes treatment within months.
- In terms of the length of time necessary to acquire relief from symptoms, the current standard achieves relief of symptoms within two weeks of daily use; whereas, psychotherapy often requires months. (This is the only advantage of current treatment over psychotherapy, but ETT® as psychotherapy can often relieve SAD symptoms within two weeks.)
- The current standard treatment creates a dependency on the treatment; whereas, psychotherapy generally does not.
- Over the long-term, the current standard costs more than psychotherapy.
- When one compares the length of time required for treatment on a monthly basis, the current standard requires approximately fifteen hours (thirty minutes per day) and psychotherapy requires only four hours.

This comparison, based on most of the important factors of treatment outcomes, shows that the psychotherapy treatment of SAD before 1984 was superior to the current standard of treatment. However, since 1984 the scientific community has rarely studied psychotherapy as a method of treatment for SAD. Millions of dollars have been spent and hundreds of published studies now exist on aspects of bright white light treatment and SAD, while the previous method that appears to be superior was simply ignored. Why?

Why psychotherapy has not been chosen for study is a matter of speculation. One reason may be that the biological clock (suprachiasmatic nucleus of the hypothalamus), a well-established concept, is apparently assumed not to interface with psychodynamic issues. If psychotherapy works to eliminate SAD symptoms, we must assume a contributing causal connection between psychodynamic issues—trauma, dysfunctional relationships, loss, and others—and the regulation of the biological clock. To date, no study has been conducted to explore this interface. The 2004 article, "The New Light Psychotherapy for Seasonal Affective Disorder," published by this author, was the first to theorize about this connection (Vazquez, 2004).

Biological reductionism refers to the concept that all human activities can be reduced to biological causes and can be explained only in biological terms such as biochemistry. By reducing all phenomena to biological explanations, it is possible to exclude any social or psychological factors as causal because it is assumed that these are a consequence of biological forces. Then, if research within this narrow range of etiology is conducted and is found to support biological factors as valid, these findings can be generalized to be the complete explanation of a phenomenon. In the case of SAD, the biological clock concept and the role of light in stimulating it are the limited domain from which biologically reductionist explanations have been drawn. This is not to say that these concepts are incorrect, because it is clear from the research that they do have some degree of validity. However, we do not know if these reductionistic biological factors such as genetics and biochemistry provide 10 percent, 90 percent, or some other proportion of etiological factors related to SAD because other psychological factors have generally not been selected for study. Therefore, the narrow range of focus produced results that created a incomplete perspective of reality.

The fact that many of these scientific studies have been funded by pharmaceutical companies and/or manufacturers of lighting devices may provide an underlying motivation for the direction of research. Scientific research can be leveraged as an important marketing tool on behalf of one's products. Through the sequence of (1) biological reductionism to narrow the focus of the issue, (2) scientific research to validate the concepts, and then (3) the use of scientific research findings for marketing, both professionals and consumers have tended to accept these concepts as a relatively complete understanding of SAD and its treatment.

INTERACTIVE IMPACT OF LIGHT VERSUS SCIENTIFIC FINDINGS

Clinicians and scientists pursue their findings in entirely different ways. The neurobiological work on attachment disorders makes it clear that a person usually needs to perceive safety in order to retrieve and process strong emotions. In psychotherapy the clinician serves as a supportive guide who creates an atmosphere of safety. However, in scientific research, the researchers are committed to being objective. By virtue of the different approaches, it is not surprising that therapists and scientists will elicit different responses from the subject. The point is not to contend that scientific findings are inaccurate or inferior, instead that scientific findings are limited in their capacity to identify aspects of emotions that are not likely to occur in a context of research conditions. Because of these different approaches, methods like ETT® discover causal factors that are not likely to be found in scientific research and consequently can facilitate changes that cannot be easily changed within a biochemical framework of intervention alone.

People tend to project attributes of others previously known to them onto currently experienced relationships. These projections are drawn from a working model of relationship experiences existing within the memory of the person's own psyche. Since the person experiencing a negative reaction to a visual environment may not be consciously aware of the source of this distress, it often falsely appears that the visual environment is the cause of the distress, when instead the visual stimulus is often merely the triggering element. Therefore, it has been observed that when light or other visual environmental stimulation activates the human psyche, certain external lights tend to evoke emotions and accompanying physical symptoms that are associated with latent unresolved emotional issues existing within that person's psyche. One type of result of this encounter is symptomatic responses to visual environments. This perspective would explain why some people react to a visual environment in one way and others may have little or no response to the same environment.

One major concern about the conventional bright white light and antidepressant treatment for SAD is that it is a form of self-treatment in which the person is alone in the process. For people who possess existential anxiety and loneliness as features of their depression, recommending a form of treatment that has little or no interpersonal component to it risks further alienation. Depression is often a consequence of perceived separation, lack of support, emotional unavailability by attachment figures, and thwarted verbal expression. Therefore, to send people away for the major portion of treatment to be done on their own would likely reinforce these core problems, even if the symptoms temporarily improve. This self-treatment that omits interpersonal processes might further alienate clients, who often appear to have the avoidant attachment pattern, from their own emotions. People with the avoidant attachment patterns seek to avoid unpleasant emotions rather than to face them and process them successfully.

Interaction with the Visual Environment

As the child grows into an adult, the person's visual environment is perceived to expand more, but the mechanisms of the internal visual system of the brain continue to be emotionally sensitive and remain available. It is proposed that eventually visual environments as a whole can potentially impact the adult as if a reenactment of the adult's parent's influence were modulating his brain and body. Other people and variations of light and color become significant environmental factors that influence the visual system in adults. Since people typically fail to recognize their relationships with their visual environment, symptoms are often attributed to other mechanisms. Seasonal Affective Disorder (SAD) is an example of such an environmental influence in which variations of light have a strong impact on moods. ETT® seizes this influence to modulate the light environment for therapeutic purposes.

If the visual environment is the external cause of SAD and mood states in particular, what are its biochemical mechanisms? "Various lines of evidence point to a significant role for serotonin in the pathophysiology of SAD, with both presynaptic and postsynaptic mechanisms . . . likely involved" (Lam & Levitt, 1999, p. 46). Since visual brain stimulation deregulates serotonin activity that affects mood states, it would stand to reason that appropriate light stimulation can activate serotonin for the recovery from pathological mood states.

The mother's influence, through mutual gaze interaction, indirectly influences the child's hormonal regulation, which affects dopamine activity. "Dopamine increases the transcription of the gene that encodes the precursor of endorphin in the pituitary, and circulating endorphins act as a controlling mechanism of the postnatal development by influencing DNA synthesis and regulating dendritic growth and spine formation" (Bartolome, Lerber, Dileco, & Schonberg, 1991; Hauser, McLaughlin, & Zagon, 1989). This is one means by which interpersonal influences elicit biochemical processes through a sequence of activities that alter genetic expression. In this example, positive emotional regulation results in processes that regulate neuronal growth and ultimately affects spine formation. While these processes largely take place during critical periods of development, by reactivating psychological states similar to those occurring during these critical periods, present-day interactions can re-activate these same potentials.

NEW TREATMENT FOR SAD AND VESS

The innovative treatment of SAD with Emotional Transformation Therapy® begins with the building of interpersonal rapport between the therapist and client. Interpersonal responses are based upon optimal responses that are congruent with the client's attachment patterns. Next, a careful assessment of the client's symptoms is evaluated. If these symptoms fit the criteria for SAD, the following treatment plan is implemented:

- If the affective or physical symptoms are intense upon the initial presentation, the peripheral goggles are used for peripheral eye stimulation to rapidly reduce intensity.
- If the presenting symptoms are not initially intense and the sources within the person's personal history regarding the present symptoms are not known, the Spectral Resonance Technique is used to access affect and insight.
- Next, specific wavelengths of light are selected to emit into the client's eyes for the purpose of matching the resonance of each affective state experience of the client while providing verbal validation, which results in rapid progression through these affective states.
- At some point during the sessions, an attempt is made to stimulate a replication of the exact SAD symptoms by using specific wavelengths of light into the eyes that produces the same symptoms (described in the book *Emotional Transformation Therapy: An Interactive Ecological Psychotherapy*). Then processes like photic release, peripheral eye stimulation, or eye movements are used to bring the affective states responsible for the symptoms to closure.

The content of the client's dialogue during these processes tends to fall into five categories (1) unresolved attachment disorders, (2) classically conditioned experiences with light and darkness, (3) unresolved trauma, (4) symbolic issues with light and darkness, and (5) psychological anniversary reactions. Any type of psychotherapy that can uncover and change the emotional aspect of these issues should accomplish relief of SAD symptoms. However, ETT® is currently the only approach that directly stimulates the visual system to shift a person's relationship with light and provides a rapid speed of resolution. Therefore, it is optimal for this purpose.

Unresolved attachment disorders related to SAD usually involve a perceived boundary intrusion by an attachment figure. This is often described as an overbearing parent. The client tends to incorporate the parent-child relationship within his or her internal working model. Then, when either other people or the environment feels invasive, symptoms of distress are triggered. This pattern is developed when the attachment figure invades the client's perceived personal space during the child's early development and repeats this behavior.

A second theme regards the classically conditioned experience of light or especially darkness. For example, if a child experienced numerous unpleasant experiences in a darkened room or at night, the negative experiences could become linked to the darkness itself. Then later in life, excessive darkness that occurs during the winter months in northern climates could trigger the association with negative affect. If negative affect goes unabated or the triggers are not repeated, a "condition" develops.

Another similar type of issue pertains to the symbolic nature of darkness or light. Many adults have not lost their childhood fear of darkness. For this reason, horror movies base many of their fearful images in scenes of darkness. In fact, one scientific study demonstrated that SAD subjects actually were significantly affected by looking at symbolic pictures of darkness and light (Bouhmys, et al., 1997). Humans are symbolic creatures and light and darkness are classic universal symbols.

Unresolved trauma may contribute to light sensitivity in such a way that extended darkness can trigger the affect from trauma without the person consciously knowing the nature of its source. Trauma can directly affect the functioning of the suprachiasmatic nucleus (biological clock) in such a way that trauma deregulates the sleep/waking cycle. Trauma is so often lodged in the primitive subcortical regions of the brain that it disrupts many brain functions.

Psychological anniversary reactions involve the triggering of unresolved emotions in association with a specific date related to, for example, the death of a loved one, a catastrophic event like the a terrorist attack, or any impactful event that possesses strong, unresolved emotions. Many times these events have left the person's conscious awareness, but the emotional responses continue to emerge on that date. This could account for many depressive symptoms that may occur during certain seasons (Beratis, Gourzie, & Gabriel, 1997). For example, if a family member died on the holiday of Thanksgiving, this event corresponds with the beginning of winter and depression at this time of the year could be accounted for by the anniversary reaction.

In addition to the classic SAD symptoms, many people possess "subsyndromes" of SAD that do not meet the diagnostic criteria for SAD but may be quite severe nonetheless. The condition I have seen the most is a response to overcast skies that meets the criteria for major depression. These conditions typically involve issues related to unresolved attachment disorders, especially perceived invasiveness into one's personal space during early development.

The treatment of "reverse vegetative" symptoms of hypersomnia, increased appetite, carbohydrate craving, and weight gain are often eliminated when the other SAD symptoms are relieved. However, in many cases these symptoms are treated separately. Hypersomnia is usually improved when the initial SAD symptoms improve. However, carbohydrate craving often bears similar psychodynamic issues to other eating disorders that involve eating food for comfort. This carbohydrate craving is responsive to ETT® addiction treatment procedures found in chapter 6.

FLUORESCENT LIGHT SYMPTOMS AND TREATMENT

Visual light stimulation not only accesses unresolved psychological material and its accompanying physical sequelae but can also potentially heal these symptoms at the same time. For example, there is ample scientific research that shows that such lighting as fluorescent lights or certain types of blue lights cause physical damage to the eyes and body (Koide, Ueda, et al., 2001; Taylor, West, Munoz, Rosenthal, Bressler, & Bressler, 1992; Young, 1988; Okuno & Saito, 2002; Shaban & Richter, 2002). However, it has been found in clinical settings that by identifying and/or processing the emotional distress associated with these lights through ETT®, both the psychological and physical symptoms are usually relinquished. For example:

Case Study: Amy

I often ask an audience if anyone feels discomfort with the fluorescent lighting in the room that we are currently occupying. Typically, many people raise their hands. For example, in one audience a person we shall call Amy raised her hand.

- First, I asked Amy to describe her reaction to the lights. She said that the lights made her feel as if they were overbearing or intrusive, provoking anxiety and physical tension.
- Then I asked Amy if she has ever been in a relationship with someone who was overbearing, intrusive, and made her feel anxious. She identified a parent.
- After this identification, I asked her if she still felt the same reaction to the lights. She reported that the lights appeared softer and that the anxiety had diminished. This change took place instantly. In her case, it resulted in a permanent change in her response to the light.

Why does this response take place? Visual light stimulation activates attachment patterns and both emotional and physical symptoms associated with attachment responses. One's response to light occurs as if one has a relationship with light that bears a strong similarity to a relationship with other people. However, the lack of awareness about this relationship with light leaves people who have these symptoms to assume that their response to light is due to the lights alone. After getting Amy to describe her current emotions and symptoms occurring in association with the light and then having her recognize a previous relationship in which she possessed the same emotions and symptoms, she recognized the light was actually a trigger, not the cause of her current symptoms. When this awareness occurs the symptoms often instantly stop. I have conducted this demonstration dozens of times with audience members with the same outcome. The rapidness and magnitude of this change is usually stunning to the recipient because the assumption had been that the light was the sole cause, not the unresolved relationship. Even though a person may have had a direct experience of this phenomenon, the person may still be confused about the event because conventional understanding about the light-human interaction cannot explain it.

If light were conceived as an external objective force and seen as separate from the person, then the symptoms would be seen as a reaction only to the light stimulus. Within this confined perspective, the only answers would be to either medicate the symptoms or remove the person from the light stimulus. While these approaches may alleviate the symptoms, they provide no long-term change and fail to provide as rapid of an alleviation as the ETT® approach. By failing to recognize that light activates the attachment disorder and its consequential emotional and physical symptoms, the person remains vulnerable to triggers of light that cause symptoms of previous relationships to occur over and over again. The objectification of light is derived from the viewpoint of Newtonian physics where one conceives of elements of energy and matter as separate entities, as opposed to that of quantum physics in which all elements of nature, such as energy and matter, exist in an inseparable relationship with each other. In the case of a quantum framework in which symptoms are seen within relationships, relief can occur in a way that an objectified context is unlikely to achieve.

Scientific research about the physical mechanisms of phototoxic biochemical effects has been done in regard to fluorescent lights. Therefore, within a Newtonian Physics frame of reference it is known that this lighting is harmful to some people's eyes. I do not disagree with these facts. However, within a quantum physics frame of reference, the interaction between the light (energy), consciousness, and matter occurs as one continuous flow of a whole. Therefore, by heightening a person's awareness of the attachment response to the human-light activity and facilitating changes in it, the physical symptoms can be changed within the quantum framework of reality and ultimately the biochemistry can be changed within Newtonian framework of reality. Regardless of the accuracy of these hypotheses, physical symptoms of the eyes are consistently facilitated to relief through dialogue about that person's relationships.

An example of connecting fluorescent light related symptoms with many of the neurobiological principles previously described is the following experience. These concepts also come into play to provide relief to people possessing these symptoms.

- An attachment disorder from which one is disassociated was activated and accompanying emotional dysregulation occurred.
- Then some of the symptoms associated with emotional reactions to a previous relationship within one's internal mental model were triggered to emerge by the visual environment.
- When specific visual stimuli resonated with specific emotional states, the person's symptoms became strongly impacted in a similar manner that the mother regulates the child's brain and body during mutual gaze interaction.
- An attachment relationship between the person and the light in the environment took place below the person's conscious awareness.
- When awareness of the related unresolved relationship was raised, the person could differentiate symptomatic responses to light from symptoms of a previous human-to-human relationship.
- This differentiation relieved fearful protective responses and promoted reduction of guardedness and resulted in relaxation. The combination of the light-human bond and the facilitator-to-person bond in this process served to both amplify and change the impact of an outside light source on the brain and body. This procedure shifted the symptomatic person into relief.

The new process for changing a person's response to fluorescent lighting is highly efficient. However, it brings up some philosophical/ethical issues. Are we teaching people to adapt to phototoxic environments? Almost all man-made indoor lighting significantly deviates from the spectrum of natural sunlight, and fluorescent lights appear to be the worst offenders. At the same time, fluorescent lights are widely used and are often the most energy efficient lights. However, my own surveys among numerous audiences show that up to 50 percent of most populations have negative symptoms in relation to fluorescent lighting. Therefore, I would first recommend natural sunlight or indoor lighting that is more closely aligned with the spectral wavelengths of sunlight to solve this problem.

However, given that these first two options may not be available to some people and that fluorescent lights provoke harmful symptoms, the ETT® process for relief of these symptoms is the next best option and is preferable to taking medications to relieve these symptoms.

There are many people for whom economic survival is dependent upon working in a fluorescent-lighted environment. Furthermore, these people may not be in a position to have a say about changing the lighting environment. Since these people cannot avoid the fluorescent lights and daily medication use may take a toll on their bodies, the ETT® approach clearly offers the healthiest option. Until more businesses can be convinced to use healthier lighting, our healthiest option is to facilitate changes within people that reduce vulnerability to photo-toxicity.

Recognizing that fluorescent lights are simply a catalyst for people's unresolved issues is potentially empowering because it potentially removes one's susceptibility to external fluorescent lights. It is valuable to detoxify people from unresolved emotions. The principle that specific types of visual stimuli can be harnessed to both evoke and assist in rapidly processing unresolved emotions to a natural completion is one of the central premises upon which ETT® is based. While fluorescent lights are unnatural to us, the opportunities to use their impact for psychological growth can be seized upon.

In addition to SAD and fluorescent-light responses, many people develop a high level of visual sensitivity to several different forms of visual stimulation. These people often describe their lives as being constantly bombarded by visual stimuli. They have often had numerous medical tests to look for an explanation, but more often they view bright lights in malls, on computer screens, and in buildings as the culprits. In these cases, I usually find that these people have often been victims during childhood of repeated intrusions of personal space by family members.

LIGHT TOXICITY IN DAILY ENVIRONMENTS

Dark sunglasses of any type can be purchased by anyone to use at anytime. In many cases sunglasses, tinted contact lenses, and an entire variety of eyewear have become fashion statements. In the Sunbelt area of the United States, many people put their sunglasses on every time they are exposed to outdoor lighting. This procedure systematically eliminates any natural sunlight from entering their eyes. Therefore, symptoms of sunlight deficiency can occur in people who live in a sunny climate. After reviewing the scientific evidence about the impact of visual stimulation, it becomes apparent that the customary use of sunglasses may pose a high risk for health and mood states. Since I do not have the power to control these potentially harmful behaviors, my next best option is to educate people about the risk of using sunglasses excessively. The overuse of dark sunglasses may interfere with ETT® treatment. On the other hand, ETT® can correct issues to which sunglasses have contributed.

There are exceptions to this prohibition about sunglasses. For example, in a snow environment such as mountain skiing, if sunglasses are not worn, the surface of the eyes can be easily burned. Therefore sunglasses are necessary in that circumstance. However, in most environments that are sunny, sunglasses are unwarranted. For people who say that it hurts their eyes to go without sunglasses, I recommend a gradual change in exposure to the sun so that one's eyes can acquire an adjustment to more light exposure. If sunglasses must be temporarily worn due to light sensitivity, a neutral gray color that allows approximately the same amount of each color of the spectrum to enter the eyes is recommended. Then a gradual exposure to a little more sunlight, a little bit at a time can, eventually lead to no longer needing to wear sunglasses at all. As this process takes place, emotions and physical symptoms may arise. If these issues are processed, the adaptation to sunlight will be easier and the response to light may stabilize.

Snow environments, fog environments, continuous rain environments, or even continuous sunny environments can all produce significant sub-syndromes or severe psychological disorders. These conditions are all treated in a similar manner as the ETT® treatment for SAD. However, the types of visual stimulation that artificially duplicate these symptoms during sessions require one type of stimulation for one sub-syndrome and a different one for another sub-syndrome. Nonetheless, the underlying psychodynamic issues evoked by the visual environment tend to be similar to the SAD issues described earlier in this chapter.

Within the last two or three decades there has been a strong emergence of other visual stimuli that are man-made, such as computer screens and television screens. The escalation of the number of children with attention deficit hyperactivity disorder within the last couple of decades may be directly related to these stimuli. While we should do all we can to educate people about these hazards, until it becomes widely known that viewing these screens for hours a day is harmful, we can use ETT® and other methods to reduce the impact of these stimuli.

IMPLICATIONS FOR DIAGNOSIS AND RESEARCH

In Michaels's case, what would normally be seen as a medical condition or hypersensitivity was processed as a psychological light sensitivity condition. There have been many other cases like these, but, to date, no scientific studies have been conducted on the treatment of these symptoms with this method. There are three areas of investigation that should be scientifically studied:

1. etiological issues
2. diagnostic issues
3. treatment issues related to the impact of visual environments

A simple scientific survey of the public could establish whether or not a visual environment sensitivity syndrome exists to a significant degree. I have noted from observing people in ETT® sessions that a high responsively to light correlates with high degrees of unresolved affect. In these sessions, people have disclosed various types of extreme sensitivity to environments, such as fluorescent lights or overcast skies, which they had not previously shared with anyone else. These sensitivities were not uncommon and were found to be reliable predictors of the existence of numerous psychological conditions. In some cases, the psychological conditions were known, but the visual sensitivity surprised the person in treatment. Sometimes they had not consciously connected the condition to their visual sensitivity. Then, this concept was extended to apply to responsivity to the visual environment in general. Surveying the general public could validate this phenomenon. Conceiving of psychological conditions within the context of visual sensitivity syndromes has the potential for providing more useful diagnostic categories.

The evocation of symptoms by visual environmental stimulation can be harnessed to provide an exceptional means for discovering etiological factors of a condition. Because visual stimuli have been observed to consistently evoke symptoms emerging from underlying psychodynamic experiences, an appropriately trained therapist can use visual stimuli to swiftly identify these experiences. When systematic visual light stimulation is used with psychotherapy clients, psychodynamic experiences tend to emerge in affective, somatic, and behavioral forms that often bypass the intellect. This emergence of symptoms can be facilitated to rapid relief by use of different wavelengths of light in conjunction with therapeutically guided expression.

3

A Quantum Leap in Emotion

Why is there a need for a new theory of emotion, in particular, the process theory of emotion? New discoveries in the sciences of psychology, physics, biology, and other fields have made profound changes in our understanding; therefore, changes in traditional theories relating to these fields inevitably must occur. Theories of human emotion are no exception. Traditional theories of human emotion are generally classifications of emotion as static entities. For example, sad-like emotions are listed in one group, fear-like emotions in another group, and anger-like emotions in yet a different group. While these classifications often satisfy our intellectual need to create order, these classifications do little to clarify how emotions actually function in daily life. Traditional classifications often fail to prepare us for how an emotion may progress to fruition. Human emotions, by their very nature, are potentially transient rather than static. Emotions are a process, not a fixed entity. Therefore, it stands to reason that we should seek to identify emotions according to the manner in which they move, progress, or change. From this perspective we will be better able to recognize both their qualities and the direction of their movement. This knowledge will assist us in predicting not only the course of emotions, but also harnessing their power and regulating them in more constructive ways.

ETT® provides a new opportunity to see the depth and process of emotions in a way that ordinary experiences rarely provide. It reminds me of the experience of looking at an ordinary leaf with the naked eye or through a microscope. The microscope offers a fresh, new, but equally valid view of the same leaf. In a manner similar to this analogy, ETT® provides a new understanding of the nature of human emotions because it has the power to expose emotions rapidly and clearly, and in the context of patterns of sequences. Just as scientists had to reevaluate their concepts of leaves after they saw them through a microscope, now it is time to reconsider the nature and classification of human emotions since we have seen them magnified and at a greater depth through the lens of visual brain stimulation.

E. L. Rosenberg described "affective traits" as stable predispositions toward certain types of emotional responding that are consistently expressed over time and across situations. She categorized emotions as "acute, intense, typically brief psychophysiological changes that result from a response to a meaningful situation in one's environment" (Rosenberg, 1998, pp. 247–270). Rosenberg places "moods" as a subset of affective traits but super-ordinate to emotions. However, within the context of ETT®, we often see long-held patterns of emotional tone rapidly shift, previously brief emotional states expanded into new depths, and less conscious mood fluctuations emerge into consciousness and undergo transformation. We are seeing more clearly how dissociation commonly disrupts the completion of an emotion, which changes the entire course of emotional activity. Therefore, I will simply use the terms emotion and affect interchangeably and the term "mood" to refer to an overall emotional state of mind.

Five major approaches offer traditional theoretical perspectives on emotion:

- psychophysiological,
- neurological,
- psychodynamic,
- cognitive, and
- evolutionary.

Physiological and neurological activities are important components in the experience of emotions. However, dissociation may significantly distort an emotional response to make the physiological aspects of it appear either more intense or absent altogether. Furthermore, subjective awareness of somatic experiences can provide far more practical feedback in regulating emotion than most of the standard physiological measures. For example, techniques in Somatic Experiencing, Focusing, and Applied Kinesiology have used subjective somatic awareness in their methods. In ETT® somatic feedback is a major means of tracking, identifying, and accelerating the processing of emotion. Somatic experiences are one of several potential sequelae of the experience of emotion.

The evolutionary perspective on human emotion is based on Darwin's evolutionary model. Through this lens, emotions act as signals of communication that ultimately are designed to assist in survival. While this concept has some validity, what happens when our entire view of evolution changes? New research makes Darwin's concept of evolution largely outmoded. If we update our view of evolution to include cooperation over competition, psychosocial genomics over random selection, and a purposive evolution over survival, then evolutionary concepts take on a new meaning.

While the aforementioned approaches have value, they each focus on one narrow aspect of emotion. I advocate that findings from each of these approaches be incorporated into any comprehensive theory of emotion. However, I believe they remain limited in their practical application to psychotherapy. Secondly, they are all largely out of date because they are based on a Newtonian physics worldview alone and have not been re-conceptualized to be congruent with the current scientific perspective of quantum physics.

QUANTUM PHYSICS AND HUMAN EMOTIONS

Human emotions can be seen within the context of phenomena described in physics. William Tiller, PhD, a Stanford University professor and an author of 250 scientific publications, proposed a model of emotional/spiritual reality within quantum physics. It is based in part upon the latent energy found in what most people would call empty space or a vacuum (Tiller, Dibble, & Kohane, 2001).

> At least 99.99 percent of all space within atoms and between atoms is vacuum. According to quantum mechanics and relativity theory the vacuum must contain $\sim 10^{94}$ grams of equivalent latent energy. This means that the amount of vacuum energy latent in the volume of a single hydrogen atom is much more than all the mass energy present in all the planets, in all the stars that telescopes would detect in a radius of 20 billion light years.

Tiller describes three layers of subtle energy that occur within a vacuum and can enter into physical reality or dense matter. He coins the term "deltron" to refer to the coupling mechanism of emotional energy that binds the dimensions of the physical world with the dimensions of consciousness and thought (Bruce, 2005, p. 149).

Tiller proposes that the magnitude of coupling increases as deltron activation increases, allowing finer waves to enter into physical reality. He proposes that only when emotions are activated can intentions alter physical matter. Tiller's model describes how emotions in the form of waves (energy) carry messages through interchanges with matter from space into matter (physical human body) into consciousness and then again through space to another person (matter) and then into their consciousness. When these emotions enter consciousness, the impact of these exchanges affects cognition, behavior, and somatic experiences.

The salient feature of this interchange is emotion. Some popular theories of the role of emotion refer to processes of similar activities in the brain as "information processing" (Shapiro, 2001). However, these conceptions objectify emotional exchanges. Objectification tends to eliminate an aspect of information that takes the humanness or divinity out of it. I prefer to use the phrase, "sentient processing," that can be described as intentional messages in consciousness that travel the space-time-matter continuum through the impetus of emotional energy. This conception neither limits emotions to a physical model nor excludes the role of sentient intention and consciousness as mechanisms of emotional functioning. This concept does, however, imbue consciousness with the richness of emotion, which contributes to both the meaning of survival and the activation of our highest potentials.

NEWTONIAN AND QUANTUM PHYSICS

Newtonian physics and quantum physics are significantly different. Almost all sciences have accepted the Newtonian model but have yet to integrate concepts of quantum physics into their frames of reference. According to Dr. Jenny Wade, the Newtonian physics model dominates psychological theory:

> Conventional psychological theories have postulated the bounded, three-dimensional representation of independently existing, separate objects in space to be "normal," mature experience of spatialization (e.g., Piaget's Formal Operations). Clinicians routinely assess patients against this Newtonian spatial orientation, using it as a yardstick of "objective reality," the standard for normal mental functioning. . . . According to conventional developmental theory, the experience of temporality is fixed after early childhood, when it culminates in the "normal" historical sense of the past, present, and future. As for the third reference point . . . clinical practitioners ask patients to identify themselves and other people and, when fine distinctions need to be drawn, to indicate the boundaries of self and other. (Wade, 1996, p. 6)

Wade goes on to distinguish Newtonian physics from post-Newtonian (quantum physics) by virtue of the three criteria of fluctuations of space, time, and sense of self. She advocates that when the three aspects of space, time, and sense of self fluctuate, expand, or change in significant ways, one's subjective experience extends from a Newtonian framework to fit more accurately into a quantum physics model of reality. These three aspects of experience differentiate transpersonal experiences from ordinary ones. The following comparative chart illustrates the basic difference between Newtonian physics and physicist David Bohm's version of quantum physics.

Newtonian Physics	*Quantum Physics*
The universe is composed of separate entities in space.	The universe is a seamless whole of fluctuating possibilities.
Space is empty.	Space is full of latent energy.
Matter exists as separate objects in space.	Matter exists interchangeably with energy, space, time, and consciousness.
Time is linear and moves from the past to the present and then to the future.	Time is all at once, timeless, and can flow in any direction.
Energy is objectified as separate from space, matter, time, and consciousness.	Energy is interchangeable with time, space, matter, and consciousness.
Consciousness is separate from space, time, energy, and matter.	Consciousness is inextricably involved in space, time, matter, and energy.

SPACE, TIME, AND SELF

My proposal is that the more intensely emotions are experienced, the greater the tendency for shifts in perceived space, time, and sense of self to occur. According to physicist David Bohm, the universe, an undivided whole in a constant state of flow and change, involves relationships among consciousness, matter, energy, space, and time (Bohm, 1980). This view of the universe allows a perceived reality where fluctuations of space, time, and sense of self potentially offer an accurate appraisal of reality. In the case of emotional experience, variations of spatial perception, subjective experience of time, and self-perception are perceived as fluctuating more when emotions intensify. For example, intense fear can evoke regression to previous fearful experiences (time), a perception of the world closing in (space), and a sense of feeling smaller (self). On a continuum of 1 to 10, with 10 being the most intense, perceived fluctuations of space, time, and self-perception become more likely when intensity of emotional experience passes level 5.

At emotional intensity levels of 9 or 10 the perception of space, time, and sense of self may shift drastically. For example, manic states, panic states, extreme states of grief, and other states of extreme emotionality typically exhibit dramatic changes in the perception of space, time, and self. On the other hand, mystical or ecstatic states of wellbeing have also been documented to possess extreme variations in the perception of self, space, and time (Wade, 2004). These transcendent states appear to be more common during ETT® sessions than in any other type of therapy. Transcendent experiences may go beyond the experience of the 1 to 10 intensity scale. Some people believe that the conventional concept of emotion is not applicable to certain transcendent states, nor are words adequate to describe them. I refer to these as states of extreme wellbeing. This will be discussed further in chapter 9.

These variations of perceived space, time, and self during emotional experiences are derived from and expressed by ordinary clients who may have no knowledge of quantum physics. However, these clients are often unknowingly describing their emotional experiences from the point of view of the quantum physics model of reality. These descriptions of perceived fluctuations can occur with or without the use of ETT®. However, since ETT® has such an extraordinary impact on emotions, some descriptions of fluctuations of perceived space, time, and self occur far more frequently during light-human interactions. For example, I hear more people report feeling "taller" or "lighter" after ETT® sessions that bolstered self-esteem than I have ever heard outside of ETT® experiences. These characteristics of emotions can be understood best in a process-focused theory of emotion.

During emotional experience, some people actually become hotter (energy), feel a sense of constriction (space), or identify with a completely different self-perception (out of control). It is certainly likely that these experiences are perceptual changes that cannot be measured to confirm actual changes in space, time, or a sense of self. On the other hand, in some cases people claim that objective measures verified their change in weight (matter) and space (dress size) without food intake or loss of waste material. However, what may be of most therapeutic importance is that these changes feel real to the client, are associated with emotional experiences, and are therapeutically amenable to change. The following descriptions represent specific examples of emotions in the context of subjective reports of space, time, energy, matter, and consciousness as they have occurred in emotional experiences.

EMOTIONAL EXPERIENCES OF TIME VARIATIONS

There are at least three "present" time contexts of emotions. The most common is the brief, fluctuating present tense of experiencing an emotion. In this case a person may feel sad, for example, about something happening now. However, sadness typically emerges briefly; a person's temporal attention moves elsewhere, and then it emerges again. Emotions often trigger memories of similar events, which tend to briefly take one out of the present moment. Therefore, this fluctuating interruption of the present tense is often only a partially present experience.

A second type of "present" time context is perceived as spatially constricting and fixated. This may occur during a perceived emergency when a person is alert to every nuance in the current time, typically because survival is thought to be at stake. For example, if a person drew a gun and pointed it at you, unless you go into shock, you would be likely to focus in a hyper-vigilant manner on the present experience.

A third "present" time context involves the numinous present in which the perception of time is expanded. The "experience of the 'numen' is characterized by awe and majesty, by a sense of being in the presence of great power and urgency" (Gentz, 1986, p. 749). During the eternal "now" the person seems to be experiencing first-hand what physicists say is the past, the present, and the future all existing simultaneously. In the expansive numinous present, people appear to perceive the reality described in quantum physics as timelessness.

Another time context may occur during the numinous present in which numerous experiences are characterized with wonder and expansions of time and space. Experiences emanating from various forms of meditation may be numinous and characterized as the timeless now. One of my clients reported an experience that occurred while she was potting a plant. This client was not trying to achieve this state nor was she familiar with the concept of the numen. Nonetheless, she reported an experience of feeling fixated in the moment in a state of awe and wonder, unlike anything she had ever previously experienced. There was not anything unusual about the actual potting of the plant itself, but the perceived expansion of the present tense into timelessness and the majestic wonder of everything altered her state of consciousness in such a way that the ordinary became extraordinary.

Daniel Stern, MD, has conducted an extensive exploration with substantial documentation about *The Present Moment in Psychotherapy and Everyday Life*

(2004). He devised a "breakfast interview" to assess the differentiation between moments experienced in the present and dissociated moments (Stern, pp. 9–24). He describes "Lived Stories," "experiences that are narratively formatted in the mind but not verbalized or told," as one of the experiences contained in present moment experiences (Stern, 2004, p. 55). Stern also identifies "intersubjective contact" as

> Two people see and feel roughly the same mental landscape for a moment at least. These meetings are what psychotherapy is all about. They also provide the happenings that change our lives and become the memories that compose the story of our intimate relationships. . . . Moments of intersubjective creating are special present moments. (Stern, 2004, p. 75)

There are at least four "past" contexts of emotion. You can experience the past as if you were subjectively in the past. This occurs during regressive experiences. There are varying degrees of emersion into these first-hand experiences of the past. Your field of awareness can be only partially involved in a subjective experience of the past or fully involved or anywhere along a continuum toward a total regression where you would be totally immersed in the past. On the other hand, you can recall emotions from your past from an observer position. This observer position of recollection can be either from a third person vantage point or an omnipotent viewpoint. In either case, the emotional experience may be vicarious.

A third type of time context of past emotion may be the "transcendent past." While I am neither confirming nor denying the phenomena of past life experiences, I am simply categorizing what clients report. Nearly half of the world's population believes in reincarnation. This type of transcendent past experience involves the perception of a previous lifetime identity where emotional experiences from the ancient past occur in the present. Whether these recollections are fantasies or memories, sometimes a perceived past life experience was reported to be the source of a disproportionate emotional response to a current situation. Therefore, it becomes of practical value to recognize the client's subjective context.

Emotions can also fit into a related phenomenon—intergenerational past emotions. These emotions are experienced as if you are feeling emotion that was experienced by your grandmother, her mother, or other ancestors that you may or may not have met. Whether these "recollections" can be verified or not is unknown, but clients report them. A third overlapping category may involve multiple transcendent past emotions. For example, different emotions from different, specific previous transcendent past experiences may be felt simultaneously. While these experiences may appear imaginary, if they are accompanied by very real emotions they could be recognized as a time context for emotion.

A third time context of emotion is associated with a perception of the future. Subjective experiences of the future fit into at least three types. The most commonly reported type occurs as worry and distress in response to an anticipated, perceived future event. A different experience occurs as precognition about one's own life or that of someone else. In these events one may feel the emotion as if one is already in the future. A variation of this theme is a future context of emotion that occurs as an awareness of collective future events such as distress about a cataclysmic event like an earthquake or a tsunami. The possibility of this future context only makes sense in a quantum physics frame of reference where the future is a part of the timeless now.

Mixed or alternating time contexts of emotion can occur. A past and present context of emotion can co-occur. For example, combinations of emotions from a future context and the present or even a past and future co-occurring experience can take place. These may occur within various ego states. Emotions of a state associated with a previous trauma may emerge along with an ego state associated with a perceived future event. For example, the sight of an injured person can trigger distress from an event in one's past that causes a spontaneous "fast forward" to fear of what will happen in one's own future.

PERCEIVED SPATIAL CONTEXTS OF EMOTIONS

Many emotions are experienced from a position outside the person or through an external locus of control. For example, some people empathize with others to the extent that they feel other people's emotions. This response should not be confused with projective identification in which other people's emotions trigger our own emotions because we identify with some aspect of the other person's situation. In the case of an external locus of control, the context of our personal space is expanded to include the other person's emotions, while projective identification involves the other person's experience as a trigger for our own experiences. The phenomena of "loading" occurs when one person takes on the emotions of others for the purpose of bearing the emotional pain of others with the conscious or unconscious intention that the person initially possessing the emotion may be relieved (Eisner, 1995, pp. 55–57). A fourth type of extended spatial context occurs when a person dissociates in such a way that he or she perceives himself to be outside of his physical body. This is known as depersonalization. This often takes place during shock or during an overwhelming emotional experience. Emotions may be totally or partially blocked during depersonalization. The perception of self outside of the body can also be associated with a voluntary desirable mystical experience.

A variety of other types of spatial contexts exist in which emotions occur along a continuum of polar opposites.

- One example is the heavier-lighter continuum in which heavier typically represents an unpleasant feeling like sadness and lighter represents pleasant emotions as the consequence of the relinquishment of unpleasant emotions.
- Another example is the larger-smaller continuum, which often represents degrees of self-esteem, with larger being elevated self-esteem and smaller representing lower self-esteem. However, "smaller" may also represent a regression to a perceived childhood state.
- A third continuum commonly reported during emotional experiences is constricted to expanded occurrence. Constricted is often related to fear, and in this continuum "expanded" often represents emotions like relaxation or trust.
- A fourth continuum reported by clients is the hollow to full experience. In this case hollow may represent a lack of sense of self or the absence of an adequate affectionate emotion. Often this is referred to as emptiness. Full can represent either excessive emotion in an unpleasant way or a pleasant experience of a sense of wellbeing.

EMOTIONS IN THE CONTEXT OF "MATTER"

Clients often report perceiving themselves in various states of what could be construed as variations of "matter." For example, people describe their body as "fluid." This fluidity is often the context in which certain emotions are experienced. Fluid could be used either as a metaphor or as a literal description. Fluidity may represent a transition from one emotional state to another, indecisive fear, or a state of shock. Whether a person is actually heavier or lighter as measured by "objective" means is a concept limited to the Newtonian of physics. I have a client who reported that she physically expanded two dress sizes but had actually lost two pounds. In this case her experience of expansion is verified, yet it is not congruent with her weight (perception of matter).

In quantum physics matter exists in conjunction with consciousness, time, space, and energy. For example, a person who resists being lifted or perceives himself as heavy, feels much heavier to others than if he perceives himself as light. These variations of qualities of matter are essentially qualities of one's emotional experience.

The Emotional Context of Energy

The heat versus cold continuum can represent fear (cold), anger (heat), or lack of affection (cold) and fulfilling affection (heat). Heat and cold can also represent a variety of other emotions. For example:

- Heat can represent arousal passion.
- Heat in the facial region can represent embarrassment.
- Heat can be perceived during relaxation.
- Cold or cooling can represent fear.
- Cold may occur during a calming down from intense emotions like anger or excitement, and the elimination of fear may feel cool.

In physics, variations in temperature are intricately associated with interchanges of energy and matter. Temperature changes strongly correlate with emotional changes. Researchers Chen-Bo Zhong and Goffrey Leonardelli conducted research with large numbers of volunteers to assess the relationship between perceived temperature and social rejection. They found that those people who perceived themselves as being socially excluded also perceived themselves as physically colder. Loneliness was found to be correlated to perceived temperature decline (Branan, 2008, p. 13).

Clients commonly describe their emotional experiences in terms of energy. Clients report intermittent high and low swings of energy that may be either temporary or represent a long-term pattern such as found in bipolar disorders. Some clients have described a calm energy that is totally different from fatigue, but is nonetheless an inactive state. Descriptions of energy quality are not often disclosed without the accompanying context of space, time, or temperature. While these perceived factors of physics are being discussed separately, they all typically occur in relationship to each other.

THE QUANTUM MODEL OF REALITY AND PRACTICAL PSYCHOTHERAPY

How are the perceptions of qualities of quantum physics valuable as practical attributes? There are several ways to use the perceptions beneficially. For example, I worked with a woman who had hot flashes and wanted them to stop. Through the use of ETT® we discovered that her experience of physical heat represented unresolved anger. Then we processed this anger to completion, which initially resulted in the reduction of heat and later in the elimination of hot flashes. This does not mean that her perception of heat was purely in her imagination, but instead that unresolved anger played a pivotal role in the heat she experienced.

A sense of heaviness may not be understood by a client experiencing it; however, when processed as sadness, grief, or a burden, it will often "lighten." People will seldom use adjectives such as fearful, sad, or angry to describe emotions. Instead, they tend to use the terms "constricted," "tight," or "rigid." If therapists recognized these terms as analogues for emotions, they could help the client become more "expanded," "loose," or "flexible." An emotional experience is often linked to cognition. One client described her thinking as blending into the background. By the time the session was over and her emotions were changed, she described her thinking as sharp and separated from its background. She felt better. People often describe the shape, density, time context, energetic quality, and temperature of their emotional experience, not just the name of it. A process theory of emotion, therefore, provides a basis for assessing the change and completion of emotional processing. In order to achieve treatment objectives it is important to ascertain constructive versus non-constructive processing of emotions.

ACTION TENDENCIES AND EMOTIONS

There is a concept that all emotions possess "action tendencies" (Kiesler, Schmidt, & Wagner, 1997). This means that embedded in the full range of an emotion is an inherent need to take action. For example, the action tendency of anger is to fight; the action tendency of various forms of fear may include the action of running away. All of these action tendencies involve the use of the physical body to carry out these action tendencies. This accounts for the specific physical sensations that occur simultaneously when an emotion is felt. However, when the person withholds the physical expression of an emotion, the person is often left with the physical symptom from that emotion. For example, if one wishes to fight but doesn't, the arms, hands and shoulders may exhibit tension, or when one wishes to run, the feet and legs are often tense. Therefore, when identifying emotions it is important to recognize the accompanying physiological sensations regarding action tendencies or therapy may inadvertently serve to further separate the person's emotions from bodily responses. If these action tendencies are repeatedly thwarted, their physical attributes may manifest in chronic physical symptoms.

Historically, many therapists have recognized these attributes of emotions and some of them believe that the only real way to access and resolve emotions is through bodywork, movement, or cathartic verbal expression. Wilhelm Reich used Orgonomy to breakdown body armor, Janov used primal scream to access the core of unresolved emotion, and Somatic Experiencing uses body awareness as the key to its interventions. Most body-oriented approaches assume that one must externally manipulate the body, encourage movement, or in some way promote physical expression in order to move or discharge the action tendencies of emotions to free the body of trapped affect. While a degree of emotional expression is certainly valid, ETT® offers an entirely different means of dislodging somatic aspects of emotion. By directing wavelengths of light into the eyes, photoreceptors convert external light into neural impulses which, if selected accurately, enter the neural circuit responsible for the emotion and action tendency. When this takes place along with appropriate interpersonal support, the physical aspect of the emotion is resonated with and brought to a rapid completion. This generally takes place without kicking, screaming, or being physically manipulated. In addition to the client undergoing less intense struggle to accomplish discharge of somatic emotion, the speed of this change often occurs within seconds. This rapidness of discharge is a drastic departure from other methods.

This approach sheds new light on the essence of emotion. It has been observed that emotion resonates with specific wavelengths of light as if emotion itself were a wavelength of light. Resonance only exists if two things are vibrating at the same rate. Therefore, by definition using specific wavelengths of light to resonate with the embodied emotion would not work unless the nature of emotion and physiology existed in a vibrating form. The speed at which resonance occurs with specific external visual stimuli suggests that ETT® offers the most direct route to accessing and healing these experiences.

Acting out Emotions

Many emotions can progress through almost all phases of escalation, peak, and de-escalation but are expressed through behaviors and words that lack an accurate recognition of their nature. This typically occurs in children and adolescents who act out their emotions without knowing the complete nature of the emotion driving their actions. If their actions are not allowed to reach completion, they are more likely to store these emotions uncompleted rather than allowing de-escalation to extinguishment.

DISSOCIATION

The use of ETT® has dramatically changed our understanding of dissociation. ETT® brought into view an entirely new range and detail of the phenomena of dissociation. Many ETT® tools, but particularly the spectral chart, have revealed an array of specific diagnostic features of dissociation that have been relatively unknown to therapists before this discovery. Experience with ETT® suggests that dissociation is far more widespread than previously thought. This new awareness can and has led to better and more rapid treatment.

We can now see dissociation in a new light. Dissociation is to "break the association of; disconnect; separate." If we stick to this basic lexical definition, there are at least thirty different types of dissociation that I have now identified. Therefore, I think the term dissociation is too vague for practical usage in psychotherapy. Instead, we need to label the type of dissociation in order to provide any relevant meaning for discussing it. For example, cognitive dissociation might indicate a form of amnesia versus somatic dissociation, which might indicate a physical numbness. One client may possess cognitive dissociation without having any somatic dissociation. Therefore, I will identify every type of dissociation uncovered so far. Next I will describe how ETT® tools can be used to diagnose each type of dissociation. Finally, I will review how ETT® is used to treat dissociation.

Dissociation can also be categorized as major (from 6 to 10 on a scale of 10) or minor (from 1 to 5 on a scale of 10) because there is a potentially great difference in the degree of dissociation. For example, a person may be amnesic regarding parts of a specific event versus total amnesia of everything of significance that occurred within the last few minutes or the last few days. In some cases dissociation is so pervasive that a person cannot function, and it appears obvious to anyone observing the person that something is very problematic. In other cases, dissociation is so hidden that neither the person experiencing it nor experienced clinicians can detect its presence. In these cases the only apparent evidence for its existence concerns the symptoms caused by the dissociation. However, the use of the spectral chart may be the one means for identifying this type of subtle, hidden dissociation. Just because it is hidden and the client appears to function does not mean that this dissociation could not be significant.

Some of these categories of dissociation to be discussed are well known, but there will also be many new categories of dissociation that I have never seen identified in the professional literature. In addition there are certain categories of dissociation that are identified in the DSM IV, but not under dissociation. However, the single common factor is that some aspect of experience is disconnected from other aspects of experience. All forms of dissociation are categorized into eight general groups.

The eight categories of dissociation also have several subcategories in most cases. Identifying each of the eight categories when referring to dissociation helps to specify a phenomenon that may show drastically different characteristics. The eight categories include the following:

1. Cognitive dissociation
2. Affective dissociation
3. Somatic dissociation
4. Behavioral dissociation
5. Identity dissociation
6. Derealization
7. Transcendent dissociation
8. Combinations of more than one type of dissociation

These categories cover every known type of dissociation. In many cases certain forms of dissociation are not observable or detectable to either the client or the therapist, but their consequential symptoms are known. In these cases the diagnostic features of the spectral chart appear to be the only means to differentiate these types of dissociation.

The first category of dissociation can be referred to as cognitive dissociation because it pertains to lack of awareness of thoughts or knowledge related to an experience. The following is a list of types of cognitive dissociation:

1. Absence of thoughts related to other experiences.
   Example: Crying without any awareness about why one is crying.
2. No thoughts (going blank)
3. Loss of cognitive awareness during a focus on emotionally intense recollections.
4. Amnesia
   a. Total amnesia, meaning unable to remember anything. This can be due to a physical blow to the head or other organic causes, or it can be psychogenic or both.

b. Partial amnesia

1. No memory before a certain age
2. Intermittent amnesia
3. Amnesia about specific events
4. Short-term memory loss

The primary form of dissociation that typically impedes psychotherapy is affective dissociation. Disengagement from emotions is a common defense that occurs in a number of very different ways. The following list identifies these different types:

1. Lack of awareness of all emotions (continuous). This could occur as intellectualization (continuous) or in states of shock (temporary), or anhedonia (temporary).
2. Lack of awareness of specific emotions. For example, some men sometimes experience anger but no awareness of sadness, affection or other feelings (continuous).
3. Temporary loss of emotional awareness. This can occur during disclosure of a painful situation when emotional contact exists and then suddenly shuts off.
4. Loss of awareness of emotion from specific events. A person may normally be aware of emotions, but when a specific event is focused on, awareness of emotion is absent.
5. Partial loss of emotion: a person may possess a slight sense of emotion but not full awareness.
6. Alexithymia: awareness of emotion is not accessible to be labeled in words. Emotion may be expressed somatically instead of verbally. This should be differentiated from avoidance, denial, suppression, or any mechanism in which emotion is consciously known but not disclosed.
7. Rapid loss of emotional awareness responsible for a behavioral drive. An example is emotional anxiety that disconnects from awareness but continues to manifest behaviorally as compulsive eating.

A third category of dissociation is somatic dissociation. This can be a disconnection from awareness of the physical body or sensations of the physical body. This is a common experience fostered by a cultural and philosophical perspective of the mind and body as two separate entities. The following are types of somatic dissociation:

1. Lack of awareness of specific physical symptoms. When medical evidence verifies the existence of a physical problem that should possess sensations but the person doesn't feel them.
2. Lack of awareness of physical sensations associated with known emotional distress—all emotional experiences should have physical sensations associated with them.
3. Lack of awareness of all physical sensations—shock, numbing are examples.
4. Experience of physical symptoms with no awareness of why they are occurring—physical pain syndromes that occur without a known cause are examples.
5. Depersonalization—lack of grounding in the physical body yet possessing normal reality testing. Perception of self as outside of the physical body. This is usually temporary but can be continuous.
6. Loss of awareness of sensory experiences:
   a. Visual
   b. Auditory
   c. Tactile
   d. Gustatory
   e. Olfactory
7. Combinations of sensory disconnection

A fourth category of dissociation is behavioral. The following types of behavioral dissociation exist:

1. Lack of awareness of specific behaviors, for example, not knowing one is twitching; not knowing one is verbally repeating; not knowing one is smoking.
2. Lack of awareness of most behaviors, compulsive or habitual behaviors (cleaning house, shopping, repeating information).
3. Lack of control of behaviors (running from a crime scene, sleep walking).
4. Dissociative fugue—leaving one's home and life to establish a new identity at a new location.

A fifth category of dissociation is classified under the term derealization. Derealization is experienced as a separation or unfamiliarity with people or objects in one's environment while remaining intellectually intact. Some examples include the following:

1. Familiar people and places perceived as unfamiliar.
2. Confusion about what is real or unreal as if one is in a dream.
3. Perceived changes in the shape or size of people or objects.
4. Feeling detached from other people.
5. Perception of people or places fading away or disappearing.

A sixth category of dissociation pertains to identity confusion or identity alteration (Steinberg & Schnall, 2001). Many forms of dissociation have a strong impact on one's sense of identity. Identity confusion often is revealed in the following issues:

1. I don't really know who I am.
2. I can change so much from day to day.
3. I have felt as if I am two different people.
4. I am confused about my sexual identity.
5. I suspect that the real me is hidden.

Identity alteration issues may be exhibited in some of the following experiences:

1. Having moods that do not match who I think I am.
2. I don't recognize things I have written.
3. At times I speak in a totally different voice.
4. My public self is very different than my private self.
5. I don't feel like I am who people think I am.

Another category of dissociation concerns transcendent states of mind. These states are not categorized in any conventional model I have seen, but they do occur. They include the following:

1. Dissociative spiritual states in which specific transpersonal events consistently emerge, but are blocked from normal functional states.

2. When previously accessible transcendent states are blocked from awareness. In religious history this is called "the dark night of the soul."
3. Transitional transcendent dissociation. This occurs in "over-focused ADD" when a person merges with other people or things, then shifts into pragmatic activities but dissociates during the transition. Losing things, forgetting to do things during transitions are examples of this type.

A final category may in fact describe the most often seen dissociation category in psychotherapy. This category describes mixed dissociative states in which more than one of the previous categories occurs together in the same person. The following list provides some of the prevalent forms of mixed dissociative states:

1. Inability to experience the present time context.
2. Cognitive and affective dissociation.
3. Affective and somatic dissociation.
4. Affective and behavioral dissociation.
5. Depersonalization and amnesia (cognitive dissociation).
6. Derealization and affective dissociation.
7. Identity confusion and somatic dissociation.
8. Sympathetic hyper-arousal followed by hyper-parasympathetic dissociation.
9. Freeze: "conservation withdrawal" (Powles, 1992, p. 213) and cognitive dissociation.
10. Other combinations of two, three, or more forms of dissociative symptoms.

Recognizing Dissociation

There are several ways to recognize dissociation. The simplest way is to inquire about dissociative experiences through either a questionnaire or an interview. I have used a Dissociative Experiences Scale and/or the Steinberg questionnaires (Steinberg & Schnall, 2001). These questionnaires are very helpful, but in many cases much more is needed. Information from close friends and relatives can add much that the client may have forgotten or may even deny. On the other hand, some clients can provide an external persona that hides dissociative activities even from their closest relatives. Of course another way to identify dissociation is by observation of the client during the interview. The more obvious characteristics of dissociation are staring off into space inappropriately, excessive intellectualization, or no awareness of bodily experiences. However, in most cases dissociation may be more elusive to recognize.

Dissociative phenomena may appear to be many other conditions or may be a part of other conditions. For example, attention deficit disorder may be the label given to a person who dissociates and is unable to sustain his/her attention. While it is accurate that one's attention is not focused, this lack of focus may be due to a disconnection cognitively rather than the classic scattering of mental attention known in attention deficit disorder. People could also be labeled as depressed because they appear listless and non-responsive to others. However, upon further exploration these people may be affectively dissociated. Then again the person may be both depressed and experiencing some form of dissociation intermittently. People who appear to be bipolar may simply be exhibiting dissociation from one state in order to escape to a compensatory state, or dissociative phenomena can be mixed into their actual bipolar condition. These are just a few examples, but the list of conditions that are actually dissociative phenomena is quite extensive.

Differing forms of dissociation are important to recognize because dissociative experiences can delay, stop, or circumvent the progression of emotion to its natural conclusion. In doing this, dissociation frequently places emotional experiences on hold and unresolved. Dissociation may have served to allow a person to survive a perceived threat or enhanced a person's ability to function at one time. However, if the current therapeutic goal is to resolve unfinished emotions that impair the client's current life, then recognition, reactivation and progression of emotions to completion is necessary. In order to do this, a means for correcting dissociation efficiently is necessary. The Spectral Resonance Technique provides a way to track both the flow of emotion and the dissociative cessation of emotional flow at the instant it occurs (a full description of this process can be found in the book *Emotional Transformation Therapy: An Interactive Ecological Psychotherapy*). Therefore, a facilitator can track the movement of emotion and enhance its flow toward optimal progression.

OPTIMAL EMOTIONAL PROGRESSION

Emotions are in a relatively continual flux. Therefore, it is their flow, blocked flow, or divergent paths that might serve as the central focus of a theory of emotion. It is this principle of process and patterns of sequences that might provide the best understanding leading to a precise harnessing and regulation of emotions.

In order for emotions to be regulated in an effective fashion, it is therapeutically valuable to identify characteristics of the optimal progression of emotions. This is particularly essential for regulating unpleasant emotions. This type of emotional regulation is most characteristic of a secure attachment pattern, which is a primary goal for the client to achieve. Therefore, it is important for therapists to be familiar with what optimal emotional process looks like. The following nine characteristics are proposed features of optimal processing of unpleasant emotions.

1. Emotions should ideally be recognized and identified.
2. Emotions should ideally be based on accurate appraisals of a situation.
3. Emotions should ideally be transient and short-lived. Brevity is a relative term in this case meaning that the emotion should progress without significant stagnation.
4. Emotions should ideally progress to total completion.
5. Emotions should ideally be expressed in either verbal, written, physical, or artistic forms.
6. Emotions should ideally be processed in the context of constructive interpersonal relationships.
7. Emotions should ideally be expressed appropriately within the social milieu.
8. The inherent intent to act, associated with emotions, should ideally be fulfilled.
9. Constructive emotions should ideally feel activating or enlivening.

These characteristics can be exhibited if people allow emotions to progress unimpeded by learned defenses and societal norms that in some cases restrict expression of emotions. Therefore, the opposite characteristics of processing of unpleasant emotions represent the least effective means of emotional processing. These forms of emotional dysregulation are usually the result of attachment disorders. They include the following characteristics:

1. Emotional responses do not occur within a constructive interpersonal context.
2. Emotional responses are based on inaccurate appraisals of the situation at hand.
3. Fixated emotions continue to be charged and endure for an extended time.
4. Emotions are unresolved and unconcluded.
5. Emotions are experienced but without recognizing their presence or being able to identify them.

6. Unexpressed emotions are withheld from any significant type of disclosure.
7. The experience of emotions may feel draining, heavy, or in some way deactivating.
8. Emotions are expressed inappropriately in such a way that their expression results in negative consequences for the person experiencing them.
9. Emotions exist for which the inherent intent to act is thwarted, blocked, or otherwise unfulfilled.

Some or all of these impediments to the optimal processing of emotions may, in fact, be highly functional during times in which the intensity of emotion, or the sheer quantity of emotions, would otherwise overwhelm the person. However, when these characteristics of emotional processing become a habitual way of operating, or when they occur as unconscious defenses, these processes tend to become dysfunctional.

Human emotions appear to be innate and universal, but their patterns of dysregulation and healthy regulation are largely shaped initially by interpersonal interactions with parents. These patterns generally operate in the following manner:

1. A stimulus such as a loud sound may provoke fear in the child.
2. This fear is responded to by a startle reaction and then crying.
3. The attachment figure acquires the child's attention.
4. The attachment figure responds to the crying with empathy and nurturing behavior.
5. This response results in emotional distress coming to closure.
6. Emotion concludes completely.

When these processes do not take place with any degree of consistency, different types of attachment disorders and emotional dysregulation result. The creation of emotions such as guilt and shame are particularly noteworthy. More than likely, without guilt and shame, people would lack an appropriate conscience that regulates ethical and moral behavior. However, when these emotions occur unabated, severe guilt and shame can become dangerous emotions. Entire cultures exist where shame is the norm and accepted as appropriate. Specifically, Japan possessed this norm. Japan has long had the unenviable distinction of having had the highest suicide rate of any country in the world. The potency of guilt and shame lies in the fact that guilt and shame are often initiated by the attachment figures on whom the child relies for protection. This situation potentially leaves the child alone to process his emotions before he is capable of healthy, self-regulation.

Ideally, after guilt or shame is produced, the attachment figure should repair the emotional distress to the point of closure. If this does not take place on a repeated basis, the high risk of negative self-perception or intense fear of failure can produce significant psychological symptoms throughout the person's life.

Fear, anger, sadness, and affection appear to be universal experiences in people, but guilt and shame are largely developed and shaped by interaction with attachment figures (Schore, 2003). Subsequent to interactions with attachment figures, children may also develop many other specific emotional patterns by virtue of their encounters with the outside world.

Pleasant Emotions

The experiencing of pleasant emotions can also be either functional or dysfunctional. Some functional characteristics of pleasant emotional experiences optimally include the following:

1. They are frequent and easily accessible.
2. Their intensity and/or duration do not contribute excessive harm to the person experiencing them.
3. They are appropriate to the time and social milieu.
4. They foster improved physiological experiences.
5. They foster constructive cognitive experiences.
6. They may be associated with a state of transcendent wellbeing.

These functional characteristics of pleasant emotions are optimal; however, very similar pleasant emotions may also become dysfunctional. The following characteristics of pleasant emotions may render them dysfunctional:

1. They occur infrequently and are difficult to access.
2. Their intensity and/or duration contribute to negative consequences.
3. They serve as an uncontrollable defense mechanism, such as excessive escape from appropriate responsibilities.
4. They foster an excessive loss of control, to the point that they become inappropriate.

These dysfunctional aspects of pleasant emotional experience may become associated with negative consequences and lose their capacity to enhance a person's wellbeing. This often fosters the generation of other emotions.

Optimal Process Sequences of Emotion

In order to understand the process of emotional progression, it is helpful to begin by identifying the sequence of the simplest emotion as it unfolds. We will start with the optimal flow of emotion and then identify numerous deviations from this optimal pattern. The following characteristics of each phase of the progression of emotional unfolding represent optimal sequences:

1. A stimulus provokes the genesis of an emotion.
2. Cognitive recognition of an unpleasant emotion occurs.
3. Emotion is verbally identified.
4. Emotion comes into somatic awareness.
5. Emotional intensity escalates to a peak.
6. De-escalation of the emotional intensity moves toward completion.
7. Emotion concludes completely.
8. As the emotional intensity completes to extinguishment, the somatic experience of it ceases and the cognitive perspective shifts.
9. The emotional experience is seen in a past context.

EMOTIONAL CHAINS

Another type of emotional pattern involves a combination of several emotions. Typically, these emotions arise in a series or a chain. Typically, one emotion arises, escalates, reaches a peak, deescalates, concludes, and then the next emotion arises to undergo a similar process. Often a third or even fourth emotion follows this pattern until the entire series reaches conclusion. This process can be seen as "layering," when each of the emotions is completely different. When one emotion arises in connection with an event and then reaches a conclusion only to have the same type of emotion occur again, but this time related to an entirely different event, it can referred to as "bridging." For example, the death of a close friend may evoke a similar re-experiencing of a completely different loss. Both layering and bridging can be construed as vertical chains of unfolding emotions. Typically, each emotion experienced in the chain leads to a deeper or earlier life experience of uncompleted emotion.

A "horizontal chain" of emotion involves the experience of simultaneously experiencing more than one emotion. For example, one can experience love and hate, or sadness and anger at the same time. Sometimes numerous emotions occur at the same time like jealousy, anger, sadness, or possessiveness. Since these emotions are experienced at the same time, they are referred to as a horizontal chain of emotions.

Both layering and horizontal chains of emotion are based on the concept that one emotion "completes" its process and another emotion emerges. However, at times an emotion does not complete before the next emotion emerges. Sometimes, this occurs repeatedly. I refer to this pattern as "branching." Branching occurs as several partial expressions of emotion take place.

It is also possible to possess both horizontal chains and vertical chains of emotions at the same time. This is referred to as complex chains of emotions. For example, one may feel a horizontal cluster of jealousy, anger, and sadness that when concluded leads to a new series of guilt, shame, and fear. Then, as this complex chain of emotions continues to unfold, the next series emerges. Complex chains of emotions are both horizontal and vertical in their process. These sequences are commonly seen in the therapeutic processes that accelerate both progress and depth awareness. When attachment disorders combine with certain extreme circumstances such as torture, childhood sexual abuse, or repeated physical abuse, complex chains of emotion often result.

When emotional trajectories change through ETT®, for example, a person whose trajectory of emotional expression is ambivalent/resistant is often at a maximal level of intensity and endures unabated for a long time. After therapeutic interventions with ETT®, the intensity level may first be reduced from a level of 10 to a level of 8 and then eventually to a level 5, which is similar to the peak trajectory of a secure attachment. Equally important is the change in the length of time to conclusion. For example, the ambivalent/resistant trajectory of panic attacks might last for fifteen hours unabated and be gradually reduced to twelve hours, then to one hour, before they disappear altogether.

In summary, process emotion theory focuses on the nature of emotional progression, characteristics of emotion based on phenomena verified by the new realities articulated in current physics, and the concept of optimal emotional unfolding, which has value for guiding emotions to fruition. Sequences of various patterns of the progression of emotion can provide new capacities for harnessing their power, regulating their course more effectively, and predicting their direction. Since emotions are not static entities, a process theory of emotion may more accurately portray their nature. It is possible to have a theory of emotion that is intellectually sound as well as practically functional. If for no other purpose, the value of this theory to psychotherapy may be enormous. While traditional theories of emotion all contribute meaningfully to our knowledge, certain aspects of these theories are simply outdated. It is time to reevaluate our concept of emotion. Process emotion theory is an attempt to provide a fresh new perspective.

4

Putting Sleep Disorders to Rest

Heather look perplexed and frustrated when she said that she wakes up during the night every night and compulsively eats. She wanted to lose weight but felt no control over this problem. Heather was a forty-year-old married woman who initially sought counseling for other issues. She didn't remember much about what happened during the night except that she knew she had an urge to eat and later regretted eating so much. This occurred for several months.

I used the photo assessment method (described in the book *Emotional Transformation Therapy: An Interactive Ecological Psychotherapy*) to systematically reactivate her nightly psychophysical state in order to process it to conclusion. After exposing Heather to a broad spectrum of colors, green was the color that reactivated her disturbing night state. This state consisted of urinary urgency, mental alertness, physical lethargy, and a compulsion to eat. After this exact cluster of symptoms was replicated, by the photo assessment procedure with the Chromapulse II, awareness of emotions began to arise. The star conversion process (precise eye movements with a constant wavelength of light) was used to extinguish all of the psychophysical symptoms. It was interesting that urinary urgency arose but extinguished without urination, but by relieving the psychological distress. This eating issue was primarily focused on lack of affectionate fulfillment for which eating food served to temporarily alleviate. As the process eliminated this problem the entire cluster of symptoms reduced.

One week later I asked Heather if the nighttime compulsive eating stopped. She looked surprised and said she hadn't thought about it but now realized that the pattern had stopped. Months later Heather confirmed that the night eating pattern had never re-emerged.

THE SCOPE OF SLEEP PROBLEMS

Approximately forty million people in the United States suffer from chronic sleep disorders. Of that number about thirty-two million have insomnia, eighteen million have sleep apnea, and two hundred thousand have narcolepsy. Sleep disorders are more common from ages eighteen to sixty-four and among people who have poor health. More women experience daytime sleepiness and insomnia, but more men experience snoring and pauses in breathing. If we simply look at the millions of prescriptions given for sleep medication, it is clear that sleep disorders comprise a virtual epidemic. Clients often reported dramatic changes in their sleep patterns after ETT® was used to change daytime distress. Therefore, I knew ETT® had the potential for affecting sleep changes, but I did not know initially how to harness its power consistently. There are numerous variables as well as numerous types of sleep disorders that make sleep disorders very complex. Therefore, it is very important to assess these factors at the beginning of treatment in order to custom-tailor treatment for each case. For example, there are at least ten different variations of what could generally be called insomnia.

- Difficulty regarding the decision to go to bed
- Inability to fall asleep either for a long time or not at all
- Inability to go back to sleep after waking up during the night
- Awakening at regular intervals during the night
- Awakening too early in the morning
- Awakening to use the bathroom too frequently
- Restless leg syndrome
- Awakening due to nightmares or other dreams
- Awakening due to night terrors
- Combinations of the above issues

Other sleep issues may not be classified as insomnia per se but are still related to insomnia. For example, some people actually sleep seven or eight hours but wake up feeling exhausted as though they haven't slept. Many people have reversed circadian rhythms in which they are sleepy all day long but cannot sleep at night. Fear of the dark is far more common among adults than most of us will admit. This issue alone is a significant factor in sleep disorders. Although night shift work and jet lag are problems, this chapter will not include those issues. Restless leg syndrome is a common debilitating sleep hazard (described in the book *Emotional Transformation Therapy: An Interactive Ecological Psychotherapy*).

In addition to insomnia, problems of hypersomnia, or too much sleep, may be a huge issue for many people. Again, hypersomnia takes place in several variations. Some examples of excessive sleep disorders include the following:

- Sleeping too many hours per day (ten or more)
- Inability to wake up for many hours
- Dread of getting up in the morning
- Inability to get up after awakening

These problems of excessive sleep are less common than insomnia but are equally as problematic. There are also sleep issues such as sleepwalking. Sleep apnea, which has become more prevalent, produces the risk of anoxia and even death. Many sleep partners complain about snoring as a major factor related to insomnia. Bedwetting or enuresis has long been a problem among children. Bruxism or the grinding of teeth during the night is also problematic.

The number of different types of sleep disorders is huge. Therefore, this chapter will focus primarily upon insomnia and the factors that contribute to it. It is important to understand what normal or healthy sleep is.

BRAIN ACTIVITY DURING SLEEP

In terms of brainwave patterns, there is a pattern that is well known that characterizes normal sleep. In stage 1, a person becomes gradually drowsy as beta brainwaves give way to alpha brainwaves. Then the brain descends directly through each slower brainwave state until it reaches the deepest part of sleep within about fifty minutes. After experiencing delta at its deepest point, the normal sleep pattern of brainwaves rises to rapid eye movement (REM) sleep at about ninety minutes after initially falling asleep. Next, brainwave patterns plunge through to the delta brainwaves again for the second and last time. The brainwaves get faster as they ascend to REM sleep again every ninety minutes. The pattern goes up and down every ninety minutes throughout the rest of the eight hours of sleep. Therefore, the brain needs to go through every different brainwave state repeatedly, except for beta, in order for the full benefits of sleep to take place.

Sleep research makes it clear that disruption of any part of the normal sleep pattern causes significant negative consequences for one's waking state. Optimal sleep occurs as a process of change through each brainwave state.

When stressful or traumatic events occur while a person is operating within a certain brainwave state, the memory of that event can often be associated with that particular brainwave state. Then, when the brain reenters that brainwave state during sleep, it risks either triggering the reemergence of the emotions related to the trauma or the defense mechanism necessary to protect the person from re-experiencing it. One defense may be to thrust the sleeping person into a waking state in order to avoid re-experiencing the pain of the trauma, resulting in insomnia. These experiences tend to occur spontaneously without interaction or control. In addition to purely psychological issues, physical pain, environmental noise, or unpleasant temperature can disrupt the sleep pattern.

FEAR AND DARKNESS

One of the most pervasive issues related to falling asleep and sleep issues in general is fear of the dark. Adults are sometimes uncomfortable about admitting how great this fear may be. Many times clients are in denial about their fear of darkness. Typically, this fear is related to a fear of loss of control. Then clients often choose to sleep in a room that is too highly lighted. The presence of too much light causes a shutting down of melatonin secretion, which results in an inability to sleep.

Nighttime has long been associated with fear and psychological distress. The fact is that more violent crime takes place at night. Events that encourage disinhibition occur most at night, such as parties. One can make a case for the existence of "night consciousness" versus "day consciousness." Understanding these differences has implications for treatment. The following is a list of the differing features of night and day consciousness (illustration 4.1):

Focus on inner world	→	Focus on outer world
Child-like views	→	Adult views
Emotional reasoning	→	Intellectual reasoning
Less inhibited thoughts and expression	→	More inhibited thoughts and expression
Experiential spiritual events	→	Conceptual spiritual ideas
Projection of meaning from within the person onto environmental events	→	Reception of information from environmental events outside of the person

ILLUSTRATION 4.1

Fear of darkness is often related to a perceived loss of control. The severity of this type of fear can vary widely from person to person. Whatever the origin of one's fear in the night, that fear is pursued via any of the four ETT® modalities.

CATEGORIES OF SLEEP DISORDERS

Researchers have divided sleep disorders into secondary and primary sleep disorders. Secondary sleep disorders account for the majority of sleep disorders. Secondary sleep disorders occur as a consequence of other conditions such as physical pain, illness, injury, or psychological disorders. Primary sleep disorders emerge from the nature of sleep itself, such as narcolepsy, obstructive breathing, or circadian rhythm disorders (Hirskowitz, 2009, p. 68). In most cases ETT® alleviates secondary sleep disorders without ever directly addressing these symptoms because the sleep disorder was a consequence of emotional distress that occurred during the daytime. In other words, the sleep disorder was secondary to the psychological symptoms, which had prevailed during waking hours. However, in the case of malfunctioning circadian rhythms, the suprachiasmic nucleus of the hypothalamus that governs circadian rhythms is itself controlled by external light. This makes light stimulation via ETT® an optimal form of treatment.

LIFESTYLE ISSUES REGARDING FALLING ASLEEP

There are several factors that contribute to different types of insomnia. Many of the factors fit into lifestyle issues. For example, a sedentary lifestyle does not allow the body to receive enough stimulation to sufficiently tire the body into needing sleep. Sedentary daylight experience appears to confuse the brain's sleep mechanisms to differentiate inactivity from sleep time. The remedy for this is physical exercise. Lifestyle habits are often deeply ingrained and may require several sessions to correct them.

On the other hand, some people live a lifestyle that is filled with continual activity and active cognition. When this busy activity extends up to the moment of the time to sleep, it often becomes difficult to transition to sleep. These people lack time to transition from being active to inactive. One remedy for this is to learn how to wind down. Some people are avoiding their own inner thoughts and feelings by keeping mentally busy. If alpha brainwave states of inner awareness and relaxation are avoided, the very states needed for a drowsy transition are omitted. This results in an inability to fall asleep.

Many people live a lifestyle in which they rarely get any exposure to sunlight. The spectral distribution of fluorescent light or even incandescent light is not even close to the type of lighting produced by natural sunlight. This abnormal exposure affects the biological clock in ways that may not be conducive to normal circadian rhythms.

Another obstacle to falling asleep is worry, obsessive thinking, and a "racing" mind. These cognitive activities may occur on occasion or almost every night. If the person is diagnosed with obsessive compulsive disorder, then ETT® can help. Peripheral eye stimulation through the use of the peripheral goggles is particularly valuable for use with the "racing mind" syndrome. In more severe cases, the therapist can prescribe the peripheral goggles for the client to use at night. Otherwise, worry can be processed to completion through the use of a light emitting device during ETT® sessions.

Adults who have grown up in chaotic households with little or no structure may lack awareness concerning the relationship between food consumption and sleep. Some people eat at a time very close to bedtime, which makes falling asleep difficult. Some people eat so much earlier before bedtime that their hunger may interfere with falling asleep. Others use food or drink as medicine to help them fall asleep.

Other food consumption issues involve the use of food or drink that alters the nervous system. Caffeine in coffee, tea, or energy drinks can contribute to difficulty falling asleep or maintaining sleep. The consumption of significant sugar too close to bedtime can disrupt falling asleep or staying asleep. Before attempting psychotherapy for sleep disorders, it is valuable to first rule out these lifestyle factors. If resistance to changing these patterns exists, treatment should focus upon motives for this reluctance.

THE PHARMACEUTICAL SLEEP REMEDY

Because of this pervasive sleep disorder epidemic, pharmaceutical companies are offering all types of sleep medications. Millions of people are using prescriptions like Ambien and Lunesta. Millions more rely on over-the-counter sleep aids like Tylenol PM. Many people, however, believe that abnormal sleep is preferable to no sleep at all and see pharmaceuticals as their only option for insomnia. However, sleep medications may not elicit the normal brainwave patterns of optimal sleep. In addition, sleep medication may develop entirely new problems. For example, Ambien users may sleepwalk and take all types of high risk actions during sleep. Mature judgment is absent for many Ambien users. Auto accidents are now accounted for by drivers being under the influence of Ambien. Several people have used it every night for months or even years, producing a serious addiction. People often become terrified by the thought of eliminating sleep medication and will not take the risk of temporary sleep loss to pursue a natural resolution. Physicians who do not monitor the use of sleep medications inadvertently support the addiction that occurs with continued use. Many people are unaware of other alternatives, so they feel compelled to take a drug for sleep.

Under normal circumstances melatonin secretion is blocked during the day if exposure to sufficient light takes place. This results in melatonin secretion during sleep at night. Melatonin is the most natural and safest substance to take for many people. However, some people complain that it lacks potency or has other side effects that may be undesirable. One must search to find the best brand of melatonin and the best amount to fit each individual. Because its use may compromise endogenous production of melatonin, it is important to use sleep aids like melatonin infrequently and to avoid dependence on any substance. Alternatives to substance use provide the best means for achieving a normal sleep brainwave pattern.

ETT® INSOMNIA TREATMENT

If insomnia persists after lifestyle issues have been resolved, the following procedures are used. The treatment of insomnia involves identifying the exact nature of the person's insomniac pattern. Then the photo assessment technique is used to reactive a degree of the psychophysical state the person is in during the insomnia. For example, in some cases there are problems choosing to go to bed and/or falling asleep and/or reawakening during the night. In these cases the issues are pursued as they occur in sequence. This begins with the problem of choosing to go to bed, which is usually resolved during one session, then falling asleep is treated in the next session, and reawakening is the focus in the third session. One full session for each component of the insomnia pattern is the typical regimen.

People who find it difficult to decide to go to bed tend to exhibit certain issues. In one case a woman believed she had a seemingly endless number of tasks to get done, which was coupled with a strong sense of responsibility. Therefore, the ETT® session focused on these issues, first by means of SRT and then with the Chromapulse II. These chronic emotions were resolved, which allowed her to go to bed at an appropriate time. When working with sleep disorders one does not know the outcome until after the person has had an opportunity to test the sleep issues overnight. In this case two days later we knew that the treatment was successful. However, the next objective was to achieve falling asleep. The photo assessment procedure (described in the book *Emotional Transformation*

Therapy: An Interactive Ecological Psychotherapy) was used to reactivate this condition. Then amplified attunement and peripheral eye stimulation with the Chromapulse II eliminated this issue in a single session.

The issue of awakening from sleep and not being able to go back to sleep is a common form of insomnia. In this case it is essential to ask numerous questions in order to acquire a clear and complete picture of all the features of the reawakening experience. Typical features are the following:

- a "racing mind" of rapid and continuous thinking
- a wide awake mind but lethargic body
- physical body agitation but a lethargic mind
- fully activated mind and body
- urinary urgency
- hunger

It is important to acquire the exact configuration of symptoms in order to target them effectively. Most of the aforementioned symptoms, especially physical agitation have been found to be associated with the brain's basal ganglia. The wavelengths of light in the red range have been found to consistently reduce the over-activated basal ganglia, which results in reduction of this type of awakening at night. However, the photo assessment procedure is used to reactivate the unique cluster of symptoms for each client. Then ETT® techniques are used to relieve this psychophysical template. This procedure consistently tends to extinguish the nighttime awakening problem. This same procedure is applied to the problem of waking up too early.

Sometimes repeated experiences of insomnia develop dysfunctional associations with anything related to the failed sleep experience. People begin to dread nighttime because it reminds them of the frustrating insomniac problem. The following case study illustrates this issue and how ETT® processes where used for it.

Julie's Case

Julie entered the session in tears as she yelled about her frustrating insomnia. She said she was overwhelmed with exhaustion. She said, "I have a headache and I cannot sleep, no matter what I do." Julie described weeks of continuous nights of insomnia. She was a fifty-five-year-old married woman who had fought nighttime anxiety for months. When she collapsed totally exhausted and ready to sleep, as soon as she lay in her bed, anxiety would suddenly awaken her. She had developed an association with her bed from the repeated frustration of insomnia that made a bed the trigger for her anxiety. I selected the SRT process to pursue this issue.

On green Julie described her fearful association with the bed but received no relief. On red Julie said, "When I lay down my brain switches to hypervigilant. I am so afraid of the anxiety. I feel fullness in my brain and every little sound in the room becomes loud!" The colors appeared stable as she clearly disclosed her emotions.

Next I asked Julie to view purple on the spectral chart. She said, "My thinking speeds up while I am in bed; all the sounds get loud and I cannot figure out how to reverse it." Then I had Julie look at orange and she said, "It feels like I get a shot of caffeine. I fought insomnia so much that I feel afraid to lie in the bed." Then she suddenly said, "It now feels less intense when I talk about it." Nonetheless, she had a headache.

Then I had Julie look at indigo. Here she said that her headache was gone. When she next viewed yellow, Julie began to yawn repeatedly. I requested her to describe her emotions regarding her bed and insomnia. Julie could barely talk about it because she became overwhelmed with repeated yawning and relaxation and then began to laugh. On blue Julie described that her exhaustion turned into a comfortable relaxation.

That night the dread of the bed was no longer present. This issue never emerged again after several weeks.

This case proceeded well, in part, because Julie was well aware of her emotions and was very able to express them. The color stimulation served as a catalyst to accelerate her progress through her distress. By processing her distress that linked her bed with fear, the association between the two was dismantled.

TRAUMA AND SLEEP

Night terrors are different from dreams in that they do not occur during REM sleep. They involve sudden jolts of terror in which the client acts out their fear behaviorally without recognizing that the danger is not present. It appears to be a re-enactment of a traumatic response that is lodged in slow brainwave states. When the brain activity passes through the delta or theta brainwaves, it risks re-awakening terror from previous life experiences that has been repressed into implicit memory. The use of flicker rates from 1 to 6 can elicit these slow brainwave states and move the frightening issue into awareness.

Trauma research clearly demonstrates that a correlation exists between those traumatic experiences that occur at night versus those that occur during the day. Insomnia is a far more prevalent experience for those people whose sleep was disrupted by a traumatic experience than for those whose trauma occurred during daylight hours. When these traumas are processed to fruition, chronic insomnia tends to cease.

Posttraumatic Sleep Pattern

What I am calling "posttraumatic sleep pattern" is a unique phenomenon. In post traumatic sleep pattern a triggering event activates a previous traumatic insomniac pattern from that person's life.

For example, women who have had children often awaken every two hours due to the infant's sleeping and feeding pattern for several months after the child's birth to care for the baby. Mothers often operate in a hypervigilant state of light sleep for months. After this phase of life ends, the mother's sleep often normalizes. Later in life, when events occur that elicit a hypervigilant orientation, the previous sleep pattern may re-emerge. However, this time once the pattern emerges, it continues without abating. This forms a pattern of insomnia in which the person awakens frequently. Therefore, ETT® treatment involves processing the hypervigilance and its underlying fear motives. Treatment often involves working through the emotions involved in the original insomniac experiences. When the work has been accomplished, a dramatic improvement in sleep patterns often results. The key is to uncover the unconscious hypervigilant emotions for which the client often possesses no awareness, and then resolve the motive for hypervigelance via ETT®. Because the linkage between the current trigger and the previous sleep pattern is often not apparent, posttraumatic sleep patterns are difficult to detect.

Gary's Case

Gary was sleepy and complained of insomnia. During the interview he appeared to drift in and out of falling asleep. He was a fifty-five-year-old, married physician with two adolescent children. His chronic sleepiness was a result of sheer exhaustion from not being able to sleep at night. In desperation he pleaded for help. His concern for his patients and family revealed the role reversal attachment pattern.

When I placed Gary in front of the Chromapulse II device to explore issues that might be contributing to his insomnia, he drifted into a brief sleep during the conversation. As I inquired about his stressors, he described deep concern about his adolescent son expressing suicidal thoughts. Almost every night his son would go to Gary's room and want to talk. These talks often involved his son's suicidal thoughts. Gary wanted to be responsive to his son, so he listened and gave advice. However, the son failed to take action.

As Gary shared his concerns about his son, I asked if he had ever felt anything like this before. At first he said no. Then Gary recalled that when he was going through his hospital residency after medical school he would often have to work thirty-six-hour shifts. During these shifts there were about ten to fifteen people per night that had to be resuscitated to avert death. He recognized that his son's suicidal thoughts triggered a re-activation of the traumatic medical residency during which he was very sleepy. Some people died and others barely survived during Gary's residency. Gary's pattern of hypervigilant survival responses was re-activated by his son's talk of suicide, and he was unable to conclude this traumatic sleep pattern.

We processed Gary's emotions about the residency experience to conclusion using the light device. The next therapeutic target was helping him release the worry about his son's suicidal thoughts. This issue was released using red-orange to differentiate him from his son. After a couple of sessions Gary's normal sleep pattern was improved. This case is an example of how an unresolved sleep trauma can be triggered. Later, I ended up working with Gary's son, and much of his distress was alleviated in five sessions.

PRIMARY SLEEP DISORDERS

Among the primary sleep disorders is sleep apnea, which involves the blockage of the airways during sleep and results in a loss of oxygen to the brain. In many cases sleep apnea is related to chronic snoring. Conventional treatment for sleep apnea is either surgery or the use of CPAP (Continuous Positive Airway Pressure) devices (Lewis, Seale, Bartle, Watkins, & Ebden, 2004). Chronic sleep apnea frequently results in excessive sleepiness during the daytime (Reishtein, Pack, Maislin, Dinger, Bloxham, George, et al., 2006). However, getting people to comply with the nightly use of the CPAP device is often an issue (Hoy, Vennelle, Klingshott, Engleman, & Douglas, 1999). Therefore, people often look for other options for treating sleep apnea. One of the other options is based on a research project that demonstrated that consistent playing of the didgeridoo instrument for four months changes the musculature in the throat passage and eliminates sleep apnea (Putham, Suarez, Lo Cascio, Zahn, Heitz, & Braendli, 2005).

During ETT® sessions with clients suffering from sleep apnea, traumatic memories of a choking experience have emerged. This facilitation to awareness of implicit memory about a choking experience was processed to conclusion by the use of the Chromapulse II device. Subsequent to the resolution of the choking trauma, sleep apnea symptoms ceased. At this time it is too early to establish what proportion of sleep apnea cases have this correlation to choking trauma, but we now know that in some cases the resolution of the choking trauma may be the route to rapid relief.

BRUXISM

Bruxism involves grinding one's teeth during sleep at night. In most cases people have no conscious awareness of teeth grinding, but evidence of the deterioration of teeth and jaw fatigue or pain confirms the existence of bruxism. If bruxism occurs unabated, it can severely affect the usefulness of teeth. Dentists typically treat bruxism by having people wear teeth guards during sleep. While conventional treatment can protect the teeth, it offers few useful approaches to end the jaw clenching. This condition has been found to be related to unresolved affect within implicit memory. Since clients tend to have no awareness of this affect, many clients are in denial of this possibility.

SRT and the Chromapulse II device have both been used for bruxism. The first task is to elevate awareness about what emotions are involved, and once retrieved, help the client process these emotions. Typically, once these procedures are concluded, teeth grinding at night ceases. Unexpressed emotions, usually anger, are the contributing factors. Discovering factors that inhibit emotional expression may be critical to the resolution.

CIRCADIAN RHYTHM TREATMENT

Circadian rhythm dysfunctions may include patterns in which a person simply awakens at inappropriate times. In some cases people stay awake at night and need to sleep during the day. However, in these cases people are not awakened by a racing mind, physical pain, nor do they even worry. This lack of accompanying psychological distress suggests a circadian rhythm dysfunction that emerges from sleep patterns instead of distress intruding on sleep patterns.

In the case of circadian rhythm dysfunction, the wavelength of light in the blue range (between 440 nm and 485 nm) has been shown to have the greatest impact (Brainard, Hanifin, Greeson, Byrne, Glickman, Gerner, & Rollag, 2001).

There is a specific ETT® procedure used to correct circadian rhythm dysfunction. First, all stressors that are potentially a factor may need to be ruled out. Then any distress about the rhythmic night/day sleep pattern is processed to conclusion. The following procedure is used to correct circadian rhythm dysfunction:

- the wavelengths of blue on the RGB system are selected.
- while the client is viewing blue, he or she is encouraged to describe the subjective experience of the errant sleep cycle.
- during this mental focus the saturation level of blue is continually slowly altered.
- when the client begins to feel sleepy, this is an indication that the specific saturation level is shifting the biological clock controlling the day/night sleep pattern.
- at the time of sleepiness, the saturation level associated with the onset of sleepiness is held constant, and the client is allowed to close his or her eyes. This sleepy response suggests that the process has changed the circadian rhythm. This procedure suggests that the suprachiasmatic nucleus of the hypothalamus (biological clock) is being modulated.

There are other circadian rhythm problems such as jet lag or issues of night shift working. At this time protocols for treating these issues have not been pursued via ETT®.

RESOLVING NIGHTMARES

Disturbing dreams may be one of the most distressing problems related to sleep. There is a range of different views about the significance of dreams. On one hand, some brain researchers view night dreams as meaningless epiphenomena of the brain. However, Freud saw dreams as the royal road to the unconscious. There are numerous forms of dream interpretation, such as the Jungian approach and the Gestalt approach. ETT® does value the importance of night dreams and views nightmares as particularly relevant to the client's issues. The ETT® perspective differs in that instead of imposing a theory and an interpretation onto dreams, ETT® technique allows dream interpretations to emerge from within the client.

Currently, dreams are understood as occurring during the rapid eye movement portion of sleep in which brain hemisphere dominance is in the process of switching from one hemisphere to the other. This activity takes place every ninety minutes (and actually continues during the waking state without dreams) in what is called ultradian rhythms. Dream content is thought to be related to the consolidation of issues that occurred in the previous day's waking state. If these issues have not been resolved, they fail to consolidate and can culminate in nightmares of various types. The ETT® approach assumes that unresolved affective issues are central to this failure to consolidate. ETT® dreamwork is called Luminous Dreamwork. It pursues resolution of the affective element of dreams. This results in cognitive changes, visual imagery changes, and meaning changes. It has been found that this type of resolution to dreams impacts client's issues at a depth level. Therefore, dreamwork is often given priority over most other issues described in this book.

Some night dream recollections may emerge during an ETT® session. Dreams may occur within different formats. Recurrent dreams are believed to be of high significance. Their general message is that an unresolved issue wants attention and has not been appropriately addressed. Sometimes flashbacks of traumatic memories may occur in the form of night dreams. However, at other times these memories may occur within symbolic representations.

Many people do not recall dreams. Other people may not recall dreams until they spontaneously occur during ETT® sessions. Other people may recall dreams only when specific procedures are used to activate dream retrieval. ETT® utilizes dream retrieval techniques. In some cases dreams spontaneously become conscious as ETT® work increases self-awareness. Lucid dreaming (becoming aware one is dreaming during a dream) can be used to assist in problematic dreams. Dream incubation technique can be used to allow night dreams to function as a means to resolve one's issues. Finally, transpersonal dreams or dreams that involve spiritual events can provide depth, inspiration, and resolution when they occur.

The objectives of Luminous Dreamwork include the following:

- Understanding the meaning of dreams
- Resolving disturbing emotion in dreams or as a consequence of dreams
- Stopping disturbing recurrent dream patterns
- Promoting increased awareness through dreams
- Advancing therapeutic goals

When disturbing dreams have occurred during the night before a session, dreamwork may become the priority in the session. If one or more dreams are long and complex, dreamwork may require the entire session. Therefore, the dream processing should begin early in a session. It is important to process dreams as close to the night of the dream as possible because if the dream is weeks, months, or years old, the person's issues may have changed to render the dream's messages obsolete.

Dream recollection during ETT® sessions often represents an emergence of implicit memory into consciousness. This is a fairly common phenomenon with clients undergoing ETT® sessions. Dream symbols can easily become unraveled by simply asking the client questions about the symbol's possible meaning while visual stimulation via ETT® tools is taking place. The therapist can make suggestions about meanings but interpretations are a mutually collaborative process.

Luminous Dreamwork involves the following steps:

First, retrieval of dreams is necessary. At times a client may recall only a dream fragment. In this case when it is reviewed during light stimulation either the meaning of the fragment may emerge or the rest of the dream may be recalled. The use of the flicker rate of eight to ten cycles per second reactivates the same brainwave state in which dreams occur. Therefore, this flicker rate can be a means of priming dream recollection. A variety of other techniques for dream recall can be used, but intention to recall one's dream appears to be the main factor.

Second, it is preferable to have the client bring a typed copy of the dream into the session. The process of writing up the dream itself may evoke further awareness. Then while the client is repeating the dream during light stimulation, awareness tends to emerge spontaneously. This allows the therapist to identify the key points of emotion in the dream that are targeted for processing.

Third, amplified attunement is conducted with each affective state, which tends to resolve emotional disturbance as well as actually change the course and content of the dream itself.

Fourth, various ETT® procedures that facilitate emotional resolution may be used to relieve the disturbance.

Often memories arise as the therapeutic process allows the dream to be unraveled. The symbolic representation of the dream may simply occur as imagery that masks the actual traumatic memories. When these unresolved memories arise, ETT® procedures of various types may be used to resolve them. Matching the wavelength of light with affective state is the first choice in the ETT® decision tree, and then peripheral eye stimulation is next.

It is usually necessary to undergo the first four procedures again as the complete dream is retold. The retelling process tends to promote more awareness of dream meanings and linkage to other issues or concepts. Spontaneous awareness of dream meanings tends to arise during this procedure, which spares the facilitator the role of dream interpreter. After the affect from disturbing dreams is complete, the client is encouraged to narrate a summary of the dream, usually with indigo stimulation, in order to consolidate the learning.

Nightmare Case Study

Natasha had a slightly confused look on her face, but was not currently upset in any way when she reported that she had a nightmare the previous night. She said that the dream did not make sense and was very disorganized. Natasha was an attractive fifty-year-old single female with long, flowing blonde hair and a classic Russian accent. I recommended that we pursue resolution of the nightmare and she said that she wanted that. I asked her to first tell me the entire dream as we sat facing each other. The following was her initial recollection of that dream.

> I am visiting Moscow where I am originally from. I am in my apartment. My best friend calls me to tell me she is in the area, but she has no time to meet with me. I am upset in the dream thinking that I have traveled around the world and she is not making time to see me. I feel I am not important. Then I find myself wandering the streets of Moscow. I am in a sporting goods store trying on shoes. Then I keep noticing a couple of people with round faces. Everywhere I go, I feel there is some kind of a connection between me and them.
>
> Then I end up meeting a friend at a downtown restaurant and that couple is there at the table next to us. My friend ends up talking to that couple next to us. I feel left out. A very dark man showed up from out of nowhere. The man is very dark (Mediterranean type). His hair, eyes, clothes, demeanor is all disturbingly dark. Then the man pulls out a Turkish sword and tries to cut me, but disappears before he touches me. I am very scared and want to scream.

Natasha was very intellectual and detached from emotion as she told her nightmare, except for the last part involving the dark man when fear appeared to briefly emerge in her voice inflection. The second step in the dream procedure involved the use of the Chromapulse II. I had her view blue-green (red-0, green-50, blue-50). As she looked at this wavelength of light she was to completely retell the dream in sequence. However, this time if emotion arose at any point, we would stop there and process that affect.

This time when she retold the dream while viewing blue-green, as she got to the part where her friend was not available to see her, Natasha erupted into deep sobbing. At that point green saturation level was slowly elevated, which resulted in lessening the intensity of her sadness. Further process occurred at red-0, green-255, and blue-0.

Intermittent weeping continued to take place as Natasha suddenly recalled a childhood trauma in which Natasha was abandoned by her mother. Intensity of sadness emerged as she recalled this painful event that occurred around age five. At this point Natasha was directed to view the periphery of the light at the three o'clock position. Here Natasha's affect initially eased but as she spoke about her feelings, the intensity elevated. Therefore, she was directed to move her visual focus to the nine o'clock peripheral position. The same experience of initial reduction of emotional intensity followed by emotional escalation took place at the nine o'clock position as well as six o'clock and then twelve o'clock position. Simultaneously the change in the saturation level of green took place to ease affect intensity at each location. Suddenly at seven o'clock sadness ended and anger about her abandonment arose. This was met by a change in wavelengths from green to yellow, where anger was processed. After expressing this anger, the peripheral position was changed to one o'clock. At that point Natasha reported an internal shaking and she described feelings related to loss of control. Yellow wavelengths were elevated and all shaking ceased.

Next the peripheral position was changed to seven o'clock. Here Natasha reported fear of dying and bodily shaking activated. The wavelengths were changed to red at saturation 100 and Natasha reported a complete cessation of shaking and a secure bodily sense of peace. It appeared that all distress concluded.

The next step in the procedure was to have Natasha look directly at the light and verbally report the entire dream all over again. This time when Natasha got to the part of the dream in which her friend did not have time to visit her, Natasha laughed spontaneously and said, "Who cares."

This time, in the dream retelling, when she was walking the streets of Moscow alone, Natasha said, "Great, I can do whatever I want since I am alone!" At the sporting goods store she saw the couple with rounded faces and described their faces as kind. "They are here to protect me and have been following me for a while." Natasha spontaneously described these people as her angels. At this point Natasha cried but reported that her tears were about overwhelming peace and joy. The brightness of the light was elevated, which strengthened her positive feeling. Next she said she met with her friend at a restaurant and her angels were close by.

Finally when Natasha's friend started talking to her angels, the dark man with the sword showed up. When Natasha's desire to scream emerged, I elevated the saturation of blue to 45 and the urge released. Then the dark evil man was "sucked away into the light" and Natasha said that she felt safe.

During this dreamwork several important changes took place. First, the dream was reported exactly as Natasha recalled it. Second, when she verbalized the dream on blue-green the emotions that occurred during the dream emerged. Third, the first emotions that emerged during the dream verbalization were processed to completion. Fourth, the meaning of the dream spontaneously emerged without any interpretation by the facilitator. Fifth, once the emotions were concluded, the nature of the dream spontaneously changed. Sixth, the meaning of the two people with round faces was revealed as "angels," which comforted her. Seventh, the most frightening aspect of the dream, the evil dark man and the need to scream disappeared into the light.

Subsequent to the dreamwork Natasha described herself as calm and light. The nightmare was fully understood. She reported that when she felt contact with her angels, it was a familiar experience that she had forgotten.

Since ETT® possesses the unique attributes of rapid regulation of emotion and the use of light (which controls the part of the brain responsible for sleep rhythms), ETT® has strengths that have a direct bearing on sleep issues. However, most people appear to limit their beliefs to the pharmaceutical form of remedy. Therefore, this issue is not about whether ETT® can work for these objectives, but instead can people open themselves, become open to non-drug answers? Sleep is of vital importance. The ETT® approach may be the most direct and consistent non-drug means for solving these challenging issues.

5

An End to Physical Pain

Generally stoic, Anita's face showed a hint of resignation as she asked for help with her lower back pain. Detached intellectualization dominated her demeanor. Anita's physician had ordered an MRI and x-rays to evaluate her pain. She was told that the stenosis could not account for the amount of pain she felt in her back. She said, "I went to a chiropractor for it and that made it worse." Anita was annoyed with the back pain because it interfered with many of the activities that she wanted to enjoy.

I requested that Anita take a seat in front of the light device. The initial focus of the session was to reduce the level of irritability concerning her lower back pain. On yellow (red-150, green-150, blue-0), Anita talked about her constant irritation with her back pain. We used peripheral eye stimulation on the light device. She had an insight that her back pain was due to all the years she felt burdened by taking care of her elderly mother, but recognized that the burden no longer existed since her mother had died months ago. At another peripheral position she described that her back pain was tiring and she had other things to do. At this point she was soothed by my responses. Then the wavelengths were changed to red-orange (red-255, green-30, blue-0) for the purpose of facilitating differentiation from her mother. The flicker rate of the light was changed to 5.0 and color at blue-green (red-0, green-100, blue-104). Here she reported that her low back pain's message was to slow down and not try to do everything, but she recalled that "to lie around was not okay." Anita was affirmed for her awareness.

However, it was apparent that Anita became self-aware on these wavelengths of light during brainwave entrainment. The back pain was a little better. Therefore, at the end of the session I recommended that she come to my office for thirty minute self-sessions. She was directed to use red-orange for fifteen minutes and blue-green for fifteen minutes, at a flicker rate of 8 cps with her attention directed to her low back pain and self-perception issues.

After one week Anita returned to a session and reported that she did not notice much effect. However, as we proceeded with a light-stimulated session, one insight after another arose and her low back pain was reduced dramatically. The focus of the session was on physical accidents that might have contributed to her low back pain. The emotions associated with each accident emerged and were rapidly processed to completion. Anita was surprised at her sudden insights and pleased with the elimination of low back pain. Her self-perception had improved. She left that session exhilarated. Anita returned the next week with even more exhilaration about both her pain-free state and her emotional state. One year later Anita reports a fun life with no low back pain.

Many people with low back pain possess little awareness of the mind-body connection as well as little self-awareness in general. These people are not in denial in the classic sense, but instead possess little or no alpha brainwave pattern (the brainwave state vibrates at seven to eleven cycles per second). By having Anita do a week of daily sessions that entrain brainwaves to alpha, her access to self-awareness became possible. This could take place during facilitator-led sessions, but frequent self-work sessions can prepare the person to make substantial gains in the next session, as it did with Anita. This frequent daily work is valuable when long-term chronic pain is entrenched as a pattern.

THE SCOURGE OF PHYSICAL PAIN

Physical pain may be the worst form of human suffering. While acute physical pain is often miserable, it is temporary. However, chronic physical pain may last for months, years, or even a lifetime. Fifteen to twenty percent of all adults suffer every day with chronic pain. Pharmaceuticals can reduce most physical pain for a short time, but pharmaceuticals are not designed to provide long-term relief of chronic pain, nor can they completely eliminate most pain without the risk of developing a dependency on the substance. Conventional medicine is not equipped to provide successful long-term relief of chronic physical pain and if it does, the process is usually a very long one. About half of primary care patients have chronic pain that does not get any better after a year (Porreca &

Price, 2009, p. 34). This situation has prompted a huge variety of alternative modalities to pursue pain resolutions, many of which prey on people in need. In many cases people are so desperate that they are willing to try extreme measures such as painful testing procedures, the surgical severing of entire nerve groups, and expensive surgical implants. In this atmosphere, a proliferation of alternative modalities like chiropractic care, Chinese medicine, and Ayurveda has become more popular, as have dozens of over-the-counter creams, pills, and gadgets.

ISSUES WITH CHRONIC PAIN TREATMENT

I spoke with an orthopedic surgeon about low back pain. He stated that he could tell by the x-rays that his surgery had corrected the spinal problems, yet in about fifty percent of his cases the physical pain persisted in spite of surgical success. At that point he told me that "we are obviously missing something because according to the physical correction, the pain should no longer exist."

While physicians usually recognize that stress plays a role in most medical conditions, they often lack the mental health training to make recommendations that possess a realistic chance to work. My clients have told me that their physicians sometimes told them to "relax," but this "instruction" does little to teach the actual skills of relaxation, especially when one is challenged by work and family responsibilities. While these physicians were technically correct that relaxation would help, clients with anxiety disorders can be highly treatment-resistant and can rarely relax by conscious choice alone.

Not only does conventional medicine often fail to alleviate chronic pain, but in many cases it worsens and/or complicates these conditions with risks of more pain, drug side effects, or prescription addiction. One of my worst fears was verified while speaking to a group of physicians who were in their residency program. When I asked them how their supervising physicians handled patients who asked for more pain medication after the appropriate amount had been prescribed, I was told that doctors should give patients what they want or they would risk losing patients to another doctor. Marketing research has found that the majority of physicians will provide a drug if the patient requests it. Therefore, widely circulated commercials now commonly add this advice: "Ask your doctor if x drug is right for you." However, I have had some patients tell me that their doctors "push" these medications on them. Whichever way it might be, there is often some type of collusion that creates unnecessary medication use because no other way to solve the pain problem is known.

Given the wide variety of conditions that cause physical pain, isolating the common denominator in all of them is important. Psychological stress is almost always present in physical pain conditions. Western medicine, which has created psychiatric medications for psychological stress, cannot, however, provide a long-term solution that does not also produce dependency. In other words, it does not cure the cause of the pain. Much of Western medicine simply attempts to manage stress with medication. Other natural methods for the relief of stress sometimes offer temporary relaxation, but also fall short in providing a long-term remedy. Even in the field of psychotherapy one may receive support and understanding for the experiences, but most psychotherapy methods do not provide a means to eliminate the stress that ties directly into the physical pain itself.

Many people who have seen psychotherapists for numerous sessions and experienced the improvement of mental health issues have still found no relief for the accompanying physical pain. Most therapists do not view symptoms of physical pain as falling within their domain. This scenario gives the patient a doctor who is not well versed on how to alleviate stress and a psychotherapist who is not well versed on the interface between psychological activity and physical symptoms. The client's issues are left "falling between the cracks" of everyone's specialty. As a result there are now multidisciplinary pain centers that attempt to provide professionals in several disciplines working together as a team. However, my experience with these centers has been that most of them are often comprised of professionals with separate specialties, but they do not often custom tailor treatment as a team.

IS PHYSICAL PAIN "ALL IN THEIR HEADS"?

Due to a lack of understanding, a lack of empathy, or a limited belief system, people who experience physical pain are often not believed by their friends, family, or physicians. In common vernacular their experience of physical pain is believed to be "all in their heads." Since it is well known that some people report having physical pain when they do not actually have it, this stereotype is often placed on people who have physical pain but are not understood, and their pain is often unrecognized as legitimate due to the limited belief system of the caregivers.

Because reports of physical pain without a confirmed physical source do occur, it should be noted that some of these people may fit into one of the following categories:

1. Hypochondria: people who obsessively worry about imagined medical problems but have no medical evidence to confirm it, may be hypochondriacs.
2. Malingering: people who fake having medical problems and know these problems do not actually exist are malingerers.
3. Somatoform Disorders: people who possess definite psychological conditions that are experienced as functional physical deficits without medical verification, such as temporary paralysis, fit into this category.

While all three of these conditions exist, my experience is that they are not the norm and comprise only a small percentage of reported physical pain conditions. If a condition does not occur within the paradigm of conventional medicine, it is far too often labeled as contrived by the patient in some way. We do have strategies to promote recovery from hypochondria or malingering conditions, but these strategies will not be the focus of this chapter. Instead, the focus will be on physical pain conditions, many of which appear to be spurious to conventional medical wisdom, but do in fact exist. Well-known physical pain conditions such as low back pain, migraine headaches, sciatica, temporomandibular joint pain, regional pain syndrome, and others will be the focus.

Even though severe depression or intense anxiety may be experienced by people suffering from chronic physical pain, most people do not seek psychological help. A motive for avoiding psychological counseling is that these people typically want medical professionals to confirm the physical existence of their pain. If they went to a psychotherapist, it could be seen as a concession to others that their pain is "not real." Therefore, these people often want a clear medical diagnosis that, in their minds, confirms the reality of the experience. This mindset places the physician in a difficult situation. If the doctor recommends any form of psychological counseling, the patient may become upset, believing that the recommendation means the physical condition cannot be verified. Due to this unfortunate misunderstanding of mind-body interactions, most chronic pain patients do not reach any form of psychotherapy until the condition has worsened over a long period time. In desperation and as a last resort, these patients may eventually attempt some form of counseling. Therefore, educating the client about emotional and physical interaction and validating clients about the reality of their pain is essential during initial sessions.

Many of the problems encountered in treating physical pain exist in part due to a limited perspective that categorizes physical symptoms as medical and psychological symptoms as separate from physiology. In spite of the fact that it is largely recognized that many medical conditions are stress-related, most treatments still treat the mind and body separately and conceive of these conditions through separate theories. Furthermore, the general public tends to divide conditions into medical or psychological even more rigidly. What is lost in these views is the interaction between psychological and physiological components.

A NEW UNDERSTANDING OF THE INTERACTION BETWEEN MIND AND BODY

Much of the research regarding physical pain has been stimulated by the gate control theory, a theory that has provided the primary perspective in the history of pain and one accepted by conventional medicine. This theory generated research that provided new information about the nature of pain. Among the findings was the concept that physical pain experienced in the body descends from mechanisms in the brain, in addition to impulses ascending to the brain from peripheral nerves. The descending neural circuits emanate from the periaqueductal gray part of the brain, which has reciprocal connections to the reticular formation and the nuclei in the rostral medulla. The periaqueductal gray has the potential for activating enkephalin-releasing neurons into a sequence of biochemical activities that can eventually lead to pain inhibition (Melzak & Wall, 1965). These neural circuits and brain mechanisms are also involved in the experience of emotion related to the fight, flee, or freeze defense responses, which can contribute to pain. Therefore, these neural circuits can be involved in either the experience of pain or its inhibition.

Much of the control of physical pain emerges from mechanisms in the brain. Therefore, interventions that can accurately target these brain mechanisms should be able to change the experience of physical pain. Visually initiated impulses in the brain can be used to target brain mechanisms responsible for the emotional component of physical pain, which appears to activate the analgesic function of brain mechanisms responsible for physical pain inhibition.

The neurochemistry of the descending system involves the norepinephrine-containing system and the serotonin-containing system, which interact with the endogenous opioid system. The serotonin and norepinephrine systems are also known to be associated with the biological basis of emotions. Therefore, physical pain biochemistry is shared with affective biochemistry. Norepinephrine, which is associated with anxiety and depression, is commonly activated in response to illness or injury. Since serotonin is replenished during sleep, if physical pain interrupts stage 1 of sleep, the regulation of serotonin is often impaired, which contributes to depression (Nevens, 1999, p. 43). Therefore, neural circuits and associated biochemical processes involving physical pain, emotion, and sleep are related.

Since the neural circuits of the experience of physical pain and emotion overlap, it appears that pain could contribute to the emergence of the emotion or emotion could elicit the physical pain. Moreover, a repeated feedback loop in which physical pain evokes emotion and emotion exacerbates physical pain appears to be responsible for increasing the intensity of both, as well as contributing to the enduring nature of chronic pain. In addition, the entwined nature of physical pain and emotion also suggests that successful interventions that stop one of these experiences might reduce or eliminate the other one.

THE ENDOGENOUS OPIOID SYSTEM

Neuropeptides produced within our own bodies have been found to bind with opioid receptor sites, resulting in both the relief of physical pain and the production of psychological states of euphoria. The first neuropeptide identified was called enkephalin (Hughes & Kosterlitz, 1977, pp. 157–161). Others have been identified since then. Dynorphine, for example, has been found to have almost two hundred times the analgesic effect of morphine. Moreover, these informational substances are not confined to the brain and nervous system for transmission but can travel throughout the brain and body in extracellular fluids. Neuropeptide receptor sites have been mapped and now appear to exist extensively throughout the brain and body (Pert, 1977). This means that relief of physical pain is not dependent solely on the circuits of the nervous system.

The placebo effect for pain includes the idea that when someone expects little or no physical pain by virtue of a belief in a medicine or remedy, in fact little or no pain is likely to be experienced. It has been found that the placebo effect can be accounted for by the aqueductal gray's stimulation of endorphins that leads to pain relief (Fields, 2009, p. 45). However, the vast majority of ETT® clients do not initially expect ETT® to stop physical pain. Nonetheless, ETT® appears to utilize the same endogenous system within the body to facilitate pain resolution (see illustration 5.1; Purves, et al., 1997).

Our Endogenous Biochemical Pain Relief System

Periagueductal gray of the midbrain activates

↓

Enkephalin, releasing neurons that project to

↓

Raphe nuclei in the brainstem, which releases

↓

5-HT (serotonin), which

↓

Descends to the dorsal horn of the spinal cord, which

↓

Forms excitatory connections with inhibitory interneurons located in the substantia gelatinosa.

↓

When activated, interneurons release either enkephalin or dinorphin, endogenous opioid neurotransmitters.

↓

Opioid neurotransmitters bind to mu-opioid receptors on axons of C and A delta fibers.

↓

C and A delta fibers carry pain signals to nociceptors that are activated in the periphery.

↓

Activation of mu-opiod receptors inhibits the release of substance P.

↓

Substance P inhibits neurons responsible for the pain signal up the spinothalamic tract to

↓

Ventroposteriolateral nucleus of the thalamus.

↓

Nociceptive signals become inhibited before they can reach cortical areas like the anterior cingulate that interprets it as "pain."

ILLUSTRATION 5.1

PHYSICAL PAIN, ATTACHMENT, AND EMOTION

Whenever physical pain is experienced, it has been consistently observed that an attachment-based emotional response is highly likely to occur. For example, some people react to physical pain by expressing emotional responses intensely and are unable to acquire closure to this emotional experience, whereas other people may deny or withhold emotional responses to physical pain. In the first case the ambivalent/resistant attachment pattern has occurred and in the second case the avoidant attachment pattern has taken place. These attachment patterns become established in enduring emotional neural networks from early life and tend to become automatic emotional responses. It appears that when these emotional neural networks exhaust the person's tolerance, these explicit emotional neural patterns re-route into implicit somatic neural circuits. The new somatic circuits tend to occur in the same "pattern" as the emotional pattern associated with attachment-based experience.

Case Study—Migraine Headache

With her stern demeanor, Suzanne looked very controlled, and her body movements were slow and rigid. She described having a migraine headache that she had had daily for sixteen years. On this day her physical pain level was at 4 (on a scale from 1 to 10 with 10 being worst), but the toll of migraines every day for so many years was wearing on her. Suzanne said, "I have tried every kind of conventional medicine I could find, as well as Ayurvedic and Chinese medicine, but nothing has worked beyond sometimes a temporary relief." Suzanne felt desperate at this point because her physician had explained that no better medication beyond the third tier, which she was currently taking, existed. This last tier of medication obviously did not have her pain under control. Her migraines occurred every morning upon waking and gradually worsened throughout the day. Suzanne felt a high sensitivity to light and sound all the time. The sunlight, even with sunglasses on, intensified her pain and sometimes made her throw up. Although Suzanne had been through twenty-five years of psychological counseling already, she was willing to try more if it might help alleviate her migraines. Suzanne's objectives were to acquire some pain relief as well as to gain some understanding of it.

I knew that daily migraine headaches were not the typical course of frequency for migraines. Suzanne's headaches were in the most severe category of migraines. I tried to demonstrate as much empathy and understanding as I could. I saw that she needed an immediate therapeutic intervention that could work, but she was not a candidate for light stimulation directly into her eyes due to her light sensitivity. Therefore, I selected the peripheral goggles because they actually reduce the amount of light entering the eyes. Suzanne reported watering in her eyes, and she knew that meant the pain was in the process of worsening.

As soon as the goggles were placed on her at the three o'clock opening for light to enter her eyes, she felt calmer. When she was asked what emotions she felt in reaction to having the pain, she said, "Scared, sad, angry, and hopeless." Then at nine o'clock she immediately reported feeling more energy in her torso and limbs. She said, "I get angry and fear never being without pain." Her pain level dropped to 3.5.

Next Suzanne was asked to close her eyes so I could change the peripheral angle. She reported feeling fearful when closing her eyes because "there was too much [she] could not see." At this nine o'clock position she felt an "energy drain," so the angle was quickly moved to six o'clock, but this time I nurtured her before moving it. However, she felt averse to this position.

At the twelve o'clock position Suzanne said she felt scared, anticipating a lot of light coming in at this position. She reported that her right eye continued to water and feel sensitive to the air. However, it was pointed out that the goggles actually protect her eyes from any breeze and we both began to realize that the sensation of a breeze on her eyes emerged from within her instead. The physical pain reduced at this position. While the peripheral angle was at twelve o'clock, she was instructed to look downward, which resulted in increasing the severity of the angle. As she did this she reported, "Energy comes back into my torso, slight pain in my left eye, and my head begins to hurt." Next she was asked to look right while keeping the goggles at twelve o'clock, which resulted in more left eye pain. Then I asked her to look left, which resulted in an instant reduction of pain in both eyes. She was encouraged to stay at this position longer. Then we continued to search for an even better response.

The next five clock positions yielded different physical and emotional experiences. At seven o'clock Suzanne described "a finer energy in [her] hands but still a little pain in the left part of [her] head." At one o'clock she felt calmer physically but her right eye felt more sensitive to air. She reported comfort here, but her sinuses began to fill up. At eight o'clock Suzanne felt fear initially and perceived of a lot of light coming into her eyes. At two o'clock she felt fear as well and pain in the right side of her head. At ten o'clock Suzanne felt less pain in the right eye, pain on the left side of her head, and pain between her eyebrows. Before the session, physical pain was constant and any changes in intensity were gradual. Suzanne said, "I have never before felt these instant changes in physical pain and emotional states." One of the therapeutic purposes of this technique is to map the variations in each peripheral eye position in order to gain information for future usage to disrupt the pain pattern.

Then at four o'clock Suzanne said she saw "a lot of light." However, she said, "I have a good feeling . . . expectant joy! This was surprising. I have no pain. It brings tears to my eyes because of the relief! I felt the headache moving to my left eye brow and it has a rolling quality. It feels like it is breaking up!"

I find it valuable to wait until physical pain is at least reduced or ideally eliminated before pursuing the underlying factors in a client's personal history that may have contributed to or initiated the physical pain. At first Suzanne was asked to simply savor her pain relief. Then she was asked when she first began to have migraines. I particularly sought to find out what emotions were occurring at the time of the origin of her pain. Suzanne said her entire pattern of migraines began when she was forty-five and her kids were leaving for college. She felt intense grief at the memory of it and began to weep with sadness. She was directed to change to the four o'clock peripheral angle by looking left. This immediately helped her to feel less sad. She said, "I felt like a parent most of my life and suddenly that job was over. I felt so lonely. I felt like I was redefining myself. Now I feel a little less sad." Then she was directed to look downward when the goggles were still at four o'clock and the sadness was gone as she felt calm. However, the excursion into her painful past provoked her headache to the level of .75, compared to 4 at the beginning of the session.

This first session accomplished six important therapeutic objectives:

1. A personal history interview provided a narrative context of her life.
2. Her physical pain was rapidly eliminated and reduced.
3. A rapport was developed that was intended to ultimately reverse attachment disorders.
4. The pattern of chronic intensity of both physical pain and emotional distress was broken up into discrete segments that brought a degree of closure.
5. Helplessness about her migraines shifted to hope.
6. An awareness of emotional responses related to a cluster of events that may have produced the migraines was identified.

Second Session One week later in the second session, Suzanne reported her pain level to be .75, and this extremely low level had been maintained since our first session. Peripheral eye stimulation was used until we identified a peaceful position. Then the events at age forty-five, concurrent with the onset of her migraines, were pursued. Overwhelm resulted from a divorce, suddenly working full time, her kids leaving home, and her mother having an affair with her brother-in-law. These events led to enormous emotional intensity. Therefore, changing peripheral positions quickly helped to de-escalate the emotional intensity that would otherwise have grown as she told her story. Physical pain also intensified at some peripheral positions, but by the end of the session it had lessened.

Then Suzanne was encouraged to review the session. As she did this, she noted that at thirteen her brother had been in an accident and had become a paraplegic. Suzanne still felt upset about this. This time eight o'clock gave her relief to end the session. This last awareness served as a segue way to the issue for the next session.

Third Session At the beginning of the session Suzanne reported that her headache had been worse for three days after the last session, but then she hardly felt it at all for the next few days. This was an entirely new pattern. Suzanne reported a couple of current stressors like automobile trouble and problems with remodeling her home. After the last session, recollections of trauma from her past began to emerge between sessions. This disruption of the migraine's pattern suggested therapeutic progress, because physical pain patterns typically show variance before they stop altogether. The awareness of unresolved memories suggested that the cluster of emotions at the onset of the migraine pattern, once accessed, opened awareness to related underlying emotions. It is important to reassure a client that any temporary worsening of physical pain should not be interpreted to mean that treatment has failed, but instead it indicates a break in the pattern of pain.

Next Suzanne reported that at age eleven her oldest brother, a huge support to her in lieu of a lack of bonding with her parents, had left home to go to college. At twelve her aunt died. This aunt had actually been the only nurturing "parent" in her life. Then at thirteen her second oldest brother had became quadriplegic due to an accident. As Suzanne reported these events she described her current emotions as irritable, hyperactive, and overwhelmed. Her pain was at the 2.5 level. After this disclosure, we immediately applied the use of peripheral goggles.

At three o'clock Suzanne felt a little calmer physically, as she reported the light shining directly on the head pain in the right quadrant. At nine o'clock she reported that she did not like this position because the light was not shining on the pain. This reveals a distinct difference in her relationship with light from earlier sessions because previously she had had an aversion to light. At six o'clock she reported diminished head pain and feeling more "grounded." After four more clock positions of varying physical pain and emotional discomfort, eight o'clock produced the most comfort. The purpose of the peripheral work was to reduce intensity of discomfort so that we might proceed to resolve the emotions of the trauma she had identified.

In order to identify her pattern of processing emotions and to acquire depth of emotional awareness, the spectral chart was employed. As Suzanne was directed to look at green, she was asked to further describe the trauma she identified at the beginning of the session. She described her household as one of chaos and conflict between her oldest brother and her father. Her father was characterized as angry and dominating, which caused her to be in continuous fear of his wrath. However, her oldest brother was the only one in the family who would confront him, and this made a fearful household into one of continuous chaos. This brother provided her with support and nurturance. Suzanne said: "I feel sad over the loss I had. I felt alone and had nobody to talk to. The green color keeps going away."

At this point the disappearance of the color indicated dissociation from emotion. Therefore, she was encouraged to look for any green she could see. As she found it, the saturation of green expanded. Once this color was retrieved, the awareness of emotion returned. Suzanne continued: "I am mad at my dad for making it so hard on him. I miss my brother. I miss the little stability the family had had. It all fell apart. Our family did not talk about our feelings period! I felt lost, invisible, alone."

Then Suzanne began to talk about how her aunt made her feel special. She was twelve when her aunt died. At this point I encouraged Suzanne to shift back to her brother so that that issue could be completed before complicating it with another one. This limitation and refocusing tends to move clients from endless intense emotion without completion to a thorough progression toward closure.

Her vision was next directed to the color red on the spectral chart, and she was asked to talk about the loss of her brother again. She continued to speak of feeling anger, sadness, and a lack of emotional closure. Next, Suzanne was directed to view purple and report the same story again. After describing it again, she reported that the intensity of her physical pain and emotion had lessened.

As Suzanne was directed to view the color orange and discuss this loss, she recalled much more detail and her headache became less intense. Then she again spoke about the loving kindness of her aunt during this time. Her aunt's death by cancer was a complete surprise to Suzanne. Next, Suzanne was directed to view indigo and reported even more detailed recollections of her brother's loss.

When Suzanne was directed to look at yellow, themes of anger, fear, and entrapment emerged. Then while viewing blue, the fear of her brother leaving emerged in a different way. Also, the loss of her aunt soon after the loss of her brother took place without her expressing it at the time. She was encouraged to express it in this session.

The retrieval of unresolved emotions and memories provoked a very intense session. This, along with the tendency to dissociate, suggested that it was a critical time for me to be available on a more frequent basis. Therefore, sessions were scheduled for twice a week until that phase was completed.

Session Four Suzanne reported that the level of her head pain had stayed the same, but it was "softer," and she felt continuing grief about her losses. She stated that her aunt "was the only adult who had ever acknowledged [her]," and she didn't want to let go of her. We initiated the use of the spectral chart for processing both her aunt's death and her second oldest brother's accident.

While viewing green, Suzanne described the trauma of her brother's auto accident, one which left him a quadriplegic. The shock and sudden loss of her perceived relationship with him evoked emotion that was processed. Then when viewing red, Suzanne processed the feelings related to her grandmother's funeral. Then her attention went back to her feeling of her brother's accident. It was as if the feelings of the two events were so similar that the focus could be on either event as the same emotions progressed. The color purple evoked a sense of "letting go" of her aunt's death. Then she recalled that it felt like the "beating" her brother took felt like a defeat. Multidimensional eye movement was used to alleviate her intense emotions about her brother.

The color orange provoked intense feelings regarding her self-perception, identity, and the shock of those losses. These desperate feeling were processed. She reported that the manner in which these two people validated and supported her were very important. While viewing indigo, emotions began to subside, and a new narrative about these losses emerged. Then while viewing yellow, fear and sadness began to shift to gratitude and a new perspective about her brother, as if the accident were "a gift" because he changed for the better. Then intense anger at her dad for what he did to her older brother emerged. This was processed into a calm confidence by slow lateral eye movement while viewing yellow. Then when Suzanne was directed to view blue, she reported feeling stronger and a marked reduction of head pain.

Session four was highly intense emotionally. It required active, immediate interventions to quickly reduce affective flooding, yet move Suzanne through emotions to completion. This was a critical turning point in treatment, and because her most intense emotions could be retrieved and processed to fruition, her tension shifted. The ultimate result of this movement was the elimination of her migraine headaches.

The next few sessions focused upon Suzanne's experience of continual terror throughout her childhood. This "terror" was in response to her violent and unpredictable father. Her recollection was that he could erupt in rage at any moment. Through work on the Chromapulse II, this intense fear was finally brought to closure. It was discovered that Suzanne's continuous fear had become implicit memory that manifested in somatic neural routes experienced as continuous head pain. As the attachment disorder specific to her father was relieved, the continuous pattern of pain stopped. It appeared that the migraine headaches were over. However, a new and different pattern of pain arose next.

Suzanne reported feeling fine for several days at a time without any medication. Then suddenly, a severe migraine would occur for a couple of days. As we explored this new pattern via the Chromapulse II and spectral chart, Suzanne recalled that her mother would be fine most of the time and then have days in which she would erupt into expressive emotional distress, leaving Suzanne reeling. This attachment pattern was specific to Suzanne's relationship with her mother. The pattern matched the migraine pain pattern that emerged subsequent to ameliorating the pathological pattern of her father. After emotional distress related to her mother was resolved, the irregular migraine pain pattern disappeared. At this point, all physical pain had finally ceased. Long-term relief from migraines has lasted several years with only occasional headaches requiring a single session of treatment.

Suzanne's treatment occurred in four phases. First, rapid symptom relief took place with heightened mind-body awareness. Second, unresolved trauma related to her pain occurred. Third, the affect related to her relationship with her mother concluded the affect related to her physical and attachment specific disorder related to her father was identified, finally, resolving the response.

In the previous case, the relationship between emotional regulation pattern and the pattern of the physical pain was an exact match. This outcome suggests that the intensity and the fluctuations in the experience of physical pain are influenced and often shaped by emotional regulation patterns derived from attachment patterns. I have found that in most cases, although organic factors contribute to a pattern of pain, the pattern and intensity of physical pain is largely dictated by a client's attachment pattern. The fact that people may have different attachment patterns explains why the same condition, such as a migraine headache, may manifest in so many different patterns from one person to the next. It also suggests that effectively identifying and treating the attachment-based emotional pattern related to the pain can lead to access and change of the physical pain pattern.

ETT® TREATMENT PROCESS FOR PHYSICAL PAIN

The following steps comprise the ETT® process for treating physical pain:

I. Diagnostic
   A. Conduct an interpersonal interview to assess attachment pattern and build rapport.
   B. Utilize physical pain questionnaires to identify the features and patterns of physical pain.
   C. Utilize medical information from previous tests or refer to appropriate medical personnel for evaluation if a current evaluation is not available.
   D. Identify the current use of pain medication and its effectiveness.
   E. Identify any co-occurring medical or psychological conditions.
   F. Inquire about the nature, frequency, intensity, and variation of the current pain.
   G. If the client is not currently in pain, use the spectral resonance assessment to pursue recollections of the physical pain. During this process tendencies of affective flooding or dissociation can be identified and modified. Emotional regulation patterns and relevant memories tend to emerge.

II. Therapeutic Modalities
   A. If the client possesses a high sensitivity to sensory stimuli, the use of peripheral goggles is recommended.
   B. If the client possesses physical pain in only one location and currently is in pain, the use of multidimensional eye movement may be selected for rapid relief.
   C. If complex physical pain is currently being experienced in multiple sites and/or with severe intensity, the use of the Chromapulse II device is recommended.

III. Therapeutic Interventions
   A. The intervention should initially focus upon the emotional response to the physical pain. Select wavelengths of light and/or peripheral positions to alter affect. The emotion should be processed until the emotional intensity is markedly reduced or eliminated. Once this occurs, it is likely that the physical pain will have been reduced as well.
   B. Issues of powerlessness, hopelessness, helplessness, or loss of control are often present, and the pattern in which these emotions are regulated must be facilitated to change for long-term outcomes.

C. When using wavelengths of light, choose light that matches with the body part according to the Vazquez system. When utilizing peripheral goggles, search for the peripheral positions that reduce the physical pain.
D. Once physical pain is reduced or extinguished, pursue exploration of psychophysical factors related to the origin of the pain. If unresolved affect exists that is linked to the pain, pursue resolution of it.
E. Pursue resolution of other factors related to the pain such as compromised identity perception, behavioral habits, or problematic beliefs about the pain.
   - Pursue identification of the symbolic meaning of the particular pain:
     - What is the significance of the physical location of the pain?
     - What is the reason for the pattern of the pain's fluctuations in intensity, time, duration, and quality?
     - Is the pain a form of somatic memory or produced by physical factors?
     - What is the meaning of the movement if pain moves from one location to another?
F. Once the pain is understood and relieved the following issues may be pursued:
   - The question and anxiety about whether the pain will return should be processed to alleviation.
   - Cognitive dissonance regarding the rapid extinguishment of physical pain must be processed and relieved.
   - Development of how to live a pain-free life can be very helpful after a change of years of chronic physical pain.
   - A narration that summarizes new learning about the pain experience is often helpful in order to prevent repeating the pain cycle.

DIAGNOSTIC ISSUES

Under normal conditions most therapists would conduct an intake session in which the client's personal history is taken and objectives for treatment are clarified. During this intake an interpersonal rapport should be developed. However, if a client is currently experiencing severe physical pain during the session, the pain tends to become a distraction, clarity of thinking may be impaired, and memory of relevant information may be temporarily limited. Therefore, intake information may need to be more abbreviated than typical sessions and interpersonal rapport may be achieved more by how much the facilitator reduces the intensity of pain than by the facilitator's pleasant and interactive behavior. Therefore, when clients enter an initial session experiencing intense physical pain, utilizing ETT® interventions to quickly reduce pain serves to achieve a higher quality of rapport than the most pleasant interactions without it. Clients in pain bond more quickly with people who communicate understanding of their pain and facilitate reduction of it.

Even if an initial session achieves reduction of physical pain and a good interpersonal rapport is developed, if the pain returns within an hour, a day, or even a week, most pain patients tend to evaluate the session as failing. The victimized perspective of many pain patients tends to automatically recur when the client re-enters the pain state again. Pain patients often think that it no longer matters what happened yesterday if one is in pain today. In many cases people lose their motivation to return to another session because they assume improvement will not be retained. Therefore, it is important to reframe the experience subsequent to the pain reduction session as "the pain reduction therapy did work, but it is not yet permanent." It is common for long-term pain relief to require a brief series of sessions from which pain relief is retained longer each time until it ceases altogether. During the initial session it is valuable to explain that it is too early to predict to what degree pain reduction will be sustained. However, the fact that pain can be reduced within a single session is a positive indicator in the prognosis of the pain reduction.

In another scenario the client may present with physical pain, but the current experience of it is not so severe that it impairs thinking or the client's ability to participate in a lengthy questioning process. In this case, current and childhood relationship information is sought as well as the origin and history of the physical pain. Then it is important to ask as many questions as it takes for the facilitator to gather enough description of the nature of the pain so that accurate empathy can be established. In many cases the process of disclosure and subsequent understanding by the facilitator may reduce the pain by this process alone. The following are some typical questions asked:

- Where does it hurt?
- On a scale from 1 to 10 with 10 being the worst, how bad is it right now?
- What is the quality of the pain—throbbing, aching, burning, etc.?
- How do you cope with the pain?
- Does it come and go or is it continuous?

Of course, proper empathy should be expressed after each response to a question in accordance with each client's attachment pattern. Pain questionnaires can be used to gain more specific and extensive information about the experience of pain subsequent to the initial session. There are numerous types of pain questionnaires available.

In an initial session it is important to inquire about any previous medical evaluations that can indicate a diagnosis. Three different possibilities tend to exist. A clear medical diagnosis may be known. More often a multitude of differing diagnoses may be known. In some cases the person has not received a medical diagnosis and has either made a self-diagnosis or simply does not know what it is. In this third case one should direct the client to pursue a medical evaluation. In most cases one can proceed toward pain reduction. However, a medical diagnosis can make a definite difference in the course of treatment. It is not the role of a mental health professional to identify a medical diagnosis, but it is within our domain to pursue the stress component of physical pain.

CO-OCCURRING ISSUES WITH CHRONIC PAIN

In addition to the client's pain problem there may be co-occurring mental health or physical disorders. For example, if a person with physical pain also has borderline personality disorder or obsessive compulsive disorder, these conditions will alter the course of treatment because the co-occurring disorder requires much attention. If a person has co-occurring physical conditions such cancer, paralysis, or irritable bowel syndrome, special attention to these conditions may be required. Therefore, the treatment plan would likely need to be adjusted to accommodate the complexity of the issues involved.

Issues of job responsibility, family pressures, and lifestyle may also complicate the treatment plan. Most of these issues involve excessive stress, which is highly responsive to ETT®. However, when perceived threats to survival or to the integrity of the self, such as financial instability or a divorce occur, these issues call for more frequent sessions in order to improve the physical pain to compensate for contamination of stressors occurring between sessions. If lifestyle issues like workaholism, sleep deprivation, or unhealthy nutrition are problematic, these lifestyle issues must be addressed in order to encourage the maintenance of pain reduction. For example, excessive caffeine or sugar intake can contribute to pain (Kaufmann, 2001, pp. 163–166). Co-occurring issues are the norm, not the exception in pain treatment.

MEDICAL EVALUATION AND MEDICATIONS

It is almost always appropriate to request that clients seek a medical evaluation for their pain symptom if a diagnosis is unknown. This request is a necessary legal and ethical request, but it might also add to the understanding that aids treatment. For example, headaches are a well-known symptom of numerous illnesses and conditions ranging from a brain tumor to cancer to simple tension. When pain is a symptom of a more pervasive problem, relieving the pain may actually be detrimental to the overall condition. Failure to relieve the head pain may be because the headache is the consequence of another problem. An accurate diagnosis might provide a different direction for treatment. However, many people endure extensive testing procedures that only lead to an unclear medical diagnosis. In those cases the search for a medical diagnosis may become traumatic in itself. Therefore, our role is simply to request and encourage a diagnosis initially, but not to prolong the process.

Many people initially attend a session already using some type of pain medication or other relevant medications that impair awareness. These clients should be queried in regard to the effectiveness of these medications and/or the side effects. In many cases these medications appear to provide little or no benefit, but medications may have been the only known option, while in other cases the side effects of medications may have compromised any benefits received. Drastic variations in medical side effects exist from person to person. A key issue for treatment is this: Do the medications interfere with a client's thinking or body awareness to the degree that they limit the client's responsiveness to ETT®? If they do, then the client is asked not to take the medication immediately preceding an ETT® session. For example, a client who takes pain medication every four hours should not take the medication for at least four hours preceding the session. In this way the client could participate with better awareness of his or her pain and the effects of the session would not be attributed to the pain medication. If the session achieves a good outcome, ETT® could be used, which would eliminate the risk of medication dependency or side effects. Medication may not be necessary subsequent to one or more ETT® sessions.

An evaluation of each individual's response to medication is conducted because we assume that each person may react differently to the same drug. However, a therapist should acquire permission from the client to confer with the prescribing physician once it is clear that ETT® is reducing the pain. The purpose of the consultation is to inform the prescribing physician about the progress so that he or she can re-evaluate whether the medication should be reduced or eliminated. This issue is made more complicated if the client has become addicted to the pain medication. If the client is addicted, the addiction recovery process described in chapter 10 should be used.

If the client is not currently in physical pain but does frequently possess a chronic pain pattern, an ETT® procedure with the spectral chart can identify attachment patterns and subsequent patterns of emotional regulation. The client is asked to recall the experience of physical pain and the accompanying emotions that occur. In some cases the physical pain may briefly recur during the session. Then procedures are used to rapidly reduce it. More often the contributing factors to the pain are brought to awareness. Therefore, many of the issues that are a part of the constellation of cognition, affect, and behaviors of the pain syndrome become known. This awareness and information provide vital awareness of the pain syndrome for use in future sessions. It is not unusual for the physical pain pattern to change as a consequence of this assessment. Dissociation from somatic experiences and unwanted emotions commonly occur in people who have chronic pain. Once these patterns of disengagement are understood, re-engagement can be facilitated in order to rapidly process related emotion and somatic memory to conclusion.

THERAPEUTIC ETT® MODALITIES

Since there are several modalities to select from within ETT®, it is important to identify criteria to differentiate choices. In many cases any of the four ETT® tools—peripheral goggles, spectral chart, MDEM, and the Chromapulse II—can alleviate physical pain rapidly. However, certain conditions cause one modality to be preferred over another. For example, people experiencing physical pain may possess hypersensitivity to light, sounds, smells, and other sensory stimuli. If this is the case, the use of the peripheral goggles tends to work best. This occurs because it is a modality among ETT® tools that reduces stimulation in the process of facilitating pain reduction. Therefore, interaction and visual stimulation are used in such a way that hypersensitivity becomes an advantage during the treatment process while pain is being relieved. It is not uncommon for the hypersensitivity tendency to be reduced as a consequence of the procedure.

Another point of differentiation of modalities concerns whether the pain is located at one specific site or at multiple sites, as well as the degree of awareness related to emotion. If the pain is in a single location and awareness of related affect is known, the multidimensional eye movement procedure is optimal.

However if complex emotions exist, multiple sites of physical pain exist, and a disengagement of awareness about the nature and origin of the pain occurs, the Chromapulse II device is preferable. The facilitator selects this device because of the availability of variable processes that allow for the precise use of wavelengths of light, peripheral stimulation, and alteration of brightness. These capacities make it easy to follow and match all of the client's experiences so that in-depth progress can rapidly take place.

THERAPEUTIC INTERVENTIONS

Once diagnostic issues are clear, an interpersonal bond is established, and the optimal ETT® modality is selected, the rest of the therapeutic process can take place. The basic ETT® approach focuses first on the emotional response to having the physical pain. Only after progress is made with these emotions is the focus shifted to the physical pain itself. An adequate identification of the client's emotional response to pain may take some time if the client has disengaged emotionally to cope with the continual presence of pain over a long period of time. In other cases the physical pain has acquired so much of their attention that emotional experiences have not been their focus.

As it becomes clear that a certain attachment pattern has been a significant contributor to the intensity and/or enduring pattern of the pain, pursuing alteration of the attachment pattern becomes important. There are at least six ways to do this.

1. Exemplify the type of interpersonal contact with the client that was deficient in each of the client's attachment patterns in early bonding.
2. When visual stimulation elicits attachment-based emotional patterns, select wavelengths of light to amplify attunement to alter the affective pattern.
3. Process unresolved affect related to attachment figures to conclusion.
4. Seek positive resources that provide secure attachment patterns to utilize when necessary.
5. Resolve specific incidents of unresolved affect.
6. Educate the client about improved self-management of affect.

When attachment patterns related to the physical pain are modified, the physical pain is likely to be modified or extinguished. This focus provides the type of change that is likely to enhance long-term change in physical pain. During the process it is important for the facilitator to continually monitor physical pain changes when emotion changes. Through this process the awareness of linkage between pain and emotion is enhanced, leading to an integration of those neural circuits.

EMOTIONAL RESPONSE TO PHYSICAL PAIN

The response to physical pain could involve virtually any emotion, but the most common responses cluster into the following groups:

- a sense of loss of control
- hopelessness
- powerlessness
- helplessness

Pain tends to render people to, at least temporarily, feel hopeless, powerless, or helpless. How these emotions are regulated is often critical to recuperation.

The ventromedial prefrontal cortex of the brain plays the key role in regulating emotions of related to perceived loss of control. "The ventromedial prefrontal cortex is a convergence zone, where the lower subcortical areas of the brain that generate emotional states interface with the higher cortical areas that regulate these states" (Schore, 2003, pp. 278–279). In conjunction with the ventral medial prefrontal cortex, the dorsal medial prefrontal cortex functions include:

- monitoring one's own mental state
- intentional speech
- self-generated thoughts and emotions (Siegel, 2007, pp. 218–219)

Therefore, the medial prefrontal cortex, if developed properly, could monitor and control primitive emotional states. Otherwise, deficiencies in these functions contribute to intensifying and extending the experiences of emotions like helplessness, powerlessness, and hopelessness. Through complex neural connections, this part of the brain plays a major role in governing the autonomic nervous system (Schore, 1994) and corticosteroid levels (Hall & Marr, 1975).

A perceived loss of emotional control over one's own body can result in anger. Dysregulation of the ventromedial prefrontal cortex is associated with rage and violent behavior.

However, evidence suggests that the range of wavelengths of light perceived as yellow correlates with functions of the ventromedial prefrontal cortex, which allows light stimulation to influence this brain function.

1. When the optimal wavelength of visual yellow light stimulation is used in conjunction with verbal processing of affect such as helplessness, powerlessness, and hopelessness, the amplified attunement tends to resonate these emotions toward empowerment and hope.
2. Then options in a client's predicament are seen differently. A view of physical pain as an opportunity to learn and grow are likely, and a confidence that pain will be overcome tends to emerge. This change tends to have an enormous impact upon how the client encounters the experience of pain.
3. When this change takes place the feedback loop between emotion and physical pain is interrupted.
4. Without the emotional exacerbation of physical pain by the emotional reaction to it, the physical pain becomes amenable to normal regulation toward reduction.

In addition to the aforementioned emotions, other emotional issues may arise and call for different wavelengths of light to be used in conjunction with specific interpersonal responses. For example:

1. When there is a loss of perceived embodiment resulting in somatic dissociation, far red is used.
2. When there is a lack of congruency of affect, the blue-green range of wavelength is utilized.
3. If a thwarted escape response is exhibited and excessive body movement occurs in anxiety, the red range of wavelengths assists in processing this impulse.
4. In many cases guilt, shame, or an excessive sense of responsibility occurs. The red-orange range of wavelengths can accelerate processing of these emotions.
5. After repeated experiences of intense emotions and/or change in lifestyle or work, one's self-perception is often altered. The orange wavelengths can facilitate improvement for identity issues.

6. Most often people report depression and sadness as a result of chronic pain. The wavelengths of green are utilized to aid in the reversal of sadness.
7. The experience of feeling "fuzzy headed, or foggy" in one's thinking often accompanies physical pain. The indigo range of color is conducive in accessing clarity.

Betty's Case: Fibromyalgia

Betty appeared warm, attentive, and at the same time worried. She was a stunningly attractive divorced single parent whose outward façade contradicted her relentless physical pain and emotional suffering. Betty described a huge array of severe symptoms diagnosed as fibromyalgia. She had volunteered to undergo a six-week protocol of ETT® and was now off all medications for this project.

The symptoms she reported included multiple sites of physical pain. She reported feeling achy all over, "stress in [her] chest like somebody was squeezing it," pain on either side of her spine, and chest pain. In addition, she felt daily fatigue and "foggy thinking." However, with fibromyalgia these physical pain symptoms tend to move to different parts of the body and can change in intensity throughout the day.

Betty felt overwhelmed emotionally with "never enough time to get everything done." Anxiety and even panic were frequent, and worry about her future was prevalent. Overall, Betty felt depressed due to her multiple issues, which left her in a state of feeling incompetence.

Betty had already been to the top medical specialists in the United States. After two years of pursuing one medical regimen after another, she volunteered for the ETT® project as a last resort.

As we proceeded with the use of light emission, each emotional state would emerge with accompanying physical pain symptoms. Through amplified attunement with proper light stimulation each intense emotional state would relinquish only to be replaced rapidly with another one. Over ten different emotional states were resolved during each session.

Betty had a combination of resistant/ambient and role reversal attachment patterns. This manifested in her assumption that when I exhibited empathy, she assumed that I was burdened with her pain to the same degree that she would have been if she were empathizing. Therefore, my empathy for her resulted in more distress for Betty. Through discussions these boundaries were clarified in such a way that Betty began to recognize her projections. However, boundary issues were soon explored because no matter what amount of relief derived from psychotherapy sessions, her porous boundaries would allow numerous issues between sessions to overwhelm her emotionally and produce severe physical pain and fatigue. Therefore, the ETT® protocol called for daily sessions the first two weeks and then fewer sessions each succeeding week throughout six weeks. The first week deleted most of the emotional distress and physical pain, and the second week focused on constructing interpersonal boundaries that protected her from allowing stimuli to overwhelm her system from entering her personal space. In the following week we pursued the core issues from which both the emotional regulation pattern and physical pattern emerged.

Betty's poor boundaries made her far more vulnerable to being traumatized. In fact, Betty was traumatized hundreds of times as she catastrophized many situations that would not be traumatizing to people with secure attachment patterns. After trauma people are often automatically left in a state of guardedness in which they brace for the next onslaught. This guardedness often produces a tension that can be experienced as physical pain. Therefore, rapid processing of both unresolved trauma and its consequence of physical guardedness is important. Once a relaxation from these experiences has taken place, treatment can proceed to building an appropriate sense of self.

Betty's lack of boundaries was related to very poor self-perception. Role reversal attachment disorder left Betty focused on others and sacrificing adequate self-focus. Unfortunately, this tends to attract other people into her life that readily accept her focus on their own needs. The range of color along the red-orange and orange continuum of light provides increased self-awareness and ultimately the capacity for self-esteem. ETT® directed along these lines soon created a better self-focus. Peripheral eye stimulation reduced overwhelm and created better interpersonal boundaries, which produced a new type of interpersonal interaction in which Betty was not taking care of the therapist.

The lightwork sessions gradually showed a reduction in both emotional and physical symptoms. By the end of six weeks all emotional distress and physical symptoms were no longer present. One year later Betty continued to report long-term relief of her fibromyalgia symptoms.

While there are variations as to the factors that contribute to fibromyalgia, many people with fibromyalgia fit a profile similar to Betty's. The six-week protocol has worked for other people. There are no side effects such as those found with medications like Lyrica, nor does the process create a long-term dependency on the remedy. At this time we are awaiting opportunities for this process to be tested under scientific scrutiny.

CHRONICITY AND THE ORIENTING RESPONSE

If the person in physical pain has been traumatized by the experience, which is likely, then the post trauma issues of the orienting response can leave the person in a psychologically guarded state that exacerbates feedback loops between pain and emotion. In the case of physical pain, instead of arousal and scanning the external environment, a person becomes aroused and scans any internal signals from the body that might indicate more physical pain. When one or more of these responses is fixated, the guardedness to protect paradoxically becomes the factor that retains physical pain.

The psychological mechanisms that are responsible for physical pain activation and prolonged intensity may simply be carrying out psychological experiences modified by attachment disorders. Attachment patterns dictate how emotions are regulated. When emotions are poorly regulated, this dysfunction may transfer to neural circuits that directly activate nerves responsible for physical pain. Pain is sensed by sensory neurons called nociceptors. These cells normally send messages to the spinal cord and brain to provide awareness of strong stimuli such as pressure, heat, or cold. This awareness appears to assist in protective responses. However, when these neural pathways become overexcited, the experience is referred to as allodynia. Physical pain can often be the result of this "protective" response (Lee, Zambreana, Menon, & Tracey, 2008, pp. 11642–11649). This psychological protectiveness mirrors the guarded over-excitedness known as the "orienting response" that typically follows the experience of psychological trauma. In the case of the emergence of pain, the surprise and loss of control that occurs preceding or during the experience of physical pain can become the trauma itself for which the consequence is the psycho-physiological response of more enduring pain emerges. "Hyper excitability within the uninjured nerves that intermingle with the wounded nerve is paramount for the persistence of pain after the original injury is gone. Many of the damaged nerves degenerate" (Porreca & Price, 2009, p. 34).

One of the best examples of how the orienting response is related to chronic physical pain is chronic pain that results from whiplash—neck, shoulder, and head pain that occurs when someone in a vehicle is suddenly hit from behind. This surprise jolt activates the primitive survival response to be on guard in order to avert further shocks. The orienting guardedness causes a bracing physical behavior in order to be prepared for further surprises. This bracing tenses the neck and shoulder muscles, feeding further pain and creating a feedback cycle that can become fixated. Although x-rays and other medical evaluations often reveal physical issues, it is the unconscious, automatic bracing response that contributes to the chronicity of the problem. This concept is supported by the fact that people who participate in demolition derbies, during which they incur an average of twelve vehicle crashes per evening, do not experience as much physical pain as does the typical whiplash victim in a car accident, nor does their pain tend to become chronic (Hall & Marr, 1975, pp. 367–371). Therefore, it can be reasoned that the surprise element of the experience contributes to the brain's reaction in the amygdala as if the event were traumatic. If it is traumatic, the orienting response follows trauma. If the orienting response is not resolved, the pain lingers excessively as a consequence.

Amplified attunement can often link the primitive brain mechanisms with executive control to process the orienting response to conclusion. When this takes place the feedback loop between physical pain and emotion is severed. Wavelengths within the red-orange range are often critical for dismantling a fixated hyper-vigilant orienting response through deactivating the amygdala. Blue-green wavelengths can assist in normalizing the functions of the thalamus, which is often largely responsible for a response becoming fixated and incongruent with other brain processing activities. Ultimately, the functions of the cingulate gyrus, activated by the violet range of wavelengths, helps people "let go" of a guarded response.

VIBRATORY INTERVENTIONS THAT ALTER BIOCHEMISTRY

One of the unique and powerful elements of ETT® pain work is the fact that specific wavelengths of light can be precisely directed to resonate with the site of physical pain. Once the related emotions are processed, the pain tends to become highly susceptible to resonance with light. This resonance results in a rapid progression of the healing sequence of physical pain that often occurs within seconds or minutes. An entire mapping of correlates between wavelengths of light and specific body parts has been developed so that facilitators can quickly select the wavelengths of light that match the physiological location. This matching can change pain without the emotional component, but trials have shown that a relapse into pain is far more frequent without processing the emotional component; furthermore, no significant learning has occurred that could serve as a preventative for possible future pain experiences. It is not widely known that vibrations such as light are converted into biochemical signals by means of integral membrane proteins on the cell membranes of all of our body's cells (Lipton, 2005, pp. 82–85). Through this process and targeting brain mechanisms that facilitate the descending portion of the physical pain sequence, pain improves on a consistent basis.

Ways that apparently activate the endogenous neuropeptide system have been developed. As the amplified attunement and resonance occur and alleviate the physical pain, the brightness of the light is elevated, and pain relief converts into states of extreme wellbeing. These euphoric states appear to be exactly like the experience known to occur when neuropeptides bind to their opioid receptor sites. This can occur at the point of either the extinguishment of affect or of physical pain. It is not unusual for clients to report transpersonal experiences. These profound experiences can become positive resources for future utilization during distress.

THE SYMBOLIC MEANING OF PAIN

It has always intrigued me that some people will feel pain emerge in their feet, while others tend to have head pain, and yet others experience pain in their hips. While it is clear that certain physical factors are responsible for the locations, such as spraining an ankle or experiencing a blow to the head, in other cases physical pain emerges where there was no apparent injury to that body part. Louise Hay has written a book that provides a list of what medical symptoms in each body part may symbolize psychologically (Hay, 1982). Her list certainly has value, but it assumes that all people possess the same bodily symbols. While I think her premise, that body parts tend to possess symbolic meanings, seems valid, the stereotypes described do not allow for individual differences. The therapeutic challenge is to help the client uncover the symbolic meanings of each body part as they apply to him or her personally. Those findings have been of enormous value in the process of recovery. For example, physical pain in the legs can represent a protest against excessive movement. The physical pain may symbolize an expression that means "stop" to a workaholic who needs to stop moving. Head pain can represent a need to stop thinking for someone who is worried or in the intellectual thinking mode excessively. People who tend to bear burdens of other people's issues often feel pain in the shoulders or trapezius.

After observing hundreds of people process physical pain, I have identified several themes that repeatedly emerge with specific regions of the physical body. These themes are usually not conscious to the sufferer initially, but emerge during sessions. When these themes are resolved, the physical pain typically is resolved.

- Trapezius, or shoulder pain: an excessive sense of responsibility; bearing a burden.

- Sciatica: conflict regarding one's direction in life. "On one hand, I wish to move in a direction, but on the other hand, I can't or should not move in that direction."
- Temporomandibular joint pain: conflict regarding verbal disclosure. "On one hand I want to disclose something to someone, but on the other hand, I can't or shouldn't disclose it."
- Morton's neuroma (feet): loss of perceived emotional/financial/relationship stability.
- Arms: thwarted fight response.
- Legs: thwarted escape response.
- Abdomen: loss of control and thwarted verbal disclosure.
- Migraine headaches: unconscious avoidance of upsetting emotions.
- Torticollis (head and neck movement pain): fixated guardedness, bracing for a potential threat.

In order to achieve long-term resolution of chronic physical pain, it is often necessary to discover the factors that contribute to its origin. By utilizing modalities like the spectral chart and the Chromapulse II, a client can seek recollections regarding the origin of physical pain. For example:

- In many cases several stressful events have occurred within a short time and the distress continued unabated.
- These multiple stressors culminated in an experience of physical pain. Then dysfunctional emotional responses to pain contributed to making the physical pain worse.
- This system of feedback loops of interaction between pain and emotion continued.
- Pharmaceuticals were used to reduce the pain, but the emotional distress was left unresolved.
- Then there may be a time of reduced pain until the activation of unresolved emotion finally overrides increasing medication to produce chronic pain.

After a long time of physical pain, some people lose their religious faith, become cynical, or have other negative cognitions. Self-perception is often impacted by chronic pain in such a way that clients may feel a variety of self-perceptions such as worthlessness, self-hate, or insignificance. People also develop habitual behavior that occurs to accommodate their physical pain. These symptoms are a consequence of the chronicity of their pain and must be addressed in the treatment process. The indigo range of wavelengths is particularly valuable to correct cognitive distortions of beliefs.

Why Does Pain Initially Emerge?

This does not explain what causes the physical pain to initially emerge. A confluence of factors may contribute to the emergence of physical pain. These factors include, but are not limited to, the following factors:

1. A genetic predisposition to certain pain conditions.
2. Repeated physical strain on certain parts of the body.
3. A single exertion on the body part subject to pain.
4. Toxic or aversive environmental factors.
5. Compromised immune system that makes one vulnerable to stimuli.
6. Physical pain as a consequence of an illness.
7. Physical pain as a consequence of an injury or surgery.
8. Extensive travel, night-shift work, or other dysregulation of day/night rhythms.
9. Unresolved resentment and/or guilt.
10. Repeated psychological stressors that overwhelm the person's ability to cope.
11. Dissociation from affect that becomes redirected into somatic neural circuits.

In the first eight factors, attachment patterns, and subsequent emotional regulation capacities influence the pain to become either brief or chronic, even if the psychological factors may not have caused its emergence. New genetic research clearly indicates that the way in which one manages responses to environmental stressors contributes to how genetic expression may take place. The second factor regarding physical strain for a body part could be psychologically related if the motivation for straining that body part is pathological. For example, if compulsive hand washing caused painful wounds, the psychological disorder preceded the pain.

Sometimes a combination of emotional stress and repeated physical exertion culminate in an event in which a single movement results in intense pain. The context in which our bodies exist may impact our experience in such a way that pain results. In the case of our visual environment, fluorescent lights often yield headaches, and in other cases allergic responses may eventuate in pain. Various forms of compromised immune system problems, which are responsible for conditions like fibromyalgia or arthritis, make people vulnerable to physical pain. Numerous other illnesses involve physical pain as a part of their symptomology. The most obvious contributor to physical pain can be accidents, injuries, or surgery. In these cases pain is expected. However, the degree of intensity from one person to the next and the enduring quality of pain often cannot be accounted for by the physical injury alone. However, where physical pain most often becomes a mystery and resistant to conventional medicine is when it emerges spontaneously without any of the aforementioned causes. Pain syndromes such as migraine headaches, sciatica, regional pain syndrome, Torticollis, Morton's neuroma, and many others fall into this category. It is this category that often possesses unresolved emotions, existing largely out of conscious awareness, which have been found to be the source of pain. These syndromes have very real physical components. By resolving the origin of physical pain that has endured for at least six months or over many years, behavior, identity, and beliefs often change.

SOMATIC MEMORY AS PHYSICAL PAIN

When emotions reach a point of intensity that surpasses the person's tolerance level, emotions may be channeled into somatic neural circuits that exist outside of conscious awareness. This often happens when a person experiences traumatic events, but people with lower tolerance levels may experience this re-routing of neural circuits due to "lesser" stress. These disengagements from consciousness are thought to occur in part due to the dysregulation of the thalamus in the brain. A function of the thalamus is to relay information to many parts of the brain. Without a functional "relay station," many experiences are severed from the frontal regions of the brain. When these somatic circuits exhibit physical pain, memories of entire experiences may implicitly be held in these neural circuits. Through the use of specific forms of visual stimulation and interpersonal guidance, these displaced experiences can be reliably elicited into explicit memory. When this occurs, the physical pain often diminishes. However, if the emerging affect is not processed to conclusion, it may cycle back into implicit memory circuits. The efficiency with which ETT® can facilitate emergence of previously implicit memory as well as rapidly resolve it is, itself, a breakthrough in treatment processing.

INTERPERSONAL INFLUENCE ON GENETIC EXPRESSION

Breakthroughs in understanding genetics occurred in the Human Genome Project when researchers discovered that social interaction has a direct bearing on genetic expression. To the surprise of the researchers, each gene is not solely responsible for the manifestation of a specific characteristic; instead, an elaborate system of genes responds to external influences by turning on and off gene expression. The implication is that certain types of interpersonal influence have a direct bearing on how genetic potentials can be either expressed, or modified, or stopped altogether. Interpersonal psychotherapy, therefore, can be used to alter genetic expression in ways that are advantageous (Rossi, 2002) identified three classes of genes that are affected by interpersonal influences:

1. Behavioral-state gene expression: in conjunction with clock genes, emotional arousal, crisis, a sense of triumph, stress, despair, and depression are all governed by this class of genes (p. 12).
2. Activity-dependent gene expression: "Vivid conscious experience can turn on genes that code for proteins that lead to the generation of new neurons and their connections in the brain" (p. 12). The expression of these genes is associated with interesting, arousing, surprising experiences. The interaction of behavioral-state gene expression with activity-dependent gene expression largely accounts for our experience of consciousness.
3. Immediate early genes can be activated within minutes and respond to signals outside the organism. These genes mediate between the mind and the physical body. Affectionate touch can also activate these genes (p. 14).

Discovery of these genetic mechanisms has overturned the idea that each characteristic of an organism is fixed and cannot be changed. For example, if a person is diagnosed with depression, arthritis, or schizophrenia, the genetic aspects that contribute to these conditions are potentially changeable. Furthermore, the means to change these conditions exist in interpersonal experiences such as psychotherapy. Specifically, forms of interpersonal psychotherapy that evoke novel experiences like ETT® have the greatest possibility for altering genetic expression. ETT® clients report the exact types of experiences that have been linked with the types of genes related to influencing gene expression. However, other neurobiological factors are involved in the interpersonal activity that contributes to the impact of ETT®. In the following case, the Chromapulse I device that possessed the capacity to combine one, two, or three colors simultaneously, was used.

Michael's Psoriatic Arthritis

Michael entered my office with a forthright intent on his face that contrasted with the limited body movement of disfigured hands and shoulders. His bright intellect made him seem younger than sixty-six, but when he described his off-and-on relationship with a woman, it seemed to make him suddenly look older than his age. He described his condition as psoriatic arthritis, a horrible combination of the worst of both diseases, a condition that he had had for forty-five years. Michael also confessed to a life-long weight control problem, but he appeared only moderately overweight. His face strained as he said, "It is the physical pain that I want relief from." Michael described a long list of treatment failures for his pain but expressed a new hope that maybe my work would provide the miracle.

He reported painful symptoms of continuous pain in his hands, arms, legs, back, neck, and scalp. Then he said his fingers were all numb. I reached out in empathy with each site of pain he reported. In order for me to really grasp what he was feeling, I asked him to rate his current level of pain, and he said "four." It was worse in some areas than others. Then he quickly changed the subject to a recent workshop that he had attended. Excitement filled his voice as he described having seen an image of a speeding cyclone that represented the fear and anger that he felt in regard to his father. When he had surrounded this cyclone with love, it appeared as a double helix in his gut. Michael appeared to sense a new hope due to this image.

During the first session with Michael we used peripheral goggles. Through this process we were able to reduce his physical pain and emotional distress substantially. In the next session Michael reported dreams about a past relationship with a woman. He awoke with left knee pain, upper back pain, and heat in both wrists, so we used peripheral goggles and the spectral chart to process those symptoms. By the end of the session his knee pain was gone and his wrists were okay. He appeared cautiously optimistic.

The third session involved the use of emitted wavelengths of light and peripheral eye stimulation. This time the focus on current somatic symptoms gave way to underlying relationship issues. After some expression about his mother, issues emerged as he recalled events that occurred at age ten. His initial image of his DNA this time appeared as if there were Monopoly pieces hanging on the strands of the double helix. Michael reported that his mother often played board games like Monopoly, but when he was ten years old, she suddenly had to go to work and was largely unavailable to him. During the lightwork, his intense emotions about this abandonment were rapidly transformed into a perception of support. Michael said that when he felt rejected by a woman, he backed off and cut himself off from his emotions. At age twenty he did this when he perceived rejection, and that was when his painful physical condition began.

The fourth session involved issues of being angrily attacked by his father in repeated incidents when Michael was a child. His father's emotional unavailability was still very painful to recall. I provided the best empathic attunement that I could as we used wavelengths of red, yellow, and yellow-green simultaneously. Michael reported intense anger and fear regarding his father and described an image of an inner cyclone throwing off massive amounts of energy. As more light stimulation and interpersonal support continued, his transformation proceeded, and he described the changing imagery as follows:

> I see it clearly as a double helix moving slowly. It is two interwoven spirals that represent the inner direction of my life. The Monopoly pieces are oblong shapes revolving slowly as the double helix is surrounded by the love of God, the Holy Spirit. I feel less intense emotions (the wavelengths were changed to orange, yellow, and blue-green). It seems to have a consciousness and it knows what we are doing. I feel I am doing the right thing (wavelengths were changed to far red, orange, blue-green). The Monopoly pieces are glowing now. I am afraid I will not be ready, but the "I" is not the scared part (wavelengths were changed to far red, orange, and violet). I am losing the blocks and parts, and I feel like I am improving! The parts are now in relationship with one another. The lines are wider and carry a lot more information. The pieces are integrating into the double helix. I feel amazed. Now it has become a more sophisticated system with a greater smoothness. I am in the space between the lines. It's incredible! I exist in pure observation—I am. I am in the space of silence. It's updating to a new form. The helix is glowing! . . . I see a double helix that is metallic with a golden sheen slowly rotating. . . . It has a very strong tensile strength. I feel no pain. It has been transformed into an indestructible, metallic double helix.

Michael reported that he believed his genetic expression was completely updated and fully "reloaded." He reported amazement about how much he had repressed about his father. He felt connected and enlivened with no more psoriatic arthritic pain. Subsequent to this session, the issue of helplessness emerged and was quickly resolved. Then physical pain emerged for the last time as knee pain. It was processed to complete resolution.

Michael's case represents how ETT® provided rapid access to previously implicit memory as well as profound change of somatic memory. Novelty is promoted consistently through visual brain stimulation. Imagery often occurs with the client's eyes open while viewing emitted light. During the process his relationship with his girlfriend changed, his mother issue changed, and his relationship with his father resolved. Our interpersonal contact appeared to allow his emotions to feel validated and heard. Ultimately, his internal relationship with himself changed substantially. All of these changes were tied into his physical symptoms as he discovered new insight.

In this case no one can say for sure if the genetic expression of Michael's DNA was actually reprogrammed, but the circumstantial evidence that it was changed is appealing. My first experience of relieving physical pain with light took place in the early 1990s when specific wavelengths of orange light were used that spontaneously and completely stopped a fifteen-year experience of arthritic pain. Most cases of arthritis that have used ETT® have eliminated arthritic pain. One case has now gone for twelve years with only one brief return to pain. It has been observed that the ultimate resolution involves issues of somatization of affect and issues regarding recovery of one's authentic self. Since arthritis has a well-known genetic component, it would stand to reason that genetic expression might be a source of change produced by the combination of visual brain stimulation and optimal interpersonal intervention.

THERAPEUTIC MOVEMENT OF PHYSICAL PAIN

One interesting phenomenon that occurs during ETT® treatment of physical pain is that the location of physical pain often tends to move during a session. The ETT® process facilitates such a direct and rapid progression of recovery that physical pain typically either extinguishes or moves to another location. One pattern involves different levels of intensity of pain being removed as if one layer at a time is being resolved. In this pattern one location of pain has little or no connection to another location. Instead a hierarchical phenomenology occurs in which pain that acquires the most attention dominates one's awareness. After that pain at the top of the hierarchy is removed, the next most intense pain comes into the person's awareness. Evidence suggests that the secondary and tertiary pain experiences were present before the removal of the top pain, but awareness was so distracted by the more intense pain that secondary pain went unnoticed. When this "peeling away" process takes place, it is very difficult to predict where pain will emerge next. Therefore, the process is to treat each new layer of pain as if it is a separate pain with its own unique history and contributing factors.

A second type of movement that occurs during the ETT® process involves what could be conceived of as purification. This type of pain movement occurs as shifts in a direction when amplified attunement with wavelengths of light resonate with the bodily region in which the pain exists. It operates as though the pain is on a path to ultimately leave the body. However, it might shift from the right side to the left side and then upward in the body. Next, it might move to the throat and then ultimately out of the body. One variation of this process is referred to as kundalini in East Indian culture because at the culmination of the pain sequence may be a purification, and profound spiritual experiences may occur in which states of bliss or euphoria are experienced. Other spiritual awareness may occur in conjunction with this purification. This process utilizes wavelengths of visual light stimulation that resonate with each new position. This second pattern is different from the first pattern in that it is essentially the same physical pain cluster of affect, cognition, and history. However, in its progression toward recovery it encounters "blockages" where various forms of unresolved somatic memory or physical problems interfere with its progress. With appropriate stimulation these blockages give way to the pain progression of recovery, which ultimately leads to the release of pain.

A third form of pain movement that occurs during ETT® sessions is less common than the other ones. In this case, physical pain is linked to ego states that may exist consciously or unconsciously. These states appear to possess an ability to move, change, intensify, or decrease. These states appear to willfully "hide" or move pain to different locations in the body. The ETT® resonance matching process appears to literally "chase" the physical pain in and around the physical body. These pain states possess very distinct psychological attributes of regressed experiences such as a rebellious teenager or a child. For example, one client possessed an ego state that was motivated by fun and manifested pain to interrupt the client when adult work was the focus, but ceased the pain when fun opportunities emerged. Therefore, in addition to pursuing resonance between light and the painful body part, resolution of internal psychological conflicts must be addressed. This form of pain movement is probably the most elusive and treatment resistant to conventional pain methods because it possesses a strong psychological component.

ALEXITHYMIA

One of the most elusive forms of the physical pain phenomena is due to alexithymia. The term alexithymia literally means "no words for moods." This occurrence may appear like avoidant attachment pattern. It may also appear that awareness of the client's emotions is simply buried in implicit memory. While these explanations may be a part of the problem, the key feature is that the person does not possess the capacity to identify, label, and verbalize some or all emotions. In many cases these patients are quite willing to face their own emotions, but due to deficiencies in their brain, they cannot identify or label these emotions with words. In many cases these emotions enter neural somatic circuits and manifest as physical pain and are resistant to any conventional means for pain inhibition. However, when these clients are provided a list of words that describe emotions and are asked to verbalize these terms, the physical pain stops rapidly when the correct emotion is verbalized. Apparently, by uttering the appropriate word that identifies the emotion, implicit somatic neural circuits convert into explicit circuits that release emotional charge. When this happens, the client is often surprised and continues to lack subjective awareness of the emotion. Then these patients are taught to map the body locations of each emotion so that they may read the somatic signal.

When people are afflicted with alexithymia, there are several tendencies to note. Physical pain may move from one location to another because unconscious emotional responses shift from one emotion to another. In cases where the origin of alexithymia emerged during ETT® sessions, it concerned a lack of validation for the person's emotional expression by caregivers during early developmental stages. The repeated omission of validation over time interrupts the brain development necessary for one to identify and verbalize emotions. Visual brain stimulation can speed up this awareness process, but verbal interaction and guidance is essential in order to reverse alexithymia. Through this process this condition can be improved.

STABILIZING RAPID PAIN RECOVERY

One of the advantages of using ETT® for treating chronic pain is that not only does the pain usually diminish rapidly, but the client is likely to have learned why and how the pain was produced in the first place. This new learning places the client in the position of having an increased awareness that might prevent the development of pain in the future. When new learning takes place, the pain experience becomes an opportunity for growth. For example, after the pain has been overcome, an increased liaison between mental processes and bodily experiences usually develops, and sometimes there is a new awareness of the meaning of the client's life. These advantages are in stark contrast to most other treatments for physical pain that simply focus on stopping the pain without addressing the avoidance of facing one's dysfunctions. While it is recognized that many people do not want to face their own issues, efficiently dealing with physical pain often helps people to overcome denial that, in retrospect, is often found to not be in the client's best interest.

One of the unique challenges for people who have had chronic physical pain for years is that when the pain is eliminated rapidly, a disorientation often results. People have often built an entire lifestyle and relationships around their physical pain. Although they seek pain relief, many people are unprepared for a rapid improvement. Sometimes people state directly that they are frightened of a pain-free life and feel unable to accept it. Others report that without the pain they would be challenged to work again, compete out in the world, and/or participate in relationships in ways in which they have no skills or comfort. After the pain is gone, many people continue to refer to themselves as an arthritic, for example. Their language often continues to reflect the pain identity with which their self-perception has been associated for so long. In addition to these adjustment challenges, the cognitive challenge of fearing if or when the physical pain will return may continue in spite of having no pain. During this phase of stabilizing the change in pain, it is important to validate the person for being in a transitional state and to encourage the person to embrace movement toward the new pain-free identity. Fears of being able to successfully encounter these new challenges that emerge in a pain-free life are one of the last therapeutic targets of treatment.

The process of change and growth often involves steps or leaps forward and then subsequent consolidation of those changes. This need for consolidation can be enhanced by having the client produce verbal or written narratives. Since ETT® often facilitates such a rapid and substantial change in physical, emotional, cognitive, and behavioral issues, a narrative often helps the person experiencing ETT® to make sense of the change. Especially after physical pain has culminated, clients are encouraged to verbally review and summarize the experience of change. Sometimes the client's memory of the process is deficient. Therefore, a collaborative process involving both the facilitator and the client might help to enrich the narrative process. The narrative process serves to integrate the client's experience and incorporate the change into his or her self-perception and autobiographical memory. On the physical level, "brain integration involves long strands of the prefrontal neurons reaching out to differentiated distant areas of the brain and body" (Siegel, 2007, p. 27). In addition to organizing the brain, narratives tend to produce new insights. Consolidation of change tends to assist in stabilizing the improvement so that the risk of relapse is reduced. Producing one's narrative of how chronic pain was overcome often feels empowering and deeply satisfying.

6

Light Years Ahead in Addiction Treatment

Jack looked fidgety and uncomfortable as he told about his cocaine addiction. He lamented that he had been in several in-patient addiction programs as well as 12-Step groups, and numerous hours of individual psychotherapy. He felt hopeless at the age of twenty-three. All he wanted was to get that high feeling but he knew his family demanded that he be in therapy. When he talked about how cocaine made him feel, he smiled and his face lit up. Then he would lapse into visible despair when he talked about treatment failure. Jack just didn't get the "higher power" aspect of 12-Step groups because he had no religious background and felt no benefit from a higher power. All he got from his parents was judgment, condemnation, and anger regarding his drug problem. Jack wanted help, but couldn't imagine living without the cocaine high. When asked about his motive for getting high, he said, "It was to get fucked up." I asked if that meant to escape. He said, "Yes." Then we pursued identifying what was driving him to escape. After lightwork it became clear that his self-perception was negative and cocaine temporarily elevated it. Drug testing confirmed that he was clean during our treatment.

While many different wavelengths of light were helpful, the orange range of wavelengths of light assisted in correcting is poor self-perception. Jack said, "That orange light is better than any cocaine I ever had!" These sessions focused on correcting relationship issues—relationship with his parents, his girlfriend, himself. These attachment issues ultimately related to his relationship with cocaine. ETT® process rapidly resolved these relationship issues so that he lost all desire to pursue cocaine as a means to elevate his self-perception. He called the light emitting device "the magic light machine." Jack didn't know that he was the first cocaine addict to lose his craving by means of ETT®. The addictive craving completely ended within four sessions and never relapsed after ten years.

This stunning elimination of all addictive craving took place in a manner unlike all the conventional addiction treatment he had been through. To most professionals in the field of addiction, the non-medication for the consistent elimination of addictive craving within a few sessions is unheard of.

THE DRUG PROBLEM

ETT® may offer the most significant breakthrough in the treatment of addictions in decades. In terms of the sheer number of cases, chemical addiction may be the greatest single mental health problem in the United States and perhaps most of the world. Alcohol abuse and addiction may be the most dangerous chemical addiction in terms of consequences like violence, traffic accidents, and family dysfunction.

- Other legally used substances such as cigarettes, food addictions like sugar addiction and caffeine, and over-the-counter drugs are the sources of millions of addictions.
- The adverse effects of prescription drugs is the leading cause of death in the United States.
- Illicit drugs like marijuana, cocaine, and methamphetamine continue to be enormous sources of substance addiction.
- Today behavioral addictions like gambling, sex addiction, shopaholics, and others have grown enormously.

We are a highly drugged society. In spite of the pervasiveness of this problem, treatment programs for addictions generally have a high failure rate. This chapter will focus primarily on the illicit drug use and alcohol. However, most of the principles for treatment of addiction bear a strong similarity and can often be applied to all other addictions.

One could view the treatment of addiction in four basic phases. The first phase involves diagnostic issues concerning the nature and extent of the addiction and the clients' issue of motivation. The second phase involves detoxification from the substance or in the case of behavioral addictions, the behavior. The third phase involves elimination of the craving for the substance or the craving for the source of a behavioral addiction. The fourth phase involves adjusting to an identity and/or lifestyle that does not involve the substance our targeted behavior.

DIAGNOSTIC ISSUES REGARDING SUBSTANCE ADDICTION

Substance abuse often occurs in conjunction with other co-occurring psychological disorders. The Treatment Improvement Protocol from the Center for Substance Abuse Treatment lists the following distinctions:

- Substance abuse can cause psychiatric symptoms and mimic psychiatric syndromes.
- Substance abuse can initiate or exacerbate a psychiatric disorder.
- Substance abuse can mask psychiatric symptoms and syndromes.
- Psychiatric and substance abuse disorders can independently exist.
- Psychiatric behaviors can mimic substance abuse problems (Flores, 2004, pp. 22–23).

Therefore, it is essential to assess diagnoses before and after substance addiction. This makes detoxification from the substance vital for a proper assessment. This also means that one must change treatment protocol based on the changes in the diagnosis. For example, substance addiction may cause a person to exhibit symptoms of borderline personality disorder while using, but the person may no longer possess these symptoms after detoxification. On the other hand, symptoms may become quite manageable if the person is using an addictive drug to escape borderline personality symptoms. However, in some cases after detoxification the borderline personality symptoms may reemerge. A third possibility is that borderline symptoms may only emerge during the phase of withdrawal from drugs. A fourth possibility is that borderline personality may occur independently of substance usage and persist with or without drugs. These complicating factors must be differentiated as early as possible. Requesting information about substance-related behavior from both the client and his or her significant others can hasten these diagnostic features.

Among the assessment issues related to alcohol is a controversy about what features define alcoholism. Research from Valliant's classic study found that the most reliable method for determining whether one is alcoholic or not is the number and frequency of alcohol-related problems or social consequences such as:

- DUI arrest
- Health problems related to alcohol consumption

- Public intoxication
- Legal problems related to alcohol consumption

Valliant showed that severity of alcoholism is most related to social consequences and less related to consumption levels or other factors (Valliant, 1983). However, measurements like SPECT (Single Photon Emission Computed Tomography) scans can show brain pathology resulting from alcohol or other drugs regardless of the social circumstances.

CROSS-ADDICTION

Another diagnostic issue is cross-addiction, which refers to replacing the elimination of one addiction with a different addiction. For example, when alcohol is eliminated, it can be replaced with cigarettes, marijuana, sexual addiction, and a long list of other addictions. Studies have shown some tendencies toward certain types of cross-addiction such as:

- nicotine dependence and alcohol dependence (Irons & Schneider, 1996)
- sexual compulsivity and cocaine use (Washton, 1987)
- compulsive spending—or compulsive gambling and eating disorders (Carnes, 1991)

In addition to cross addictions, many clients have multiple addictions at the same time. Multiple addictions take place for several purposes. For example, one addiction may be used to excuse another, or more than one addiction must be present for the other one to work. According to Flores (2004), other reasons for multiple addictions are as follows:

- One addiction is part of a ritual for another addiction.
- One addiction can be used to numb the feelings of shame for another addiction.
- One addiction may lower inhibitions so that another substance can be used.
- One addiction may be alternated with another.
- One addiction may intensify the effects of another.

For example, one might need to drink alcohol in order to be inhibited enough to act on a sexual addiction. One might smoke cigarettes to inhibit consequences of alcohol use. One might need to combine the use of prescription medication in order to acquire the greater effect of alcohol, and on and on.

Therefore, it is important to seek information about prescription drugs, over-the-counter drug use, illicit drug use, and legal addictions such as caffeine, cigarettes, as well as non-substance addictions in order to understand the pattern of each client's addictions.

BRAIN DAMAGE AND CHEMICAL ADDICTION

Research evidence shows that prolonged periods of substance use can produce physiological brain destruction (Heyman, 1995). This can make people more vulnerable to addiction. In the case of alcohol, for example, consistent use of alcohol may convert a non-alcoholic into an alcoholic who acts out dangerously. Both the director of the National Institute of Drug Addiction, Alan Leshner, and the director of the National Institute of Mental Health, Steve Heyman, contend that once a person crosses a threshold of excessive use of certain drugs that the neuro-physiological damage cannot be reversed. Prolonged use of substances can alter neural synapses and the endogenous production of certain neurotransmitters that eventually result in permanent alterations in brain functioning. These alterations in turn affect the reward centers of the brain resulting in (reward deficiency syndrome) making addiction a brain disease (pp. 114–115).

This physical brain damage from prolonged substance use make slow down effective treatment or limit treatment from working at all. However, to assume this prognosis too readily may play into a victimized hopelessness that is characteristic of addicts.

THE SELF-MEDICATION HYPOTHESIS

Research in both mammals and humans has shown that we regulate each other physiology and psychological states through the exchange of emotions. Research has shown that gene expression occurs largely due to psychosocial influences. Attachment in early childhood develops the characteristic pattern by which one regulates one's own emotions during challenges in later life. When there are significant deficiencies in one's manner of regulating emotions, the person is compelled to use whatever means available to repair the problem and avoid painful emotional distress. Adults in modern society have a vast array of options available to temporarily reduce the pain—both legal and illegal. When substances are used to attempt to repair attachment deficiencies their usage often exacerbates the problem by deteriorating the existing physical and psychological resources within the person.

Khantzian (1982) first hypothesized that addicts were drawn to the specific drugs that appeared to repair their attachment deficits. Examples are as follows:

- Narcotic addicts are drawn to opiates because they tend to relieve aggression, anger, and rage.
- Chronic depression and self-esteem deficits are often temporarily aided by cocaine.
- Boredom, emptiness, and fatigue are compensated for by stimulant use.
- Inhibited, restricted clients are attracted to alcohol.
- Anxious, fearful people are attracted to Valium and minor tranquilizers.
- Type-A workaholics are relieved by marijuana use.

These uses of substances allow clients to become their own "physicians" by selecting the drugs that temporarily provide the need fulfillment they seek. These remedies are childlike in that they are immediate and temporary. Children want their needs met immediately with no long-term perspective about the overall benefit and consequences of their behavior. These factors make it fairly apparent that a regressed emotional state is in charge of the adult user at the time of selecting these drugs to solve their issues.

ADDICTION AND ATTACHMENT

One of the more typical disclosures by addicted clients is that the substance "is like a friend." Then they often elaborate on this "friend" by explaining, for example, that it is reliably always available when it is needed; "it" makes me feel better when I am anxious or sad and "it relieves me when I feel lonely." Others may state that it makes them feel confident. These comments make it obvious that addicts use substances as a relationship object. Deficiencies in one's early bonding with attachment figures are attempted to be alleviated through a projected relationship with a substance that temporarily yields the emotional benefit that an ideal attachment bond would yield. However, a person in a regressed emotional state fails to recognize the risks and shortcomings of these remedies. These choices often ultimately interfere with enhancing actual human relationships. These unmet emotional needs provide such intense drives to be at least temporarily relieved that evidence suggests that people will do almost anything to relieve them. Therefore, while there are numerous factors and contributing causes for drug addiction, my hypothesis is that deficiencies from attachment disorders are the central motivating factor that accounts for most substance addiction.

This attachment feature of addictions makes ETT® the prime means for alleviating drug addiction at a speed and depth that is unprecedented. Attachment disorders emanate from early childhood bonding experiences that are often either not remembered or unclear. Therefore, a method that can rapidly achieve depth and clarity about events lodged in implicit memory is ideal. However, once these primitive emotions are recalled, it is essential to possess a means for rapidly processing these deeply imprinted emotional patterns to completion. These tasks are central to ETT® capacities.

Different types of attachment disorders contribute to different choices for drug usage. For example, persons with an avoidant attachment disorder may either select drugs to further their need to distance themselves from emotions by choosing drugs that (1) numb, or (2) aid in an escape from reality, or (3) compensate for their distancing. On the other hand, people may take drugs to compensate for their attachment disorder. In the case of avoidant attachment, one may take substances to help them feel when they are unable to feel. The use of stimulates or ecstasy might contribute to this quest. One of the classic symptoms of depression is not wanting to get out of bed in the morning. This symptom is remedied by caffeine in coffee or tea, which stimulates a person to feel active. Therefore, morning caffeine use may mask this symptom of depression.

In terms of the addiction or compulsive behaviors being used to fulfill some functions of a projected attachment object, what relationship function or functions does the compulsion serve?

- A friend
- A reliable available relationship
- A substitute spousal relationship
- A substitute parental relationship
- A substitute safe relationship

In conjunction with these attachment projections, substance addictions often serves as a means to regulate emotions. In this context the craving may attempt to acquire the following forms of emotional regulation.

- To acquire escape from one's present experiences
- To relieve anger
- To relieve depression or sadness
- To relieve boredom

- To relieve anxiety
- To relieve loneliness
- To relieve negative self-perception
- To acquire states of extreme wellbeing
- To acquire engagement
- To acquire comfort or nurturing

These emotional deficits are targeted for therapeutic relief. Spontaneous recollections often occur during ETT® sessions that reveal specific incidents of attachment deficits in one's family of origin or in one's current constellation of relationships. When this occurs, new objectives emerge that should change treatment to target resolution of these emotions and the attachment deficiencies from which they are derived. When these issues are resolved, long-term change tends to be more likely.

TREATMENT OF ADDICTIONS

Treatment for chemical addiction requires very different strategies for each stage of recovery. The first step is convincing the client to detoxify from the substance. The benefits of abstinence from the substance must be clearly recognized. Achieving a good therapeutic alliance is the first key to resolving this issue. There is an extremely high probability that an addict will drop out of treatment during this initial phase because of cognitive distortions, rationalizations, and denial. In addition, self-esteem has usually become compromised in many addicts. Therefore, a strategy to communicate the benefits of getting off the substance involves at least four factors:

- a strong therapeutic bond between the therapist and the client
- supportive persons like family, friends, and others who might appropriately support this change
- methods to overcome denial
- improving self-esteem

There is a strong tendency for addicts to lie to family, friends, and therapists in order to avoid giving up their addictive substance. Therefore, it is required for at least one family member or close friend to be involved in the treatment as soon as possible. One purpose of this requirement is to help verify that the client's claims are accurate. Also, a client-signed agreement is recommended that agrees to providing the results from random drug testing for any session that the therapist requests.

During the first week of therapy, when detoxification is being evaluated by the client, clients are directed to look at indigo and/or orange for thirty minutes per day to overcome denial and self-esteem issues. This exercise has surprisingly powerful effects in overcoming denial and bolstering self-esteem to the extent that the client continues to remain in treatment.

DETOXIFICATION

There are several options for detoxification. Specific ETT® procedures can be used to aid detoxification for some substances. Cranio-electrical stimulation works for some people. This device is leased to the client to neutralize cravings by using it each time cravings emerge. Other options include an in-patient detoxification program, a carefully planned retreat, and sometimes daily 12-Step programs. The least preferred method is medication because it risks becoming another form of cross addiction.

Initial bonding and detoxification are very important. In order to insure the greatest chance of success, the therapist should attempt to explore the client's history of drug use and identify any patterns of drug use. The appropriateness of a 12-Step program for each client should also be assessed.

Should 12-Step Groups Be Used?

Participants of 12-Step programs are well known for promoting them as the one and only way to recovery. There are also many therapists who do not advocate them. I have selected a position in the middle. I have had clients with years of severe alcohol and drug use who recovered with therapy alone. On the other hand, I have had clients who recovered by participating in 12-Step programs. The following are criteria I have found to be helpful in evaluating the use of these groups:

- When clients are single and isolated, 12-Step groups can help.
- When financial limitations are restricted, 12-Step groups are free of charge and offer help without cost.
- When denial is unusually significant, 12-Step programs can be helpful.
- Some people simply do not gain from group environments.

The AA twelve-step proponents often advocate identifying oneself as an alcoholic for life. This may not be true for some other drugs or even alcohol. With ETT® we are often able to achieve complete resolution of the addiction, elimination of cravings, and an end to the addict identity. This concept is blasphemy to most AA proponents. However, ETT® was not available when the 12-Step programs were developed, so there is generally no awareness of this possibility. Most clients are instructed to attend AA, NA, or CODA, depending upon their unique needs, but clients are cautioned not to buy into the philosophy that one will be an addict for life. These 12-Step programs can be helpful for the first two or three phases of chemical addiction treatment.

CO-ADDICTION

Where there is an addict, there is likely to be a co-addict. Co-addicts are people in relationships with addicts who inadvertently contribute support or otherwise enable the addict to further his or her addiction. Typically, co-addicts bail the addicts out of difficult situations and "protect" the addicts from descending into chaos. This attempt at protection actually helps the addicts avoid the natural consequences of their behavior and the potential realizations that may occur when they "hit bottom." Parents often assume too much responsibility for their teenager, which just adds to the teenager's irresponsible behavior. Co-addicts look the other way, excuse, or even provide money for addicts in hope that these behaviors will help. Sometimes a significant portion of treatment time is focused on the co-addict, not the addict. Al-Anon assists co-addicts with their excessive caretaking addiction. This issue should be addressed in the first two phases of treatment.

POLITICS AND ADDICTIONS

Drug addiction issues are, unfortunately, often highly political. Historically, the prohibition against alcohol in the 1920s illustrated how this issue divides and polarizes people. In that culture and era conservative religious groups attempted to legislate morality. More recently, this polarization has taken place with marijuana, ecstasy, and other drugs that are categorized as illegal. Some people think these drugs are either harmless or could even be beneficial. It seems that once a drug emerges outside of accepted pharmaceutical companies and is labeled evil, the prospects of it becoming legalized and regulated are dim. This political polarization impacts funding for research and often compromises objectivity. Pharmaceutical companies can become focused on looking for negative consequences and not benefits or vice versa. Then research findings can be made to support a case for or against a substance. It took enormous government pressure and disclosure from an insider to uncover the fact that tobacco companies developed hybrid plants to increase the addictive potential of cigarettes. What follows will serve as an example of how the political aspect of drug use affects the counseling process.

Case Study

A young man, about thirty, came in to see me for a session. I had seen him some years before when he was an adolescent, and I had also counseled his parents. He was a very successful, upper-middle-class, type-A business executive. He reported that he had smoked marijuana for years with his friends, all of whom were now married and had children. One day the wife of a lifelong friend found his marijuana roach. She convinced her husband that those marijuana-smoking friends should no longer be around my client. Therefore, the client came in to see me to get clear on this issue. He appeared to think I would probably side with him to continue its use. Was I going to be cool and tell him pot was harmless, or was I going to be an uptight anti-drug person? In order to function as a therapist and avoid the political polarization, I asked him if he was aware of the research facts about the medical consequences of smoking marijuana. He said no. Then I asked him if he was aware of the legal consequences if he was caught? He thought it was a fine, but he didn't know for sure. I recommended that he find out these facts, and then he would have a basis for making a decision.

Possession of small amounts of marijuana in Texas is a class B misdemeanor, which is more than a fine. However, Texas politicians had passed a law to suspend the driver's license of someone caught with any amount of marijuana for six months. In addition, anyone found guilty of possessing marijuana is prohibited from a government educational loan for life! Therefore, the misdemeanor itself is not the most significant consequence. Who can go without driving for six months in Texas? In addition, after a conviction for possession one can be expected to be watched closely. I simply asked this client to become educated about the potential consequences and then to evaluate whether smoking marijuana is worth these risks.

The most recent statistics and research information on marijuana come from the National Institute on Drug Abuse. I have found that marijuana users generally tend to believe that there is no danger in its use, but these people rarely seem to have any knowledge of the facts. This behavior is seen as only a legal risk, and the belief is that only uptight authorities and conservatives oppose it. Marijuana is the most commonly used illicit drug in the United States. In 2004, 14.6 million Americans ages twelve and older used marijuana at least once a month and the numbers have grown since then. Marijuana was the third most common substance reported in hospital emergency visits in the United States, which suggests that it is significantly more dangerous than commonly believed (National Institute on Drug Abuse, 2010).

- Marijuana has been found to contribute to the onset of schizophrenia and psychotic states (Moore, et al., 2007).
- The risk of heart attack quadruples in the first hour after smoking marijuana (Mittleman, et al., 2001).
- Marijuana smoke contains 50 to 70 percent more carcinogenic hydrocarbons than tobacco smoke (Hashibe, et al., 2006).
- Marijuana users in the work force have a 55 percent higher rate for industrial accidents, 85 percent more injuries, and 75 percent more absenteeism.

ETT® has been successful in the treatment of marijuana abuse. One of the factors that makes marijuana disengagement difficult is the fact that tetrahydrocannabinol (THC) resides in the fatty tissues of the body, unlike most other drugs, and takes as long as twenty-eight days to exit the system. This retention causes it to have the reverse tolerance effect, meaning that less and less use of marijuana is necessary to attain its effects. When these facts are coupled with the "it doesn't matter; I will make changes later" attitude fostered by the drug, it often results in impaired motivation to eliminate marijuana use. Therefore, once a client seeks extrication from the drug, more intense sessions provide a greater chance of success. Specifically an extended hour and a half session using Spectral Resonance Technique is recommended if the substance exists in the system at the time of the session. This approach tends to overcome the lack of detoxification during a session.

THE REWARD DEFICIENCY SYNDROME AND ETT®

New findings have shown that the brain's pleasure centers are at the base of addiction. Scientific research suggests that the nucleus accumbens in the ventral striatum of the brain is the central mechanism responsible for our experience of pleasure or lack of pleasure. Increases in the activity of the nucleus accumbens has been found to occur when expectation of rewards or the experience of rewards occurs (Adinoff, 2004; de la Fuente-Fernandez, et al., 2002). Neuroimaging research has shown that increase in nucleus accumbens activity occurs during euphoric responses (Drevets, et al., 2001), cocaine-induced euphoria (Breiter, et al., 1997), monetary reward (Cohen, et al., 2005), pleasurable responses to music (Blood & Zatorre, 2001), and when viewing attractive faces (Aharon, et al., 2001). Since seeking pleasure plays a central role in addictive behavior, the nucleus accumbens has been a focus of addiction research.

The D (2) dopamine receptor (DRD[2]) has been associated with pleasure and the DRD (2) A1 allele has been known as the reward gene (Bowirrat & Oscar-Berman, 2005). "The reward cascade" involves the release of serotonin, which in turn at the hypothalamus stimulates enkephalin, which in turn inhibits GABA at the substantia nigra, which in turn fine tunes the amount of DA (dopamine) released in the nucleus accumbens or "reward site" (Blum, et al., 2000). In the reward deficiency syndrome there has been found to be a breakdown in the reward cascade. This results in a craving for an external source of pleasure and a simultaneous loss of voluntary control of one's behavior.

Many parts of the brain contribute to the activity of the nucleus accumbens and then it projects to brain mechanisms that carry out activities to block or activate pleasure. Evidence suggests that drug addicts and/or behavioral addicts have the DRD2 gene activated in such a way that leaves them unable to experience pleasure naturally, thus placing them in a position to crave a means to pleasure and a dependency on the external pleasure source that reactivates their ability to temporarily experience pleasure.

The sequence of the pleasure/lack of pleasure experience appears to occur in the following manner (see illustration 6.1):

1. Attachment disorders dictate affect regulation triggered by a stressor (Sinha, 2001; Saal, Dong, Bonci, & Malenka, 2003).
2. Emotional processing involves the amygdala, the orbitofrontal cortex, and the medial prefrontal cortex, which affects:
   - stimulation of dopamine by the ventral tegmental area,
   - memory via the hippocampus, and
   - motor control involving the dorsal caudate and the globus pallidus (all of these mechanisms provide direct input to the nucleus accumbens).

How the Brain Activates Pleasure

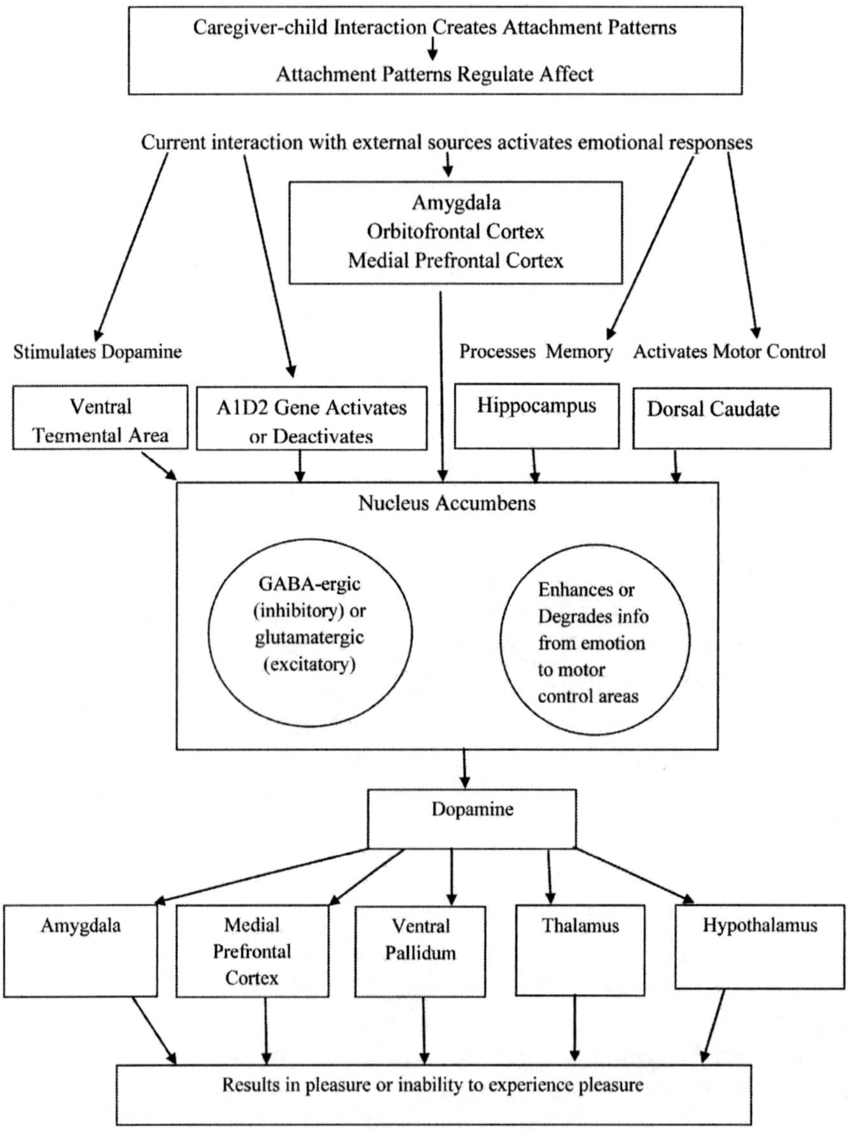

ILLUSTRATION 6.1

3. Emotional processing activates or deactivates the DRD2 gene, which makes it either possible or impossible to experience pleasure.
4. The nucleus accumbens can:
   - either enhance or degrade emotion to motor control areas
   - project to other brain mechanisms that inhibit (GABA-ergic) or excite (glutamatergic) the nervous system
   - project dopamine to other brain areas
5. Brain mechanisms receiving input from the nucleus accumbens after activities from 1, 2, 3, and 4 occur are:
   - Amygdala: activates emotional responses
   - Medial Prefrontal Cortex: central emotion processing mechanism
   - Ventral Pallidum: activates motor activity
   - Thalamus: distributes information to several parts of the brain
   - Hypothalamus: integrates emotion and physiology and stimulate enkephalins
6. Projections to these brain mechanisms results in either pleasure or inability to feel pleasure.

The complex cascade of activity initiated by attachment pattern response to stressors, and consequential dysregulation of affect, ultimately results in the experience of pleasure or lack of pleasure. This suggests that patterns of addictive craving develop from a susceptibility made possible by dysfunction in attachment patterns. Addicts are usually attempting to repair attachment deficits and the emotions produced by them by pursuing substances that at least temporarily alleviate the disturbing affective states.

When a person loses their capacity to experience pleasure by means of one's own endogenous mechanisms, there is a tendency to seek it externally. An entire lifestyle based around this external pleasure seeking may take place.

- If a person finds an external source of pleasure such as alcohol, cocaine, nicotine, etc., then the skill of seeking pleasure through one's own inner resources may eventually erode.
- When this occurs, the dependency on external substances tends to increase.
- Addiction treatment programs that utilize psychiatric drugs to assist in treating addictions may serve as socially acceptable cross-addiction sources that do not address the acquisition of skills for accessing pleasure endogenously.

If it is an illegal or prescription substance, an end to availability is eventually likely. When a loss of availability to an external source of pleasure that one has become dependent upon, is gone, extreme dysfunctional high risk behavior may take place to acquire it. Therefore, a therapeutic goal would be to enhance one's skill at regulation of emotion and activating the ability to access internal resources for producing pleasure naturally.

By providing a means to rapidly alleviate disturbing emotions as well as to eventually transform the attachment disorder, addictive craving can cease. By specifically matching the exact resonance of the psychological and physical component of the particular addictive craving state with ETT®, a rapid dismantling of that state frequently occurs.

The addictive craving state is the central component of any addiction. It includes a constellation of behaviors, cognitions, social environments, etc. Conventional addiction treatment attempts to teach all the appropriate ways to cope with every aspect of the addiction, but does not generally change the addictive craving itself. ETT® procedures typically eliminate addictive craving in one to five sessions. The addictive template itself can be changed. When it is changed, euphoria often ensues. This suggests that the dysfunctional reward cascade is reversed. If this concept is correct, it suggests that the DRD2 gene's activity is also reversed. This rapid change from craving to euphoria correlates with the change in function of the nucleus accumbens from inhibiting pleasure to producing pleasure.

RAPID ELIMINATION OF ADDICTIVE CRAVING PROTOCOLS

ETT® provides an unprecedented breakthrough in treatment. Many people have experienced treatment for detoxification from a substance only to relapse over and over. These failures occur largely because most treatments cannot access the depth of attachment disorders, nor can they facilitate rapid and complete change of the unresolved emotions involved. Some clients demonstrate a dramatic change in personality after detoxification. Substance use immediately after an ETT® session is one of the few things that can undo the work of ETT® sessions, but when ETT® is used after detoxification the magnitude and speed of change with ETT® is often quite dramatic.

At the center of problematic addictions is the phenomenon of craving. Addicts tend to build an entire lifestyle around addictive craving. Therefore, most treatment programs build an entire treatment plan that alters this context. For example, twelve step programs offer an alternative social context, and in-patient rehabilitation programs provide an entirely different lifestyle for a while. While there is some success in altering the context of addictive craving, there has been no single, swift and non-pharmaceutical process for consistently directly accessing and transforming the addictive craving itself. ETT® offers such a process. Addictive craving can be changed within a range of just a few seconds to just a few sessions depending on several factors. These factors include, but are not limited to the following issues that are pursued in the following sequence:

1. Poor relationships: establish strong interpersonal rapport by using the attachment focused responses identified in the Vazquez protocol.
2. Dysfunctional personal history: identify personal history, addictive history, recent addictive behaviors and relationship history as well as current relationship issues.
3. Identify detoxification issues regarding substance use. Provide detoxification plans if necessary.
4. Issues related to secrecy and fear of disclosure about the addiction might need to be identified and resolved before the treatment can take place.
5. Identify cross addiction issues. This may include the transfer of sexual addictions to illicit substances like cocaine or legal substances like caffeine, sugar, or cigarette. If one craving is resolved, does it actually resolve the pattern? Focus treatment on all addictive cravings.
6. Identify multiple addiction issues. If one addiction supports or makes possible a second addiction, the craving of two or more addictions might need to be resolved. For example, if one uses alcohol in order to act on a sexual addiction both cravings need to be resolved.
7. Identify potential co-addicts and involve the co-addict in the treatment process if necessary. Generally speaking, if enabling behaviors can be identified and stopped, pursue appropriate support by the co-addict for the addict's treatment.
8. Identify the potential social implications that my cause disharmony when the craving is changed. Focus on this adjustment in treatment if necessary.

Once these factors are identified and appropriately ameliorated, procedures for the rapid relief of addictive craving can be pursued with a greater likelihood of long-term success. In some cases the addiction may be relieved first. There are several different states of craving that would call for varying procedures within the ETT® repertoire. Some examples of these different states of craving include, but are not limited to the following:

1. If the person is not yet committed to resolving the addiction due to denial issues and for lack of adequate self-esteem, these issues must be resolved first, to prevent the client from dropping out of treatment. Either an intense and lengthy session to reverse these issues can be used or daily homework using indigo for denial and orange for self-esteem can take place until the second session.
2. If the person does not understand the nature of his or her inner drives that fuel the craving and desires, this would call for certain procedures to promote insight.
    A. If the inner drive is currently intense, the use of peripheral goggles would tend to provoke clarity through evoking previously implicit memory related to motives or emotions fueling the craving while reducing the intensity simultaneously.
    B. If the inner drive is out of one's current conscious awareness, the spectral resonance technique can be used to rapidly access relevant motives and/or emotions.
3. If the person is currently craving and wants immediate relief, several options are available within ETT® to stop the craving immediately and often long-term.
    A. Multidimensional eye movement (MDEM) can be used to provide quick (within seconds or minutes) relief of craving on a long-term basis.
    B. The use of the Chromapulse II light-emitting device can be used to provide wavelengths of light that precisely resonate with the craving feeling, which often results in the elimination of craving within minutes.

When addictive craving is eliminated within a few minutes the client reports a change in the intensity of the psychophysiological state from level 9 for example, to 0. As the craving intensity diminishes a spontaneous state of euphoria often emerges. If a person is used to an alcoholic high, the euphoria feels like drunkenness. If a person is used to a cocaine high the euphoric state is reminiscent of that type of state. The euphoria is likely to feel like whatever type of euphoria that person has experienced. In some cases euphoria is a completely new type of feeling. Sex addicts report feeling like they just had sex. Most often people reported feeling loved. This euphoria is consistent with the reversal of the reward deficiency syndrome in which the nucleus accumbens shifts from inhibitory to excitatory activation of the experience of pleasure.

4. If the person is not presently craving but wishes to pursue relief of the craving state, there are optimal ETT® procedures to consistently achieve this on a long-term basis.
   A. Through the use of the photo assessment technique, the addictive state can be isolated, reactivated, and then quickly extinguished.
   B. Through the use of the spectral resonance technique the addictive state can be reactivated and brought to conclusion.
5. If one origin of the addiction is known to be a trauma, use MDEM for rapid relief.
6. If the person wants to acquire long-term relief of the addictive drive in general and emotional regulation is particular, ETT® processes can be used to correct underlying attachment issues from which these cravings emanate through the following processes:
   A. The optimal response to each client's attachment pattern in the interpersonal client-therapist bond should be pursued.
   B. The resolution of specific attachment issues and events via a variety of ETT® procedures can conclude these unresolved distressed issues.
   C. Using ETT® to resolve attachment problems from early childhood can change an attachment disorder on a long-term basis.

Cigarette addicts, for example, must learn how to regulate their own emotions. Nicotine possesses the unique attribute of either calming anxiety or activating fatigue. Cigarettes are second only to heroin in their capacity to make the user an addict. However, because cigarettes are legal, attempts to quit are often not pursued with a powerful program. People underestimate the challenge of overcoming cigarette addiction. Even if they do quit, people often experience what AA calls a "dry drunk." This means that they have detoxified from a substance but not processed the issues and emotions that motivated its use. Since cigarettes numb emotions, without cigarettes these emotions are likely to surface without any skills to regulate them. This results in a very unhappy person whose relationships often become disturbed without cigarettes. Of course, another answer is to teach emotional regulation through the use of ETT®. Then the need for a crutch to numb emotions becomes unnecessary. Although this may take several sessions, if you have ever watched someone die of lung cancer or emphysema, a few sessions to learn emotional regulation seems to be a small price to pay.

Of all the different types of substance addiction and abuse, in my experience alcohol is definitely the one responsible for the most tragic consequences. Statistically, alcohol accounts for more auto accidents, more death by cirrhosis of the liver, and more dysfunctional family issues than any other substance. People who are at a high risk for abuse find that alcohol's easy availability and social acceptability make abstinence more difficult. In the case of alcohol, people often need to learn how to shift from one state of mind to another more efficiently. Tension reduction is essential. Unresolved attachment disorders are usually at the heart of the problem. When these issues are resolved rapidly and at a depth level, the attraction to alcohol diminishes. So many different types of psychological disorders may co-occur with alcohol addiction that treatment length is highly variable. In addition, relationship losses and dysfunctions may co-occur, increasing treatment complexity because more than just alcohol addiction is being treated. It is often long standing relationship issues that are the core problem.

Even when the addict abstains from alcohol, the problem is not over. At this point the most critical part of treatment is implemented—containing chaotic emotions, while at the same time processing the depth of the client's issues rapidly. For those reasons ETT® is the optimal method for achieving these ends. ETT® can contain affect intensity through peripheral eye stimulation, pursue depth through the use of color, and process disturbing emotions rapidly through the combination of several ETT® techniques.

Treatment for each substance addiction varies, and treatment of cross addictions is necessary. The length of treatment will vary based on the existence of co-occurring disorders and the complexity of relationship issues occurring at the same time. Without these complicating issues, long-term addiction relief often occurs in just a few sessions.

KEY POINTS IN TREATING ADDICTIONS WITH ETT®

Focus on relationship deficiencies.

1. Explore the relationship between the client and the substance. Does it provide:
    a. nurturance when lonely?
    b. elevation when depressed?

   c. relaxation when tense?
   d. escape when perplexed?
   e. ego inflation when self-esteem is low?
   f. other?
2. Process these types of issues in current relationships.
3. Facilitate appropriate emotional regulation. Then teach clients healthy emotional regulation.
4. Identify previous relationship deficiencies and relieve unresolved affect related to it.
5. Reverse attachment deficiencies from family of origin.

Another challenge of addiction treatment regards stabilizing the change in identity. This often involves changing the people surrounding the addict. This may mean acquiring appropriate support from friends and family or eliminating them from the client's life. A new life must be built in which addictive or behavioral sources of addiction are not involved.

OBESITY AND DIABETES

The role of obesity in the condition of diabetes is highly significant.

- 23.6 million children and adults in the United States have diabetes.
- 57 million U.S. citizens are pre-diabetics.
- 23.1 percent of people over sixty years old have diabetes.
- Diabetes was the seventh leading cause of death listed on U.S. death certificates in 2006.
- Adults with diabetes have heart disease death rates about two to four times higher than adults without diabetes.
- Diabetes is the leading cause of new cases of blindness among adults twenty to seventy-four years of age.
- Diabetes is the leading cause of kidney failure.
- $174 billion is the total cost of diagnosed diabetes in the United States in 2007 (from 2007 National Diabetes fact sheet).

The correlation between diabetes and obesity is so strong that significant weight loss has been the only intervention that has actually eliminated this otherwise lifelong condition. Motives for weight loss for diabetics extend beyond vanity and self-esteem to actual survival. Despite this fact, diabetics appear to be no more successful in losing weight than anyone else. In the case of diabetes quick-fix commercial gimmicks that foster repeated weight loss and weight gain may actually risk lethal consequences. Diabetics need and effective life-long means for resolving obesity. Sugar craving becomes a significant death threat to diabetics.

Carla's Sugar Addiction

Carla looked helpless when she asked to work on her sugar addiction. She was willing to work on it but acted as if it might be a fruitless endeavor since it was a life-long problem and she had already spent numerous sessions in different kinds of therapy to resolve it. Carla was a fifty-five-year-old, Caucasian, divorced female.

> Carla (face to face interaction): I became aware of my sugar addiction when I was a child, probably age nine or ten. I may have been addicted before that but became aware of it this because my mother would make candy for Christmas and she would store it in little coffee tins and then at Christmas time she would pull it out. Well, I compulsively snuck into the pantry where she had it stored and I would eat one or two pieces at a time and at Christmas went she when to get it, there was none there because I had eaten it all.
>
> Therapist: That is helpful. Please tell me more.
>
> Carla: I would eat on the way home from school in elementary school. I could stop at the grocery store and she had a charge account there and I could have a coke and a candy bar after school on the way home. I enjoyed doing that!
>
> I remember that when my mother was sick in bed with emphysema and I was about five, I would steal money from her purse. Then I would go to the store and by candy with it.
>
> Therapist: What about today? How is the addiction today?
>
> Carla: Well today, if I keep it out of my house I go out of my way to stay clear of it. But if it presents itself to me (like if I am at a party) I will have to have some. It's almost like I am powerless over it. I got to have it! Sometimes there have been periods of my life that I have been able to eliminate it from my life. Those periods don't last. If there is any anxiety that stirs in me the first thing I want to do is eat. I just bought some M&Ms. And that's what I wanted was sugar.
>
> Therapist: Okay. Do you have the craving now?

Carla: Not now because I just had the M&Ms.

Therapist: Alright. What would you like to happen?

Carla: "I would like to be free of that draw to it. I would like to have it not be an issue.

Therapist: You do remember what the craving is like?

Carla: Yes. But sometimes I just want it even, though I don't crave it. It's like there is a memory there. . . . I remember what that feels like, even if I am not craving it.

Therapist: I would like for you to rate the craving experience from 1 to 10. You will be exposed to each color one at a time to see what the closest match to your craving experience is.

Carla: Far Red—doesn't seem to be there. The word that comes to mind is brownies. And when I see brownies it is almost impossible for me to resist it!

Therapist: What does the craving feel like?

Carla: The feeling is excitement, anticipation!

Therapist: What about your bodily sensations?

Carla: I don't know.

Therapist: Red—pretty low craving now.

Carla: Red-Orange—I am thinking about the plate of chocolate chip cookies that would be on the kitchen table when I came home from school. They would be warm, so there would be a warmth feeling to it. I would feel loved. With a plate of chocolate chip cookies, that is how my mother would show love. I would rate it a 4.

Orange—4
Yellow—about a 6
Yellow-Green—about a 7
Green—about a 5
Blue-Green—about an 8
Blue—probably a 5, a calm 5.
Med Blue—probably a 4.
Violet—probably still a 4

Therapist: Blue-green is the color that matches your craving state

Therapist: Using the RGB system, blue-green was used. Red-00, green-81, blue-81.

Carla: I feel more intense craving. Driving to the ice cream store as a family on a Saturday when it was warm and we got ice cream.

Therapist: Look at three o'clock.

Carla: That lessened it.

Therapist: Go to nine o'clock.

Carla: In seventh grade I was at a new school and on the way home we would stop at the restaurant and I would get a small candy bar and a coke. And there was a social aspect in that.

Therapist: You see a connection between the eating and the social aspect. Did they both feel good?

Carla: Yes. The craving is not as intense.

Therapist: Go to six o'clock two inches outside of the light.

Carla: It really doesn't have anything to do with sugar. I recall my father making pancakes on Saturday mornings for the family. The thing that comes to mind is the family together. Craving isn't there but there is some sadness.

Therapist: Is there a sugar craving when you think of that?

Carla: No. I just like the feeling of the family being together.

Therapist: Red-00, green-255, blue-72.

Carla: Sadness is a little stronger.

Therapist: Red-00, green-185, blue-00.

Carla: It's easing at the six o'clock position.

Therapist: The relationship and feelings were the connection to this food and sugar.

Carla: Yes.

Therapist: Look at twelve o'clock two inches outside the light.

Carla: Probably about a 3. Preoccupied with the candy. There is some fear that I am not able to resist. Fear in upper part of my middle back.

Therapist: Red-00, green-185, blue-44.

Carla: The fear is gone.

Therapist: Now go to seven o'clock.

Carla: Craving decreased to about a 3. Sweets are still more important to me than other foods. I feel a reward of some kind; pleasure.

Therapist: Red-82, green-80, blue-00.

Carla: I feel more attached to chocolate!

Therapist: Look at one o'clock.

Carla: It's easier to think about not having it, if it's there. The problem is if it's there I see it.

Therapist: Red-81, green-80, blue-88.

Carla: Not as appealing.

Therapist: Go to eight o'clock.

Carla: Now what comes to mind is wedding cake and how much I enjoy eating wedding cake. It feels fun. I feel like I could be a lot of fun. Sensations in my face.

Therapist: Still looking at eight o'clock. Red-81, green-80, blue-255.

Carla: The facial sensations have stopped. I don't need food to have fun.

Therapist: Good, go to two o'clock.

Carla: It's more manageable. About a 2. I feel a little anxiety in my stomach about seeing it.

Therapist: Red-214, green-208, blue-234.

Carla: I feel a greater anxiety about seeing it and how I am going to react to it. . . . That's interesting. I have a choice as to what I am going to do about it.

Therapist: Red-10, green-11, blue-234.

Carla: I feel more grown up. I feel more adult about food and responding to food.

Therapist: Now go to ten o'clock.

Carla: I still have anxiety about seeing it and what will happen when I see it.

Therapist: Red-00, green-00, blue-192.

Carla: More tension in my stomach.

Therapist: Red-205, green-60, blue-16. What about the sugar craving? How do you feel?

Carla: I am thinking about the plate of brownies and thinking about how I would respond. It just feels like I don't need them as much.

Therapist: Red-205, green-60, blue-15, brightness-84.

Carla: I feel lighter, brighter, and happier. Craving is not there.

Therapist: Tell me about the original sugar craving.

Carla: When I am presented with a plate of brownies or a plate of cookies or a bowl of candy, I find it difficult not to choose to pick up and eat the sweets. The craving is about a 3. I still have something for it.

Therapist: Go to eight o'clock. What do you have here?

Carla: Probably a 2.

Therapist: Red-255, green-27, blue-00, brightness-51.

Carla: I am thinking about Oreo cookies. Still associates with my childhood. I love to take them apart and eat the stuff on the inside. I am now feeling that it is fun. That was really fun to have Oreo cookies! But I didn't have just one or two Oreo cookies; I wanted to eat the whole bag.

Therapist: Red-255, green-146, blue-00, brightness-51.

Carla: It calms the urge to eat the Oreo cookies and I can remember that I enjoyed that. I can also leave that in the past. And know that that was a part of my childhood. That is not a part of my life now. I can think about the brownies and chocolate chip cookies that way as having been a part of my childhood that way. There is a separation in my awareness that that was then and this is now.

Therapist: Red-255, green-146, blue-00, brightness-60.

Carla: It is like there is an unhooking from the needs of childhood and the needs now. The unhooking is a freeing kind of experience. It is an unhooking awareness that I am no longer that child and don't have to feed my needs that way. There were a lot of reasons, good reasons why I used food back then. But I don't have those same reasons today.

Therapist: Summarize what you think happened in this session. When you started and where you are now.

> Carla: I think I dipped into the sadness, the emotions of childhood from which I used food to deal with, to compensate for, to comfort myself, to help myself as a child. And that I have been clinging or connected to that child state, that need. It's like there was a connection with the child state, emotions and the childhood way of coping. And now it is like I am unhooked from that. I can have an awareness and appreciation for that. But I don't have to do it anymore.

Carla's case illustrates the ETT® procedures for the extinguishment of addictive craving. In the case of food addiction, one must eat food that makes detoxification or complete omission inappropriate. However, one can single out a type or category of food as the target of treatment. Due to this context and the legal availability of food, food addictions may be as difficult or more difficult to resolve than illegal drugs. The association between the pleasure of social interactions and food was illustrated throughout this case study. Over time the sugared foods alone appeared to produce the pleasure (consistent with oxytocin production) that social bonds produced. Evidence of addictive characteristics appeared early in Carla's life when she stole food and stole money to buy sweet food. It was evident that regressive psychological states emerged to dominate Carla's behavior as an adult.

It was necessary to re-activate the addictive template in order to effectively extinguish it. By systematically identifying the exact wavelength of light that re-activated addictive craving in spite of the fact that the craving had been satisfied immediately before the session provides an illustration of the power of light stimulation to precisely target and activate a given psychophysical state. Then via peripheral eye stimulation and amplified attunement specific emotional and physical states emerged from implicit memory and were extinguished one at a time. After systemically extinguishing each component of the emotional change that culminated in the addictive template, Carla described an "unhooking" from the memory and the craving for sugar products. This unhooking is consistent with reversing the inability to experience pleasure through endogenous means. This shift suggests that the pleasure center of the brain (nucleus accumbens) reversed its function, which must mean that the DRD2 gene expression was changed because research has concluded that these mechanisms are responsible for addiction.

The bottom line in addiction treatment is, does the change last? In this case and in most ETT® cases when the craving is extinguished, a long-term change takes place. So far this has occurred with Carla. However, if a relapse were to occur, it typically requires only a session or two to complete the change. While Carla can eat food and even eat sugared foods the "draw" toward sugar no longer exists. This change restores voluntary control to the adult ego state. Of course a different means for acquiring affection constructively could now take over, which makes addictive craving unnecessary as an adult.

This same procedure has worked equally effectively with other food addiction, illicit drug addictions, over-the-counter drug addictions, prescription drug addictions, anorexia nervosa, bulimia, and alcohol addiction.

Since commercial weight loss programs of all types claim high success rates, it makes it difficult to acquire unbiased information. For this reason a *Consumer Reports* study was selected to focus on for the ETT® program. The *Consumer Reports* study is the largest study ever done on obesity and weight loss. It surveyed 32,213 participants. This study provided information about people who successfully lost weight and kept it off for years as well as those who failed. The successful losers exercised regularly three times a week and listed exercise as their number one strategy. Only 10 percent of dieters lost weight and kept it off. Over 80 percent of the successful losers lost weight entirely on their own without any commercial programs. However, when the successful weight losers did seek help, it was a form of one-to-one counseling such as seeing a psychotherapist or nutritionist. Of course the successful weight losers selected healthier foods.

In addition to these factors the central focus about dysfunctional eating behavior is that compulsive eating is driven by an attempt to "stuff, block, or otherwise cope with unwanted emotions." The biological fact is that oxytocin (the cuddle hormone) is secreted after eating, which provides a soothing effect. When people do not possess the ability to regulate unwanted emotions, eating food is an easily accessible means to at least temporarily modify emotional distress. When the current food advertising market (about 75 percent of television commercials concern selling food) and the social association with food are added to the influence, eating strays far from its function of survival to a means to feel good and to fit in socially. When eating becomes compulsive, excessive, and preoccupies the psyche, it becomes an addiction, not a health activity. All of these challenges are psychological ones. Therefore, when psychological disorders such as depression or anxiety are present, one becomes extremely vulnerable to dysfunctional eating and obesity.

These profiles of people who successfully lose weight and keep it off, and profiles of people who continuously fail, present an entirely different challenge than most commercial programs address. Ideas such as "lose 30 pounds in 30 days by taking x chemical" appeal to the quick-fix allure without addressing the fundamental causes of the problem, nor the long-term lifestyle necessary for a change in eating behavior to endure. ETT® possesses as one of its greatest strengths the capacity to uncover hidden motives and the power to regulate distressing emotions. Therefore, in the ETT® program the following issues are targeted. This yields a high success in improving eating behavior and long-term weight loss.

- Rule out medical issues.
- Identify and pursue blockages to physical exercise.
- Identify and pursue issues that interfere with one becoming self-motivated.
- Assess for psychological disorders that limit a person's ability to regulate emotions.
- Involve potential co-addicts or other people in relationship with the client for proper support.
- Identify and pursue lifestyle issues and dysfunctional habits.
- Convert dysfunctional emotional regulation into constructive emotional regulation.
- Consult a nutritionist or nutritional books if necessary.
- As weight loss occurs, process appropriate adjustment of self-perception.
- Prepare the client to override or mentally counter the social challenges, societal advertising impact, and/or the atmosphere that promotes dysfunctional eating.

In every case treatment is individualized to fit the needs of each person. Instead of a hit-or-miss program that assumes the same strategy will work for all people, assessments allow a custom-tailored plan to yield a higher probability for success. Approximately 50 percent of overeaters possess psychological disorders like depression and/or anxiety. Therefore, in these cases attention should focus upon correcting these disorders first and then a change in eating behavior has a much higher chance to succeed.

Many people (particularly men) are unaware that their perceived experience of "hunger" is not actual hunger, but instead an emotionally driven experience that culminates in perceived hunger. Then the prospect of taking away food may activate a starvation threat resulting in an aversion to changing one's eating behavior. Aversion to changing can appear as a lack of motivation that is contradictory to one's logical conscious desire. Then failure to correct eating behavior is likely. This predicament can then impact self-perception in a negative way, which reinforces the same ineptness. The distress of ineptness may promote "hunger" and the need to acquire relief. Then this cycle has begun all over again.

The key to this fear of not getting the hunger feeling satisfied is often that emotions have become dissociated from conscious awareness but still surface in the form of perceived hunger. In this way people may not be aware that their compulsive overeating is an emotional regulation phenomenon. Therefore, it is difficult to conceive of a constructive change in eating behavior as something other than denying oneself pleasure. However, if awareness of emotions is increased and regulation of emotions improved, manifestations of emotional experiences into perceived hunger is unlikely to occur. This averts perceived self-denial, starvation, or the omission of pleasure. ETT® possesses the distinct capacity to elicit one's own endogenous pleasure without the necessity of an outside substance. Furthermore, this pleasure capacity can eventually be activated by oneself without ETT®.

The 10 percent of the participants in the *Consumer Reports* study that succeeded in weight loss and kept the weight off for five years advocated exercise as the best strategy. A thorough assessment of potential blockages to exercise has been helpful to identify the exact reasons why people do not exercise effectively. This custom-tailoring pursuit of blockages yields a high level of results. The issues identified are usually emotionally driven. For example, for someone to state, "I hate exercise," suggests very strong emotional issues related to exercise. Through ETT® processing when "hate" can be understood and neutralized, the idea of exercise may no longer oppose pleasure, which makes the choice of exercise easier.

Ultimately most dysfunctional eating is essentially a dependency issue. The successful weight losers in the *Consumer Reports* study were by far self starters that used no commercial weight loss program. Often when people could not get their emotional needs met effectively during development, they learned to resort to something they could reliably depend on such as food. Therefore, uncovering any issues that contribute to dependency or the lack of self initiative often proves to be very important.

The challenge seldom undertaken by most commercial weight loss programs is that of a life-long cure for obesity. In fact most commercial weight loss programs become financially successful because they can count on people relapsing and returning for another attempt. The "yo yo" experience of losing and regaining weight several times is the norm, not the exception. It is intriguing that people typically pursue a rapid weight loss and either naively assume it will last a lifetime or simply do not envision the long-term possibilities after an initial weight loss. The most common occurrence is that after two or three weight losses and regains, people become discouraged and digress into helplessness, which often becomes self-denigrating in the form of "lack of willpower." The flaw in this thinking is that a careful plan that pursues the fundamental causes of food addiction has not been resolved, so the relapse is highly likely.

In the ETT® program it is expected that as the person successfully loses weight, entirely new issues will emerge that must be overcome in order to stabilize long-term success. For example, if a woman loses 50 lbs there is a greater chance that men will make sexual advances. If this takes place and the woman is unprepared to manage it effectively, the discomfort might encourage a relapse into previous eating patterns in order to cope. If an ETT® therapist continues to monitor these issues months after initial treatment, the chances of stabilization are drastically improved.

When people have over 100 lbs to lose, that challenge is greater and requires more resources. Since medical issues may become more complex in these cases, medical monitoring is more important for safety. The amount and type of exercise is different with extreme obesity so a good personal trainer becomes necessary. Nutritional guidance may be more essential depending upon the person's knowledge. This chapter is focused on people with weight loss issues from 15 lbs to 100 lbs overweight.

Research has confirmed that calorie restriction or under eating, but not to the level of malnutrition, promotes anti aging. It appears to oppose cancer development, alter genetic expression and slow aging by reducing free radical damage to tissues (Lee, Klopp, Weindruch, & Prolla, 1999; Weindruch & Sohal, 1997; Sohal & Weindruch, 1996).

7

Healing Sexual Addictions

After my PowerPoint presentation at an international conference of addiction specialists, I asked for a volunteer who was currently experiencing addictive craving. A man quickly stood up and walked rapidly to the front of the audience of about eighty people. Bart described himself as a sex addict and crack-cocaine addict who had been through years of in-patient, out-patient, and 12-Step treatment. As my eyes met his, he looked intensely pre-occupied with his concern. He was asked to be seated in front of the Chromapulse II light device. When I asked him to describe his craving level, he said it was 7 or 8 on a scale of 10 (with 10 being most disturbing). He was asked to describe what the craving felt like. He said, "I feel intense anxiety all over but mostly right here" (pointing to his chest).

Then I turned the light device on and selected green on the RGB system beginning at 25 degree of saturation. He was asked to look at the light. His description was paraphrased back to him and he was consoled about his desperate plight. Then I said, "Let's see if I can help. Please let me know if you notice any change in your addictive craving as you look at the light." Then I began to elevate the saturation level of green. Within seconds Bart began to report a lessening of the degree of intensity of his addictive craving and a "lifting" of his chest tension. As I continued to slowly elevate the green he continued to report a lowering of addictive craving level. After a couple of minutes (with saturation at 162) he finally said that "the craving was completely gone." He said, "I can't believe it!" He had a facial countenance of euphoric peace.

Later he reported that he couldn't even bring up the craving when he focused on the image associated with the craving. The next day he reported that the change had sustained. Eight months later Bart told me that the addictive craving had never returned, and he disclosed that his original intention for volunteering was to show that the ETT® method was a hoax!

Many attempts to eliminate addictive craving have encountered an inability to alleviate addictive craving on a rapid and long-term basis. Pharmaceutical agents such as methadone and buprenorphine have been used to block neurotransmitter receptors to manage addictive craving (Thomas, Reif, Haq, Wallack, Hoyt, & Ritter 2008; Connock, Juarez-Garcia, Jowett, et al., 2007). EMDR has been used to process the trauma associated with sexual addiction to relieve addictive symptoms (Cox & Howard, 2007). Cognitive and behavioral therapy have long been used in addiction treatment. 12-Step programs provide group support for addicts but the first step implies that addictive craving may be a life-long identity (Alcoholics Anonymous, 2002). According to William Moyers, vice president of one of the world's largest addiction-treatment centers, roughly 50 percent of patients remain abstinent in the year following treatment (Weiss & Male, 2009). Long-term cessation of addictive behavior has a low success rate, even with the best inpatient treatment. Most addiction treatment assumes that addictive craving is a long-term brain dysfunction that cannot be eliminated. Therefore, the vast majority of treatment programs focus on managing the addictive craving. The non-pharmaceutical cessation of addictive craving, long-term within a single session, has not yet been consistently accomplished heretofore.

SEXUAL ADDICTION

Sexual addiction is one of several different types of behavioral or "process addictions" that is differentiated from addictions to a substance. However, sexual addiction has been described as similar to alcoholism (Carnes, Delmonico, & Griffin, 2001). These hypersexual experiences can become mood altering and craving for this form of perceived satisfaction often becomes the central focus of the person's life (Carnes, Delmonico, & Griffin, 2001). This problem of compulsive sexual behavior has escalated in conjunction to the growth of the use of pornography via the internet (Carnes, 2001). Stimulation and pleasure often become substitutes for emptiness, emotional pain (Carnes, 1997; Senay, 1998). Dysfunctional family dynamics in both one's family of origin and one's current relationship constellation have been found to be related to the etiology of sexual addiction (Carnes, 1997). Ineffective attachment patterns from early bonding experiences can make people vulnerable to addictive compulsions late in life to compensate for their attachment deficiencies (Flores, 2004). If the availability of a sexual behavior or a range of sexual thoughts and actions temporarily satisfies a specific deficiency, it can develop into a compulsive behavior. While debate exists about whether sexual activity can actually be defined as an addiction, this behavior can at least be characterized as hypersexual compulsivity that can become dysfunctional with costly consequences.

DIAGNOSTIC ISSUES RELATED TO SEXUAL ADDICTION

There are several diagnostic issues that should be addressed (Sealy, 1999). The following list identifies diagnostic issues related to sexual addiction.

- Differentiate recreational use from addictive sexual activity.
- Are there legal, occupational, or financial consequences from hypersexual compulsivity?
- Differentiate other psychological disorders from sexual compulsivity.
- Does sexual compulsivity contribute to other psychological disorders?

If addictive craving is just one focus of an overall obsessive compulsive disorder, a different four-week protocol is used for treating this obsessive compulsive disorder. The appropriate interpersonal rapport between client and therapist is a factor in therapeutic success and must work well before ETT® succeeds.

PROCEDURES FOR TREATMENT

The following procedure works well under certain circumstances. If the client is not feeling the craving currently and is unable to consistently retrieve the experience, the spectral resonance technique is the preferred approach. Under these conditions it is valuable to retrieve implicit memory and emotions that involve the experience of the craving. Once the craving experience is somewhat reactivated and can be retained, the following procedure is used. It involves a systematic preparation and search for the optimal resonance between visual brain stimulation and the craving state in the following sequence.

1. A history of the client's family of origin, current constellation of relationships, medical and psychological symptoms, etc., is taken.

2. Identification of the client's attachment pattern is assessed. Attachment-based responses are provided throughout the procedure.
3. Communicative rapport development based on his/her attachment pattern is facilitated.
4. Co-occurring disorders must be identified because treatment of other disorders accompanying addiction will modify the treatment plan.
5. Assessment of the client's readiness and objectives for treatment takes place including potential perceived safety threats, positive resources, and possible co-addicts.
6. Perceived safety is facilitated and positive resources may be accessed.
7. The procedure selected for the immediate objective and expectations for participation are explained.
8. If craving is currently present, the client is asked to rate its intensity from 1 to 10 (with 10 being most intense).
9. The client is asked to identify the degree to which each wavelength of light matches the craving state. The client provides a rating from 1 to 10.
10. When the ideal match between visual stimulation and craving state occurs, the craving usually extinguishes within seconds or minutes.
11. If the optimal match does not occur, the client is asked to view twelve peripheral eye positions one at a time, while rating the match. When the match occurs, craving is relinquished.
12. If a match has not occurred, several oscillating rates of light are provided until a match with the craving state takes place. When the match occurs, craving is relinquished.
13. Stabilization of the change from craving occurs through client narrative, education, or facilitating comfort.

There are at least two differences in the treatment of behavioral addictions and substance addictions. Detoxification from the substance in order for treatment to work is more necessary in substance addictions. There are specific ETT® protocols used to rectify denial and compromised self-esteem that often undermine the detoxification process. Chronic, long-term use of substance possesses a greater possibility for the development of organic brain dysfunction, which may limit recovery. There are specific ETT® procedures that have been beneficial for re-establishing compromised brain function that had previously been thought of as lost forever. Therefore, these two factors may require an alteration in treatment planning between behavioral addiction and substance addiction. Issues of lying and shame about the addictive behavior may be a greater challenge in sexual addiction treatment than in substance addiction.

ETT® has been shown to repeatedly eliminate addictive craving long-term within a single session. While in most cases, elimination of addictive craving by ETT® occurs in a single session, it is not unusual for a series of a few sessions to be required to achieve elimination of craving in complex cases of addiction.

Case Study: Joe

Joe felt uneasy but pushed himself to try whatever was suggested to get over his sexual compulsion for little girls. Joe was thirty and knew it was wrong and that he risked going to jail if he could not stop the compulsion. He volunteered to work with me in front of the staff of about thirty people. Joe was nervous but he still felt an intense sexual craving that wouldn't leave his mind. He was nearing the end of his ninety-day stay in this expensive in-patient addiction facility and after trying EMDR, neurofeedback, individual counseling, group therapy, 12-Step groups and other things, he still felt the craving.

I tried to create a bond with Joe by asking a few questions and attuning to his experience. Joe described a distinct fixation on young girls whose breasts were just beginning to develop. He spoke with an intensity and then a frustration about his helplessness. Joe said he felt intense anxiety all over but especially in his chest at a level 9 (with 10 being most intense). He was asked to look at the light as I slowly elevated the green saturation level upward from 25. Gradually his hypersexual craving level became less and less. Within about three minutes, it finally reached zero intensity. At that point Joe's voice got very excited as he described a state of euphoria unlike anything he could remember. He said, "I thought that maybe that neurofeedback was helping but it was nothing like this! This is a complete change and I feel so good!"

I checked with Joe's therapist the next day and craving cessation was sustained. I checked with her again a month later and she reported that no sexual craving existed still. Logically one would think an organization claiming to advocate state-of-the-art therapy would be excited to implement this method into their program. Sexual craving ceased within three minutes through ETT® when it couldn't be stopped with around-the-clock treatment for eighty days. After a couple of inquiries I never heard back from that organization. It appeared that these professionals could not accept what their eyes had seen, which is a common experience with ETT®.

Why would wavelengths of light that appear in the green range facilitate such a dramatic change? Through hundreds of observations of the effect of different wavelengths of light on psycho-emotional states, consistent effects of each band of wavelengths have been identified. These "green" effects match with the functions of the paraventricular nucleus of the hypothalamus under conditions of the loss of a primary source of affection. The paraventricular nucleus of the hypothalamus through its connections to the dorsal vagal complex (DVC) can shut down organic systems in lower mammals for the purpose of conserving energy when a perceived loss of oxygen occurs. In humans when the loss of primary sources of affection or the lack of these sources occurs, the same conservation response occurs in humans. The paraventricular nucleus produces the neuropeptiades oxytocin and vasopressin, which affect the DVC (Landraf et al., 1994). Oxytocin is associated with pleasurable feelings after feeding, during breast feeding, during sexual climax, and during affectionate touch. Vasopressin is associated with physical experiences occurring due to the loss of affectionate experiences. Visceral, bronchial and especially symptoms in the cardiac region often occur during experiences of losses of affection (Bray, 1985). When symptoms in the cardiac region occur, it is often an indication that the range of wavelengths that appear green can be used to resonate with the emotions associated with that symptom regardless of whether the person is aware that those emotions are represented in that somatic symptom. The use of green to resonate with these fixated emotions tends to rapidly acquire conclusion of the psychophysical intensity. When this takes place the secretion of oxytocin can partially account for the experiences of a euphoric peace.

This does not mean that wavelengths of green are always the choice for the resolution of addictive craving. The fact that in the aforementioned cases the subject was currently experiencing intense craving was a factor in the selection of wavelength. In other cases the craving may not be continuous and/or may be dissociated at the time of a session. This calls for a different strategy and the selection of a different band of color. There are now pre and post SPECT (Single Photon Emission Computed Tomography) scans from the use of ETT® with clients who had severe anxiety disorders in which changes in the thalamus and basal ganglia improved dramatically.

It should be taken into account that this man had been in addiction treatment programs previous to this session and was motivated to acquire relief. This preparation may have contributed to his rapid relief from addictive craving. However, similar relief from addictive craving has occurred with other people who were not as prepared. A dramatic change in the central focus of one's life can disorient the subject of this change. Therefore, other sessions may be necessary to stabilize this change. For example, if all of one's friends are addicts, one may no longer have a social network if the addiction is gone and other addicts may no longer be attractive to the non-addict. Support for this adjustment would be helpful.

The use of ETT® for the treatment of sexual compulsivity was first discovered in 1999 when this author was asked by a colleague to work with an adult male who possessed life-long obsession and compulsions to participate in sexual acts with children. This man felt tortured by his sexual compulsions and sought therapy on his own volition. The referring colleague was a psychologist who had conducted talk therapy, bioenergetics, EMDR, and other types of therapy for over a year without success. Within the first session ETT® achieved complete alleviation of the sexual obsessions and compulsions. Since this was a new application for ETT®, two follow-up sessions were conducted to be sure that the change was sustained. Several months of further contact with this client revealed that this change had been sustained. However, years went by before another opportunity to use ETT® for the relief of sexual compulsion occurred again. More recently advances in the treatment and the technology used for ETT® treatment have increased the efficacy of treatment.

The following case study was selected because it occurred under very limited circumstances demonstrating the consistency and effectiveness of the approach. The power of the method prevailed with a therapist who had just learned the ETT® techniques. The fact that this case took place by a clinician new to the method demonstrates that the protocols for treatment are replicable. If an opportunity to work with these cases under normal private practice circumstances, a more controlled situation would still be preferred. However, life circumstances do not always provide us with optimal conditions for treatment. Therefore, these examples have positive value. Of course none of this would have been possible without previously observing dozens of clients overcome craving in individual sessions.

Case Study: John

To illustrate the efficacy of the use for ETT® for the resolution of sexual compulsion, the following case study was conducted by Ann M. Kirlin, Psy. D. Psychological Intern, who at the time of the case completed the second level of training in ETT®. She invited a volunteer, who was already in treatment with two therapists and attending weekly 12-Step Sex Love Addicts Anonymous (SLAA) meetings, to use ETT® for his compulsion.

The client was a forty-eight-year-old male, divorced, Caucasian who was well groomed and a successful financial advisor. He initially volunteered to decrease his obsessions over a former girlfriend for which the breakup occurred two months previously.

John experienced a breakup with his girlfriend at about the same time his mother died, which was a few months previous to this session. John reports emotional and physical abuse in his family of origin. John had been involved with a well known in-patient treatment center that focused on relationship and sexual addiction after the break-up of his marriage that resulted from his wife's discovery of hypersexual behaviors acted out during his marriage. John experienced a high degree of obsessive behavior resulting in an increase of hypersexual behaviors after the breakup of his marriage. This similar obsessive behavior increased after the recent breakup from his recent girlfriend. John rated his obsession about his girlfriend at 10 on a scale from 1 to 10, with 10 being the most intense. John looked at her picture almost continuously and, even brought it in at the beginning of session. However, John agreed to give the picture to the therapist during the ETT® procedure. He reported continuous checking of e-mails, telephone texts, and Facebook multiple times per day. His obsessive compulsive behavior severely impaired his ability to sleep, which required prescription medication. Interpersonal rapport was developed and perceived safety was achieved to Johns' satisfaction.

John was instructed to view a series of different forms of light stimulation on the Chromapulse I light-emitting device as he focused on his obsession. When the proper wavelength of light, angle of light into the eyes, and frequency of oscillation took place, all obsessive experiences ceased almost immediately. Then the facilitator utilized all previous stimuli in an attempt to evoke the obsession as a means to test the degree of extinction of the craving obsession. The craving appeared absent. By the end of the session John was no longer interested in his ex-girlfriend's photograph and volunteered to give it to the facilitator, stating he'd rather use the frame to put his dog's picture in it. John reported to be in a state of euphoric peace, calmness, and happiness for a short time before the end of the session. Six months later the elimination of craving for his ex-girlfriend continued to be sustained.

In his second session John identified a desire to eliminate the sexual craving and arousal of imaging men as objects for his craving. An empirically based screening, "The Twenty Questions for Compulsives" from Sexual Compulsives Anonymous yielded sixteen out of twenty responses that validated his sexual compulsivity (Sexual Compulsives Anonymous, 2009). He also met the criteria for hyper sexual behavior on the majority of questions on the HB1–19 item questionnaire produced by Rory C. Reid, MSW and PhD candidate (Carpenter & Lloyd, 2009).

As the photo assessment took place certain wavelengths of light evoked strong and immediate arousal. During the session John felt an intense desire to masturbate while viewing certain wavelengths of light. He reported that outside of the session he felt compelled to make contact with others for the purpose of having a sexual encounter. Again a specific wavelength of light was found that resonated with his compulsive sexual craving. When this took place peripheral eye stimulation was used and all craving extinguished within minutes. The arousal template was attempted to be reactivated to evoke his response but now there was no reaction to it. Subsequent to this session all sexual craving was absent but non compulsive sexual desire were intact. John realized that he was not gay and reported only heterosexual desires. Eight months later John reported that the extinction of his sexual craving had been sustained. In two sessions both his relationship obsession and his sexual craving had been relinquished long-term.

In this case the principle of resonance was utilized with the craving state, which resulted in rapid extinguishment of the craving state. In addition to this change, the entire constellation of thoughts, behavior, emotions, physical experiences, and social interactions changed. Even though he no longer possessed addictive symptoms he continued to attend his 12-Step group and to see both of his therapists because it was implied that he is and will always be an addict by those authorities.

An unexpected change occurred when John became clear that he was not bisexual, but heterosexual. No attempt was made to encourage John to identify himself as gay, bisexual or heterosexual, nor was this change typical of ETT® work with sexual addictions. The intensity of John's sexual compulsion was so high that he appeared to generalize his sexual drive toward either gender. In this case, the elimination of sexual compulsivity resulted in clarification of his sexual preference.

Hypersexual addictive craving can be viewed as one particular form of affect dysregulation derived from attachment patterns that becomes fixated in association with an object or action perceived to satiate longing for relief of this state. This craving experience is a specific psychophysiological state that can be seen in the context of the concept of state-dependent learning and memory (Rossi, 1986, pp. 36–45). If an external means for accessing and facilitating a psychobiological "resonance" with the craving state is used, rapid change of the entire craving experience has been observed to consistently take place. The means of attachment based interpersonal interventions in conjunction with precise visual stimuli often creates such a resonance.

The presence of attachment disorders allows a person to be more vulnerable to the experience of trauma and posttraumatic stress disorder (Allen, 2002, pp. 61–71). Trauma is highly associated with addictive craving (Cox & Howard, 2007, pp. 5–6).

MECHANISMS FOR CHANGE OF HYPERSEXUAL ADDICTION CRAVING

The psychophysiological state of addictive craving serves as the cohesive force for a number of related thoughts, emotions, behaviors and social dynamics that are collectively known as addiction. It is proposed that the most therapeutic benefit might be achieved if the addictive craving state can be viewed within the context of state-dependent learning and memory. This concept involves the principle that the distinct pattern of arousal present in specific neural circuits in the brain at the time of memory formation may become an integral component of the stored information. Learning that occurs at the time of the memory formation may also become an integral component of the stored information. Learning that occurred during the experience of this memory may be limited to recall and use to only those times when those same neural networks are re-activated through re-experiencing the memory (Rossi, 1986, pp. 36–45). This state-dependent learning and memory, or psychophysiological template, may be embedded in implicit memory and triggered into awareness by internal or external cues. In some cases of hypersexual compulsivity the psychophysiological craving state may also become fixated in activation on a relatively continuous basis. Theoretically if the discrete psychophysiological state of compulsive craving could be accessed and rapidly transformed, craving could be extinguished and the constellation of related thoughts, emotions, behaviors and social dynamics would also be dramatically impacted. This precise access and removal of the craving state has now been consistently achieved with ETT®.

Should other issues in the constellation of addiction continue to exist when the craving state is eliminated, ETT® possesses procedures that have been observed to eliminate these symptoms. For example, these related symptoms might be specific traumas, intense shame, loneliness, or other affective states that are often responsive to ETT® interventions that reduce them within a few minutes or within a single session. Without addictive craving or the presence of the constellation of the related issues, by definition, the condition can no longer be classified as an addiction. The ramifications of this use of ETT® for rapid elimination of compulsive craving could conceivably revolutionize addiction treatment.

When addictive craving becomes extinguished through ETT®, the subject often experiences a state of extreme wellbeing. In the case of hypersexual compulsivity, subsequent to ETT® these clients report a sense of affectionate sexual bonding without the compulsive quality to it. In many cases clients report that the state of extreme wellbeing extends far beyond any previous drug or sexual state of wellbeing. One possible explanation for the frequent experience of extreme wellbeing occurring when ETT® eliminates addictive craving may be reversal of the "reward deficiency syndrome."

DISCUSSION

Is has been reported that in cases in which addictive craving involved a substance or a behavior for which it was healthy to continue to partake in the activity, this procedure eliminated only the compulsive component. For example, when appropriate sexual activity was desirable after the compulsive sexual quality was removed, appropriate affectionate sexual activity remained intact. Therefore, it appears that the compulsive quality is the cohesive force that binds the cognition, affect and behaviors together, and if it is eliminated the healthy components remain.

Subsequent to the demonstration in Bart's case at the beginning of this chapter, I found three typical responses from the professionals observing it. One group was clearly excited and recognized that what they saw was a breakthrough in treatment that far exceeds any previous attempts at craving cessation. The next group experienced cognitive dissonance and could not assimilate the demonstration into their experiences of how addictive craving could be alleviated. Some people thought they were duped by a magic trick, others reconnected it as the result of the placebo effect, and still others assumed that even if it worked the benefit would not last long-term. The last third of the audience was both excited and highly skeptical simultaneously, and wanted more explanation of the mechanisms responsible for the change in order to reconcile their cognitive dissonance. Nonetheless, the audience response was active and vociferous and numerous people personally asked the person who volunteered for the demonstration about his experience subsequent to the demonstration. These responses by the observers reflect common reactions by professionals when presented with the concept that addictive craving can be alleviated long-term in one session.

Sexual addictions occur with women as well as men, although the manner in which they manifest is often different. There are clearly more male sex addicts than females. Since similar brain functions are involved in either case the potential for hypersexual craving exists despite the fact that our society does not provide a context for this pathology to be produced in women as frequently as men.

Case Study: Nora

Nora came into this session with a look as if she had just seen a ghost. Her voice was intense as she described a recent encounter that scared her. On a weekend she went to a large retail store, where she encountered an attractive man who boldly struck up a conversation and asked her to go to lunch with him. Nora informed me that she is a sexual abuse survivor and attends a sex and love addicts anonymous group weekly. She said that she felt "high" during the encounter with this man and came very close to having sex with him. Nora was confused as she said that she was not dressed well at the time so as not to broadcast her availability, but his boldness was attractive to her. She was moved by his "genuine" interest in her, but at the same time she knew she was in a committed relationship and did not want to act on this impulse as she had in her past. Nora was an attractive, divorced, forty-year-old woman.

We utilized a blue-green at (red-0, green-27, blue-22). She became aware of gut tension, and tension in her chest as she recalled the experience. The color was changed to orange (red-255, green-30, blue-0) and Nora reported a physical release. However, I asked her to tell her story again to test whether the change remained. As she reported how flattered she felt an "adrenaline rush" took place. The color was changed to yellow (red-255, green-205, blue-0). While some reduction occurred she continued to feel emotionally triggered and sexually aroused.

Therefore, the strategy was changed to peripheral eye stimulation on the Chromapulse II. At three o'clock she described the event as a "temporary escape." The light was changed to more red at (red-255, green-183, blue-47). She immediately felt better. At nine o'clock Nora said "it really caught me off guard and it felt like it could get out of control" as her stomach tensed. When the light was changed to (red-255, green-255, blue-0) her stomach tension released. At six o'clock she remembered that she had had an experience like this before and it took her a long time to get over it. As the light was changed to a less saturated yellow (red-190, green-189, blue-0) Nora felt better. At twelve o'clock she continued her story, "He was a drug and alcohol guy who needed rescue," she lamented. Her throat tensed as she spoke. The when the light included more blue (red-190, green-189, blue-53) her throat tension released and she reported a soothing feeling.

At seven o'clock Nora reported sexual abuse by her grandfather that she recalled as an adult. She was eight years old when it happened. Then Nora remembered that she acted out sexually in high school and suddenly felt "a draw to escape." When the light was changed to (red-244, green-288, blue-0) she totally relaxed. At one o'clock Nora reported colon tension that resolved on red-orange (red-255, green-15, blue-0). At eight o'clock she described her conflict about keeping this recent event secret but resolved to disclose it.

At two o'clock Nora said that throwing away his number was the best thing she did. "The sex addiction protected me from abuse memories by deadening me." At this point Nora reported a complete elimination of all sexual craving for the first time ever. Nora understands all the dynamics of sex addiction and did all the right things, but her sexual addictive craving did not end until this session.

In this case one can see the gradual unfolding of the addictive template as it was dismantled step by step. As the current hypersexual craving incident was discharged, historically related affective memories emerged. This served to neutralize affective states that were unresolved and plentiful during the process. Nora completed the session with a new sense of pleasurable euphoria that often replace when compulsive highs.

This breakthrough can potentially revolutionize addiction treatment because most addictive treatment programs are based on ways to manage addictive craving. By eliminating addictive craving rapidly, treatment can shift its focus to other lifestyle issues, relationship dysfunction and other ways to experience wellbeing.

IS IT TIME TO REVISE CONVENTIONAL ADDICTION PHILOSOPHY?

Decades of addiction treatment in which addictive craving could not be extinguished led to an entire philosophy about addictions. In addiction treatment one of the difficult initial issues for addicts to overcome is denial that he or she is in fact an addict. Therefore, the first step in the 12-Step program advocates not only that one should own that he or she is powerless over the addiction, but also implies that one is and always will be an addict. This treatment principle is vital in order to assist the addict to overcome rationalizations and to prevent relapses.

However, if a means to rapidly and permanently eliminate addictive craving and the dysfunctions accompanying it existed, the new reality would be that the person is no longer an addict. Therefore, if we advocate facing reality, shouldn't we advocate a self-definition as a "non-addict" when the addictive craving has been eliminated?

Massive research evidence in the fields of brain science, cognitive science, and developmental psychology suggests that self-perception is largely formed by validating responses to the child by the caregiver (Schore, 1994). Therefore, it is important that therapists provide validation of a person's ego identification that is consistent with the factual evidence. For example, if symptoms provide enough evidence that one is an addict, this fact should be confirmed by the therapist. In some cases the majority of addictive symptoms may be extinguished but remnants of the constellation of addictive symptoms may continue to exist. In these cases recognition of a transitional ego identity may most accurately portray the client's self-perception and should be validated by the therapist. Likewise when all addictive symptoms are extinguished, it is valuable to validate the client's new self-perception of a non-addict. This approach allows therapists to be consistent in confirming the client's reality in relation to addiction. This validation would be consistent with the "spirit" of the first step in the twelve step program in that the client is owning-up to his or her actual position as a non-addict or a person in a transitional state.

Viewing addiction through this perspective would, of course, make "cures" of addictions appear incompatible with all of the vast accumulated knowledge of addiction from thousands of previous treatment attempts. However, in all of those years of addictive treatment, no one had utilized this new method. Therefore, these new outcomes have not yet been integrated into conventional treatment conceptions.

If research verifies what has been observed in ETT® sessions, a reformulation of addiction treatment should take place. This might mean changes of long-held beliefs about addiction treatment to be updated to our current skills. When these new outcomes are recognized, a reformulation of our perspective of addiction should take place. The following is a possible reformulation of addiction conceptions and treatment:

- Addictive craving can be permanently and rapidly eliminated.
- When addictive craving is eliminated, a person can no longer be categorized as an addict.

- Most addicts have dual diagnoses. Therefore, when the addictive craving is eliminated, the focus should shift to the other diagnosis or issues of lifestyle and/or relationships.

Any major change in treatment might threaten established systems. It may be more than a statement of levity that when the audience was asked how a means for eliminating addictive craving in a single session would affect treatment, the first response by a therapist was "I'd go broke." Even if research verifies this breakthrough, adjustments would need to be made that involve financial vested interests.

These case studies and all of the ones done in private sessions provide an apparent breakthrough in addiction treatment and should be a high priority as a research topic. In fact, any approach that can put a rapid end to addictions in general and sexual compulsivity in particular should be scientifically studied under controlled circumstances with large number of people. Long-term follow up after treatment needs to be done to ascertain if these treatment results do not have relapses over many years. The procedures have been perfected and it is awaiting scientific research as of the writing.

This new approach offers a radically different speed and outcome to the resolution of hypersexual addictive craving. Viewing the addictive craving state through the context of state dependent learning and memory provides a fresh approach to an otherwise therapy resistant condition. The fantasy of a treatment that could rapidly end the struggle over addiction appears to be here now.

8

A Breakthrough in Couple Therapy

Jacob and Jana walked into the room separately and sat apart from each other in our first session. The tension in the atmosphere was palpable. Although they were cordial to me, they both had a tense, serious look on their faces and had nothing to say to each other. I first faced Jacob to ask him some personal background questions. He provided minimal responses but alluded to having had a stepfamily in his family of origin. Jana reported that she had thought that she had grown up in a happy family, but in recent individual counseling realized that there was a lot of intense arguing at times. Jacob and Jana were in their thirties and had two children under five years old.

I told them that I like to ask each party what they think the problematic issues are. It was apparent that Jacob was less verbally disclosing than Jana. I had each one of them face me not each other. Jacob said the problem was endless arguing that never got any better. Jana reported that when Jacob's grandfather died, Jana miscommunicated with Jacob, leading him to believe that she wouldn't support him during his grief. Jana said Jacob shut down and became cold toward her from that point until the present (two years later). During these two years Jana believed Jacob was having an affair with the woman who was their best friend. Jana cited telephone log data as corroborating evidence that an affair took place and acknowledged that Jacob denied the affair. I initially viewed Jacob as avoidant attachment and Jana as resistant/ambivalent.

I asked Jana what her objective for this couple therapy would be. She said, "For us to be able to be in the same room together." She described a continual, intense hostile conflict. Jacob agreed that relief from the continuous arguing would be a goal. Then suddenly Jacob asked me, "What in the world is that?" and pointed to the Chromapulse light device. This gave me an opportunity to briefly describe ETT® and the power of visual brain stimulation. Then I told him that he might have a chance to see it in action that day. I assured him that it would be interesting. His question allowed me to prepare both of them for an ETT® intervention and provoke his curiosity. Then Jana confessed that she had texted a sexual picture of herself to a man to get back at Jacob. At this point I knew it would be unwise to allow them to talk directly to each other on their own because they had repeatedly demonstrated an inability to resolve hostile conflict. It was clear that they needed to learn to interact better. Therefore, I told them that I wanted to conduct a verbal interaction with each other in which I told them exactly what to say. They both agreed. Through this technique I could accomplish several objectives:

- Demonstrate much-needed empathy from me to each partner through my verbalizing each person's perspective.
- Demonstrate attunement to each partner through guided dialogue between the two partners via verbalized empathy for each other.
- Demonstrate validation, soothing, and/or praise via having each other voice constructive feedback to each other.
- Demonstrate a fair and equal exchange without monologues or lack of response.
- Provide support by my standing behind each person as they spoke my words to the other person.
- Control verbal exchanges so that dialogue would be constructive.

I had Jacob say that he felt frustrated and wanted relief from the conflict. Then I told Jana to verbally recognize his frustration with empathy. Jana said that she was also very upset about the hostility and concurred with his objective. I had Jacob say he understood her hurt feelings, wished it had not taken place, but didn't know what to do. Then I had her let him know that she regretted his distress and would like peace between them. Jacob was told to empathize with her, but then told her that he remained upset about her "sexting" to the other man. At this point Jana broke down in tears and I allowed her to speak freely. She said that she "felt horribly guilty and deeply regretful for doing that." At this point I asked Jacob to move closer to Jana, hold her hand, look at her in the eyes and say, "I'm sorry you are so upset and I accept your apology." When he did this, Jana wept and reported being deeply moved and feeling better for the first time.

Jacob was confused about why this worked and said to her, "I have told you that before." I asked Jana to explain to him why this experience was different. She said, "You held my hand and looked me in the eye, which made me believe you." I emphasized to Jacob that this type of engagement can accomplish far more than words. At that point in the session the tension had largely been eliminated.

During our intake interview both parties reported that they had been through five sessions of couple counseling with another counselor that yielded inadequate results. Jacob said it didn't help at all, but Jana said it provided some benefit. However, they had made no progress in breaking their impasse. After the aforementioned intervention, I asked if the benefits of this approach were different. They both instantly said yes. Then I asked how it was different. Jana said that the previous therapists listened to them and told them helpful information but no face-to-face dialogue with hand-holding took place that changed their emotions. Even though the dialogue with each other was directed by me, it still impacted each partner by simulating attunement to each other. Both parties appeared more relaxed. I asked them to review the difference between their usual exchange and the one I guided them through. They both stumbled through an attempt to explain it and reported feeling amazed and unsure about how it affected them so much. Then I explained how their communication could be different.

At this point I told the couple that I would like to see each of them individually while the non-involved person went to the waiting room. I explained that this was a standard procedure that allowed each person to share anything that was more comfortably said in private. The procedure establishes the process of moving people in and out of the therapy session for strategic purposes and allows the therapist to improve the bond between the therapist and each party. Jacob had very little to say during our individual dialogue, but Jana disclosed about Jacob's rage states and her fear of him. Jana also suggested that she believed Jacob had unresolved emotions about his parent's divorce when he was a child and that issue might be crucial to his recovery from extreme hostility during their conflict.

Next I invited both of them into the room and asked if either of them still felt discomfort. Jana said that although she felt relief, anxiety was still present in her chest and neck. I viewed these symptoms as an opportunity to use ETT® techniques and respond to Jacob's earlier curiosity about the light device. Therefore, I asked Jana to be seated in front of the Chromapulse II where neither of them could see each other's faces. The light was calibrated at red-0, green-25, and blue-25, and I gradually elevated the saturation rate while maintaining blue-green as I had her focus on her discomfort. Within seconds her chest anxiety abated. Then I showed Jacob how I used the dials. Jana reported a little anxiety remaining and described it as related to not being willing to put her guard down because Jacob may text the other woman. At that point I recommended that she ask Jacob if he intended to text her. Jana asked him and he said he would not text her unless Jana texted the man. Jana agreed not to do so. Anxiety remained in Jana's jaw. Blue was slowly elevated and all anxiety in her jaw abated within seconds. The light was turned off and both partners reported peace as they left the session. The following week Jana reported having had a smile that wouldn't stop after that session.

Blue-green was used because I hypothesized that a loop of emotion repeated over and over and was fixated by her thalamus. Blue-green would alter the thalamus. Blue-green also targets the bodily vicinity in which her physical symptoms existed. This change facilitated their first agreement of peace in months! Since both parties repeatedly triggered each other's anger, these visual and auditory triggers were reduced by eliminating visual contact of each other's faces initially and controlling verbal contact to optimal attunement. My empathic response to each of them was accepted as being understood. When the lightwork was done, their visual ecology was controlled in such a way that seeing the other's face was not an available trigger. One week later, both parties continued to report substantial improvement.

In addition to the constructive use of verbalized attunement, the visual ecology of this couple was precisely managed. In the first phase each individual faced the therapist while constructive empathy responses took place. Secondly, the couple faced each other while guided empathy and constructive expressive took place, which provided their first healthy interaction in two years. Third, empathic verbalization took place during optimal guided contact when Jana became emotionally vulnerable. Fourth, Jana viewed the light while her face was not viewable to Jacob. This situation reduced her anxiety and involved a mediated verbal exchange that resolved their ongoing conflict.

THE SCOPE OF COUPLE CONFLICT

Couple relationship conflict and break-up occurs at a high rate in America. Approximately 50 percent of marriages end in divorce. First-marriage divorce rates are from 45 to 50 percent, second marriages are from 60 to 67 percent, and third marriage divorce rates are from 70 to 73 percent. One in four women has experienced domestic violence (Elliot, Simmons, & Lewis, 2010). It is believed that the success rate of marriage counseling has the lowest success rate of any form of therapy. On the other hand, couples typically delay an average of five years before seeking counseling. By then the disturbing issues are usually entrenched and resistant to change. This problem is in need of better counseling resolutions.

THE NEURO VISUAL ECOLOGICAL MODEL

The "neuro visual ecological model" of couple therapy is a therapeutic system that focuses upon rapid and precise change of the affective pattern of couple systems. While this model incorporates systems concepts and cognitive learning, it focuses upon attachment-based interpersonal patterns and the visual ecology of each client. Attachment patterns have been found to be the source of emotional regulation dysfunction and the basis for significant brain regulation and biochemistry. Therefore, the term "neuro" refers to the impact of attachment-based interaction on brain neurological functioning. "Visual ecology" refers to the ecological psychology concept that the brain and the visual environment operate as a single unit composed of mutually interacting feedback loops. Elements of the visual environment can be used to activate specific neural networks in the brain to amplify emotional progression. Together these two principles provide the primary components of a powerful therapeutic model that can rapidly change the affective/cognitive patterns of couple relationship systems.

This neuro visual ecological approach to couple therapy focuses upon managing and resolving emotional distress between partners in a couple relationship. Since depression has been shown to be a function of relationships, this can mean that this approach can resolve depression within the relationship (Atkins, Bortnik, Hahlweg, & Glann, 2011). It could involve processing emotions that are the consequence of a perceived infidelity or a confirmed extra marital affair. Couple emotional distress could involve coping with loss of a family member. It could involve issues of finances, lifestyle, and parenting. Violence prevention can also be a focus. However, the common theme in all of these issues is the challenge of regulating emotions within the context of relationship interaction. It is this function for which the use of client visual ecology and attachment-based interactions provides a rapid means for achieving relationship harmony. When the function of regulating emotions within a couple relationship context can be rapidly and consistently facilitated, issues such as depression, infidelity, finances, parenting, and conflict have a much greater chance to be resolved.

The neuro visual ecology (NVE) model has an attachment-based interpersonal approach to couple therapy in common with Susan Johnson's Emotionally Focused Couple Therapy (EFT). However, there are at least two major differences between NVE and EFT. First, NVE uses several subtypes of the four basic attachment patterns that allow more precise individualization of attachment patterns to apply to each person. Secondly, it uses a visual ecology component that substantially amplifies the speed and depth of emotional processing. The NVE approach is systemic in that it focuses upon the attachment pattern clashes that form unique matrices. While the cognitive aspect of couple issues is dramatically impacted, instead of using cognitive behavioral approaches, therapeutic change is largely a consequence of using the visual ecology and attachment pattern of the clients. Solution-focused therapy does not focus on couples problems, but instead on solutions for the future (Lee, Selbod, & Uken, 2007). ETT® is not exclusively solution-focused because it can directly engage disturbing affect and rapidly change it. Therefore, there is often no reason to avoid facing the disturbance because through NVE solutions typically result rapidly from the process. It is often not necessary to focus on trying to provoke understanding about Bowenian concepts because when emotions resolve with NVE, insights about the couple and family of origin systems frequently spontaneously emerge with clarity. The NVE approach focuses primarily on processes and secondarily on content issues.

THE USE OF ATTACHMENT-BASED RESPONSES

Attachment patterns originate from the relationship between the infant and the caregiver. Then each person's relationship pattern develops from the prototype. These patterns of interacting govern the manner in which one's emotions are regulated and are the basis of much brain growth and biochemical activity. Attachment patterns emerge later in life under circumstances of stress. As adult partner relationships encounter stressors within their interaction, attachment patterns along with any associated emotional dysregulation are likely to emerge. This attachment-based interaction is believed to be the basis of disturbing emotional interaction patterns between adult partners. Therefore, if each partner's attachment pattern can be identified, a specific strategy to correct specific attachment pattern deficiencies can provide a powerful means for changing intense, fixated emotional impasses between partners.

Abundant research has identified four basic attachment patterns. However, Brisch has identified what I view as several subtypes of the basic four patterns. By using these subtypes in addition to the basic four patterns, it allows for a broader range of patterns that more accurately fit specific behavior. These more specific patterns allow us to formulate more individualized responses that provide a greater therapeutic impact on each person (see the book *Emotional Transformation Therapy: An Interactive Ecological Psychotherapy* for a related description). For example, "role reversal" can be seen as a subtype of avoidant attachment in which a person tends to avoid one's own emotions in order to take care of another person's emotions. This unique form of avoidance serves to distance one from one's partner. However, it operates very differently from other forms of avoidance. People with role reversal attachment patterns may be highly emotionally expressive, but these emotions are on behalf of others, whereas other forms of avoidant attachment show little or no emotion at all. Therefore, role reversal requires a different therapeutic response in order to move toward correcting the deficiency.

In the neuro visual ecology model, the unique configurations formed by each clash of partner's attachment patterns forms the dysfunctional system targeted for change. Since this model uses eleven different attachment patterns, the total number of potential combinations of couples' attachment pattern matches is 121 different configurations (or sixteen if one uses the four basic patterns). If a therapist possesses a high familiarity of these attachment patterns, extending this knowledge into each couple's attachment matches is relatively easy. Then the use of the specific interpersonal responses for each attachment pattern provides a powerful means for re-regulation of disturbing emotions. In addition to custom-tailoring responses to each person's pattern, there are some general principles for optimal interpersonal responses to disturbing affect that tend to be applicable to most people. These can be applied to couple counseling. Strategies for using these concepts include, but are not limited to the following:

- The therapist can serve as a role model by using optimal interpersonal responses to each person's attachment pattern.
- The therapist can use the specific responses optimal for a client's attachment pattern, thus reducing disturbing affect and making the client more constructively responsive in couple sessions.
- During individual sessions the therapist can teach each partner how to respond better to the other partner.

In order to step out of a spontaneous reactive attachment response, the alleviation of the intensity of these responses often needs to take place between the therapist and the client first. When optimal attachment-based responses are learned for use with the absent partner, the knowledge and skill to appropriately assist in regulating each other's emotions during stressful encounters can occur. The objective is for each partner to effectively respond to the other partner on a long-term basis, which not only resolves the presenting issues but also prevents relapse.

One of the most common attachment pattern clashes occurs when one partner possesses resistant/ambivalent attachment (RAA) pattern and the other partner possesses avoidant (AA) attachment pattern. In this case the more avoidant one partner behaves, the more emotionally reactive the other partner becomes. When this occurs, emotions escalate into severe intensity for the RAA partner. Repeated experiences of this disturbing interaction create the maintenance of a dysfunctional dyadic system. In this case the therapist's role is to interrupt the excessive intensity of the RAA client for the purpose of providing a "secure" response to each emotion expressed, one at a time. One the other hand, confrontation about the avoidant's emotions will likely cause him or her to further distance from emotions. In this case the therapist must become a patient listener to the avoidant partner. When the avoidant discloses any hint of emotion, the therapist might pursue elaboration of this disclosure. This strategy encourages emotional expression from a person who might otherwise withhold. The result of these interventions is a soothing of both partners toward a systemic harmony.

Although the RAA and AA pattern of clash between partners can be expressed in either gender, the commonly observed pattern is an RAA female and an AA male partner. In order to implement optimal responses to people with attachment disorders, therapists are in a position of continually individualizing responses. In addition to attachment specific responses, there are some general principles for optimal interpersonal responses to people experiencing disturbing affect that tend to be applicable but are not limited to the following:

1. Identification of relevant emotions: One must first accurately identify what emotions are being experienced. With avoidants this task may require a patient search, but in resistant/ambivalent one may need to sift through a variety of intense emotions in order to identify the key emotion to target.
2. Empathize: When a client's emotional expression is responded to by communication of empathy, the client often begins to move toward resolution.

Attunement to emotions via empathy is often the key omission in partner conflicts. Good empathy insures that people are understood.

3. Validation of emotions: One of the most destructive consequences of dysfunctional emotional exchanges concerns its impact on the self-perception of the recipient. Validating or honoring another person's emotions is a potent message that can quell distress as well as enhance the recipient's self-perception.
4. Soothing (comforting or nurturing): Comforting responses to the other emotional partner can serve to de-escalate the intensity of emotions and promote resolution of emotional distress, especially if validation and empathy have taken place as well.
5. Praising: Praising a partner for how that partner has provided beneficial responses can lead to emotional resolution and promote further constructive responses in the future.

THE ROLE OF THE THERAPIST

Therapists conducting NVE couple therapy must become masters of multiple roles and possess several skills. These include but are not limited to the following:

- Mediator: Approach the couple with equal concern for both parties and be able to effectively communicate this fairness.
- Assertiveness: Be willing and able to assert control over the direction of activities and, in some cases, not allow certain behaviors.
- Orchestrating each partner's visual ecology.
- Responding in a custom-tailored manner to each partner.
- Demonstrating empathy and advocacy for each partner.
- Simultaneously monitoring the content of issues while focusing on the process of the therapeutic strategies.

One can take complete control of the visual ecology and couple interaction while simultaneously demonstrating empathy, patience, and respect for each partner's position. This is the art of couple therapy in the neuro visual ecological model.

There are certain factors than can limit the effectiveness of couple therapy. If one or both partners withhold significant relevant information from the therapist, the effectiveness of any therapeutic strategy can be compromised. For example, only 6 percent of couples report that violence has occurred in the relationship, but it has been found that 53 percent of couples in therapy have been violent at one time (O'Leary, Vivian, & Malone, 1992). Another factor that limits effectiveness is the tendency to resort to pre-counseling behavior between sessions and omit most or all knowledge and awareness gained during sessions. This factor can at least be addressed in subsequent sessions, but lack of disclosure is a severe handicap to success.

CONFLICT AND VIOLENCE

While marriage and family therapists are often taught to deal with a couple's anger, blame, escalation, and contextual patterns, it has been questioned if therapists can adequately identify the dynamics of conflict (Jory, 2004; Knudson-Martin & Mahoney, 2009). Traditional treatment for violence between partners in couples separates the male batterer into anger management education type programs and females into support groups (Gondoff, 1995). However, batterer intervention programs have generally shown high rates of recidivism and dropout (Babcock, Green, & Robie, 2004). Some researchers have identified different types of violent couples. According to M. P. Johnson, there are four:

- Intimate terrorists: "Intimate terrorism tends to be one-sided violence, characterized by coercive control and escalation of violence. Intimate terrorists are usually dependent or antisocial in orientation. . . . These types should not be treated in couple's therapy."
- "Situational couple violence is characterized by mutuality of violence and lack of control or domination of one partner . . . this type of violence is less likely to result in injury and might be characterized by poor self-regulation skills and escalation" (Johnson, 2008; Oka & Whiting, 2011).
- Violent resistant: "Violent resistance refers to the partner of an intimate terrorist (usually female) who may react to violence but not in a controlling manner" (Oka & Whiting, 2011, p. 36).
- Mutual violent control: "When both parties are violent and controlling. This typology comprises a very small portion of violent couples" (Oka & Whiting, 2011, p. 36).

While ETT® could be used on an individual bases for intimate terrorists, all of the other three typologies could be processed in conjoint couple therapy. However, the ETT® approach uses both individual and conjoint sessions as a standard means of operating within the context of couple therapy. Couples are seen individually for a variety of purposes that can enhance the couple relationship without the risk of inflaming each other during the session. Individual sessions provide an opportunity for the therapist to bond with the client by appropriately responding to each client's attachment patterns as well as to educate each partner about how to interact optimally with the other partner.

THE POWER OF VISUAL ECOLOGY

> Over the first year of life visual experiences play a paramount role in social and emotional development. In particular, the mother's emotionally expressive face is, by far, the most potent visual stimulus in the infant's environment, and the child's intense interest in her face, especially in her eyes, leads him to track it in space, and to engage in intense periods of mutual gaze. The infant's gaze, in turn, reliably evokes the mother's gaze, and this dyadic system forms an efficient interpersonal channel for the transmission of reciprocal mutual influences. (Shore, 2003, p. 9)

This primitive foundation system of interaction later extends to include verbal communication. However, this fundamental visual, facial interaction is well established in the visual neural pathways of the brain as primary to all later relationships, but has often become omitted from our adult awareness as an adult's focus moves to verbal/auditory and intellectual cognition. Therefore, when communication goes awry, adults often look to rational understanding and verbal communication alone as the means to resolve an experience that is primarily emotional and visual in nature. Of course, these rational/verbal means are limited in the speed and efficiency of their ability to change emotional issues.

In addition to these dynamics, of all of the potential traumatic events, those that take place in conjunction with people we consider closest to us are among the most severe to impact us. For example, the consequences of a father raping his daughter are far more pervasive than if a stranger conducted the same act. These interpersonal traumas are often associated with visual images such as "the look in his eyes," "the look on her face," or "his face," which can become triggers to evoke an intense psychophysical response. Then if these occurrences are repeated, a consistent psychological visual trigger can be established. Traumatic triggers are often spontaneous and automatic, which often leaves the person experiencing them helpless to change them.

Recent research supports the visual trigger concept. Scientific research has been conducted in which individuals with PTSD and people with a "normal" psychological profile are interviewed with direct eye contact as well as with an indirect gaze. This takes place while the participants' brains are being monitored with an fMRI. The results show that in normal subjects the dorsal medial prefrontal cortex (DMPFC) is activated. The DMPFC is known to be involved in the brain function of self-reflection. However, the PTSD subjects' brains did not activate the DMPFC, but instead activated the superior colliculus. The superior colliculus of the brain is associated with eliciting the startle response, cowering, or escape and does not lead to affiliative responses (Lanius, 2011). Therefore, if hostile conflict has occurred between the people in a couple relationship, it could be traumatizing, and direct eye contact between them is likely to promote detrimental outcomes for couples counseling.

By appropriately managing the visual ecology of the therapeutic experience, these visual traumatic triggers can be avoided, thus reducing the possibility of hostile escalation of conflict. On the other hand, constructive visual contact can drastically enhance couple therapy. When visual ecology and optimal attachment-based interpersonal contact are combined by careful and precise selection, evidence suggests that neural brain patterns are rapidly changed. Pre and post brain scans of ETT® clients validate this outcome. This new model of couple therapy includes the conventionally used forms of therapist observation of couples, interpersonal dialogue, and basic cognitive conceptualization of issues, but radically enhances couple therapy by the precise use of the visual ecology of the couple.

The Lanius research on direct eye contact has additional implications. If one of the partners in a couple has all the symptoms for PTSD, from events outside the relationship, the therapist should also limit direct eye contact with this client in order to gain therapeutic benefits. If a person is a PTSD client due to events outside the relationship, the partner of this client can be coached about constructive gaze aversion contact. As the traumatized client becomes more responsive when PTSD symptoms are reduced, direct eye contact can be valuable again.

One of the central foci of the NVE approach is the therapist's awareness and control of when and where both partner's eye contact is directed. At early phases of therapy when hostility between partners is intense, avoidance of direct eye contact with each other is usually valuable. Then at key moments when positive affection is evident, direct eye contact can be a potent factor to shift the affect of the dyad into constructive strength. At times when an interventions such as multidimensional eye movement or light emission with one partner is used keeping the other partner out of the client's visual field is often helpful in order to maximize the intervention. However, if a situation in which one partner has rarely seen the other partner disclose emotion, it may be valuable for the observing partner to see the other express emotion or confide mistakes. Generally speaking the more the affective interaction improves, the more the therapist encourages direct eye contact between both partners. This approach is very different from previous methods in that eye contact is micro managed by the therapist.

Managing the visual ecology of the therapeutic milieu involves two major categories within the visual environment of the session. First, managing with whom each client is in facial contact during each verbalization. Secondly, managing which of the ETT® tools is selected and for which person, while facial contact is being managed. The following are the twenty-two options for the therapeutic visual ecology of the participants and the rationale for selecting them (see illustration 8.1).

Legend of Symbols

Direction of vision ——→

Direction of verbal dialogue represented by - - →

Partner A represented by "A"

Partner B represented by "B"

Therapist represented by "T"

ETT® tool represented by:

Wand for MDEM "W"

Peripheral goggles "P"

Spectral Resonance Technique "S"

Light device "L"

ILLUSTRATION 8.1

THERAPEUTIC COUPLE VISUAL ECOLOGY

1. A faces therapist while B views A and therapist (see illustration 8.2).

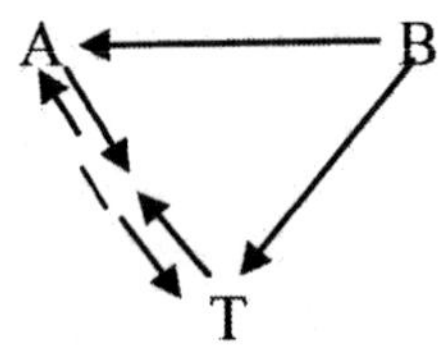

ILLUSTRATION 8.2

When "A" faces the therapist and "B" watches the interaction between "A" and the therapist, several benefits can occur. First, facial bidirectional contact between the partner and the therapist and no contact between partners reduces the possibility of triggering either client into distress. Secondly, when "B" is watching the interaction between "A" and the therapist, it provides an opportunity for "B" to observe constructive attachment-based interaction with "A" that the therapist is modeling. In many cases the therapist must tell "B" directly to pay attention to the interpersonal means of communication being used between the therapist and the other partner so that "B" can replicate the way "B" and "A" interact. This format is very important when the couple is highly reactive to each other because it eliminates direct contact between the partners that prevents continuation of the conflict.

2. B faces therapist while A views B and therapist (see illustration 8.3).

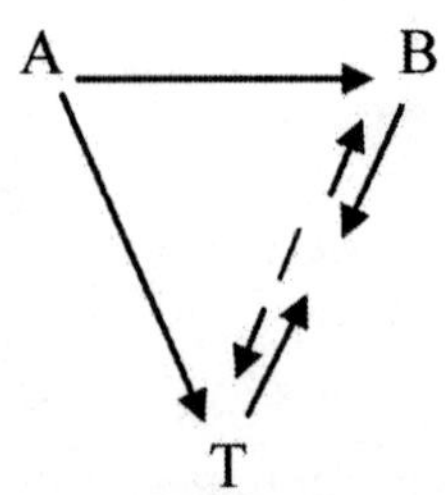

ILLUSTRATION 8.3

When "B" faces the therapist and "A" watches "B" and the therapist, the same principles apply as in scenario 1.

3. A faces B and B faces A while therapist views A and B (see illustration 8.4).

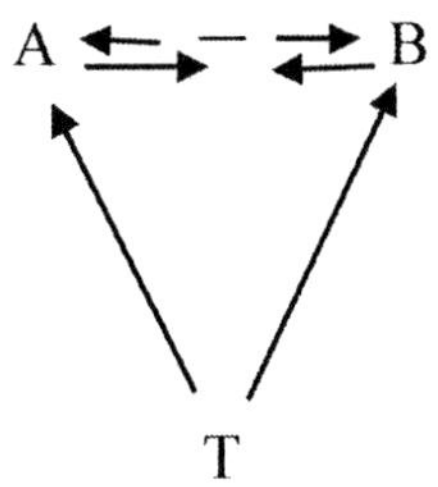

ILLUSTRATION 8.4

When "A" faces "B" and "B" faces "A" while the therapist watches "A" and "B," some of the most powerful negative effects can occur. Therefore, selection of this option is critical. First, if there is a relatively safe level of interaction between the partners, having the couple discuss issues allows the therapist to observe how the couple's interaction becomes dysfunctional. This observation provides data for the therapist to formulate a treatment strategy and appropriate education for the couple.

Secondly, if the couple is at risk of triggering each other, and the therapist fully understands the position of both parties, a therapist-directed dialogue can occur in which clients agree to say only what the therapist tells them to say. This procedure (1) insures constructive dialogue, (2) demonstrates that the therapist understands each party, and (3) contains empathy for the other party, (4) contains expression of each party's position and feelings and (5) finally, contains a positive expression of what each party wants. This verbalization is custom-tailored to the other person's attachment pattern. This process was illustrated with Jana and Jacob.

On the other hand, whenever the therapist is convinced that the couple is in harmony, this face- to-face format can serve to deeply enhance positive interaction. In the case of Jacob and Jana this took place at the end of the first session.

4. A faces therapist while B is absent (see illustration 8.5).

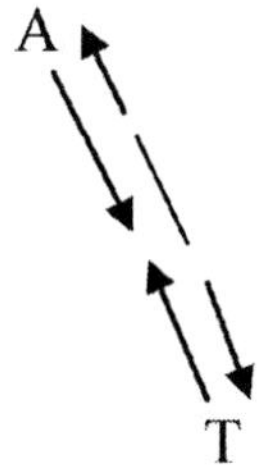

ILLUSTRATION 8.5

During the first session it is helpful to send one person out of the room while the therapist works with the other partner of the couple alone. In this case "A" faces the therapist while "B" is absent. This provides an opportunity for the therapist to conduct interpersonal dialogue in a manner that is optimal for the client's attachment pattern.

5. B faces therapist while A is absent (see illustration 8.6).

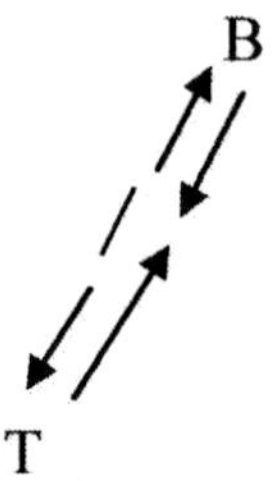

ILLUSTRATION 8.6

When "B" faces the therapist while "A" is absent, the same strategies from scenario 4 are used, but with person "B."

6. A faces spectral chart, therapist faces A, but B cannot see A (see illustration 8.7).

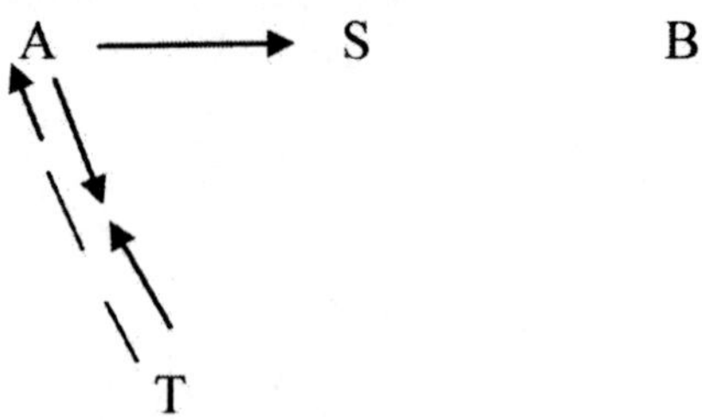

ILLUSTRATION 8.7

If it becomes suspicious to the therapist that one party is dissociated and/or emotionally flooding in such a way that is contributing to an impasse, SRT can be used with partner "A" in such a way that visual facial contact between the parties is blocked. In the case of dissociation within one party, the use of the spectral chart may bring awareness to person "A" about emotions, which can be used to facilitate a more emotionally enriched verbal exchange. In the case of emotional flooding SRT can reduce the flooding so that a more beneficial verbal exchange can occur. Blocking visual facial contact during this process can eliminate mutual triggering and this SRT process can substantially change the course of the dialogue.

7. A faces spectral chart, therapist faces A, and B faces A (see illustration 8.8).

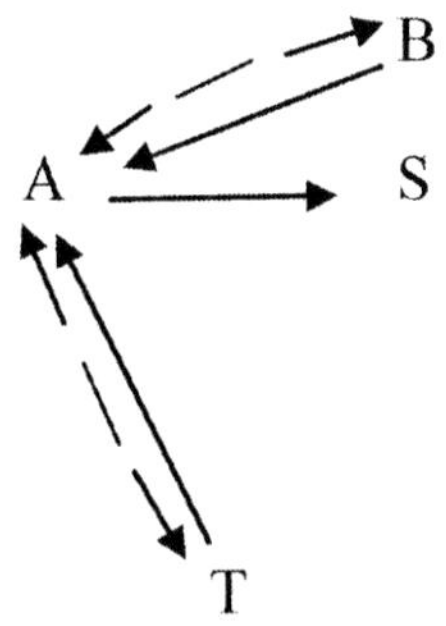

ILLUSTRATION 8.8

The same process described in scenario 6 can be used with the other partner.

8. B faces spectral chart, therapist faces B, but A cannot see B (see illustration 8.9).

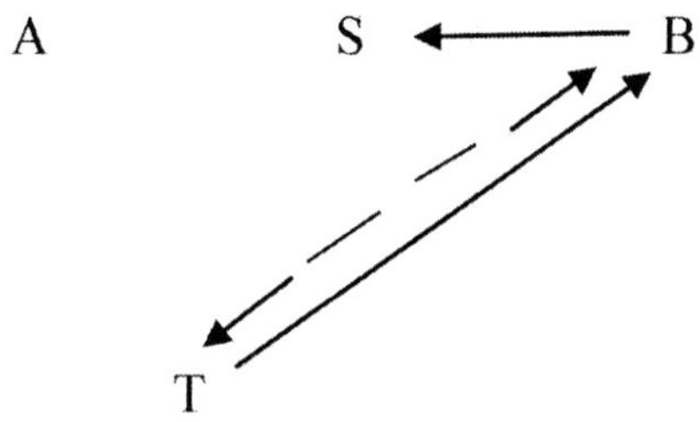

ILLUSTRATION 8.9

If it is therapeutically desirable, the spectral chart can be used with "A" while "B" can see "A's" face. This format may be valuable when "B" needs or wants to see "A's" emotional awareness increase. It is also necessary for "B" to have or need comfort by "A" watching "B." This process can be valuable when both parties want one person to be in touch with emotions. The bond between both parties can be strengthened by this process.

Having one partner undergo SRT while the other partner cannot see the first partner's face can provide certain distinct advantages. In the case of Jana and Jacob, Jacob was very withheld verbally and had never been willing to do individual work within a couple session. Jana was delighted and surprised that Jacob was open to the process. However, their conflict was so intensely negative that I believed facial contact was a high risk. By using SRT Jacob was open and disclosing about his emotions in a couple session with Jana for the first time. This process provided a breakthrough in this couple's relationship impasse during their second session.

9. B faces spectral chart, therapist faces B, and A faces B (see illustration 8.10).

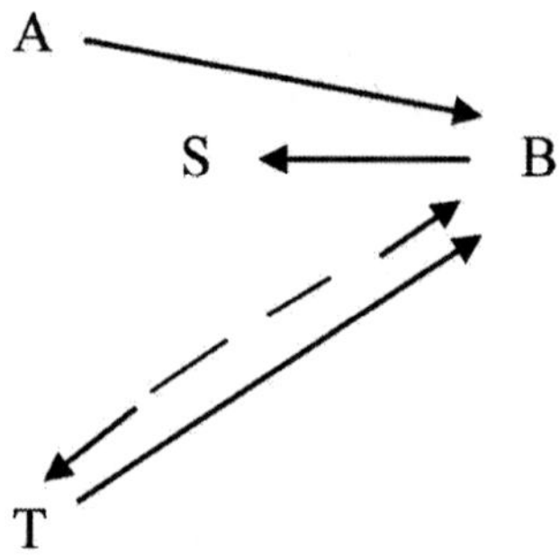

ILLUSTRATION 8.10

This visual format can be helpful in certain cases in which one partner is significantly dissociated and the other partner could benefit by seeing that partner access emotions again. If the dissociated partner wanted to eliminate dissociation and sought the support of the other partner during the procedure, it might enhance the relationship. This choice requires the therapist to be aware of the relationship dynamics in order to correctly select this strategy.

10. Procedures from scenario 8 and scenario 9 can be used with "A" facing the spectral chart and would have the same rationale.

11. B views wands, but cannot see A, but A can see therapist and B (see illustration 8.11).

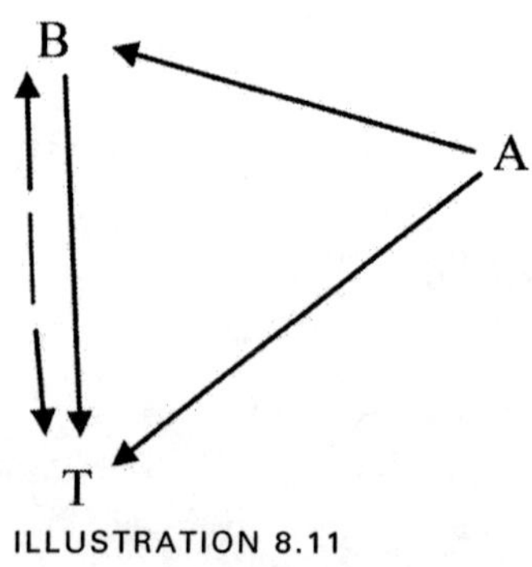

ILLUSTRATION 8.11

The use of MDEM with one partner during a couple session possesses the possibility of producing a dramatic rapid change of one partner's emotional state. MDEM can be used to completely break an impasse in a couple conflict within minutes. It is also helpful because it requires the therapist to identify one partner's eye scanpath, which can help by using that eye scanpath during couple interaction. For example, if partner "A" possesses an eye scanpath from center to nine o'clock (looking left) at a time of high emotion, the therapist can arrange seating and movement in order to avoid partner "A" viewing partner "B" from the nine o'clock angle."

Harry and Alexis

Harry and Alexis volunteered for a live demonstration of couple therapy at a professional training when their therapist suggested it, even though they had never met me. After developing rapport and identifying this couple's attachment patterns, it became known that Alexis was deeply in love with Harry and while Harry loved Alexis, he was anxious about the relationship. Alexis did not disclose to Harry that she worked as an exotic dancer by night until months after their relationship had deepened. Of course, when Harry found out about her work, he became very upset and could not get the images of her lap dancing with other men out of his mind. Alexis had committed to giving up that job as soon as she was financially able to do so. However, she made as much as three thousand dollars per night. Therefore, she needed a few months to save money. This couple's impasse was that Alexis wanted to have sex when she came home, but Harry couldn't get images and accompanying distress regarding her job out of his mind. After an exchange of sharing and listening to each other, they remained at an impasse. Harry was clearly the more distressed of the two, so I conducted MDEM with him while blocking his facial contact with Alexis. Even though it was reasonable for him to be upset, all of his distress rapidly changed within a couple of minutes while using MDEM. The impasse was broken. Harry now felt relaxed and trusting. As the couple exchanged feelings it became clear that their relationship entered a state of harmony by the end of the session.

The use of MDEM can drastically break couple impasses within minutes when one partner is fully aware of his or her emotional distress and is ready for it to change. After interpersonal exchanges have not accomplished resolution, MDEM can easily be brought in for rapid results. This intervention represents a powerful change in the impact of couple therapy.

12. B views wands while therapist views B, but A cannot see B (see illustration 8.12).

ILLUSTRATION 8.12

The same procedures described in scenario 11 can be used with the second partner.

13. A views wands; A cannot see B but B can see A and therapist (see illustration 8.13).

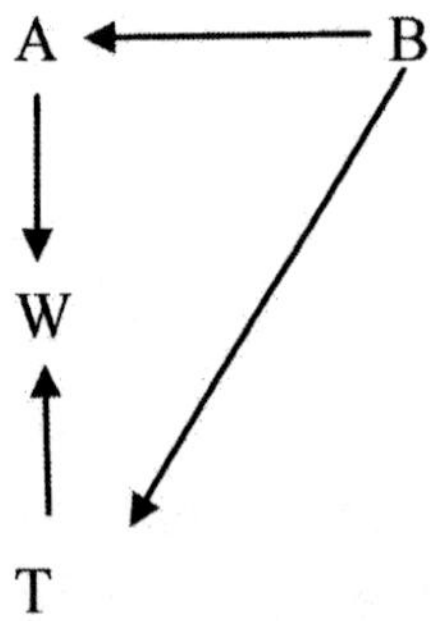

ILLUSTRATION 8.13

It may be determined that if "B" watches "A" go through MDEM, "A" could feel supported and "B" could be pleased and closer to "A" by having watched the procedure. Otherwise, the procedure is very similar to scenario 11 and scenario 12 process.

14. A views wands while therapist views A, but B cannot see A (see illustration 8.14).

ILLUSTRATION 8.14

This procedure is the same as scenario 13 except that it is done with the other partner.

15. A views light device while neither therapist nor B can see A. Dialogue is only between therapist and A (see illustration 8.15).

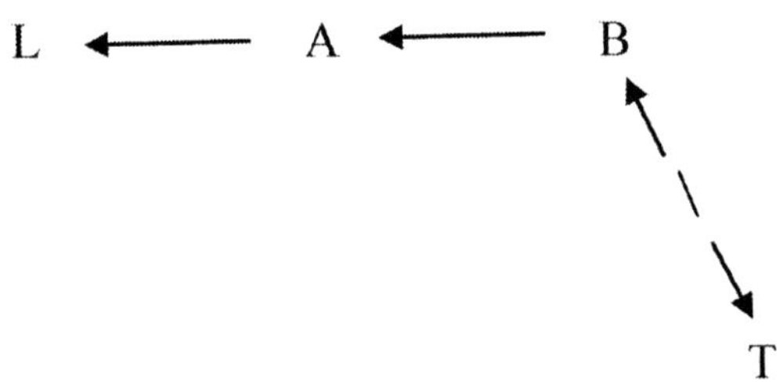

ILLUSTRATION 8.15

At the end of the first session with Jana and Jacob, Jana was placed in front of the Chromapulse II device. This procedure eliminated facial contact between these partners. However, the procedure allowed Jana to rapidly process her emotional distress about Jacob and moved them from angry, blocked contact to expressive, open communication.

This strategy eliminates the risk of facial contact while simultaneously facilitating rapid, in-depth change of one partner's emotional disturbance. The emotional change can rapidly change the interpersonal system between both partners as it did with Jana and Jacob. In this case the dialogue was initially only between the therapist and Jana (scenario 15), but once the emotional disturbance changes both Jana and Jacob were encouraged to verbally interact without facial contact (scenario 17).

16. B views light device while neither therapist nor A can see B (see illustration 8.16).

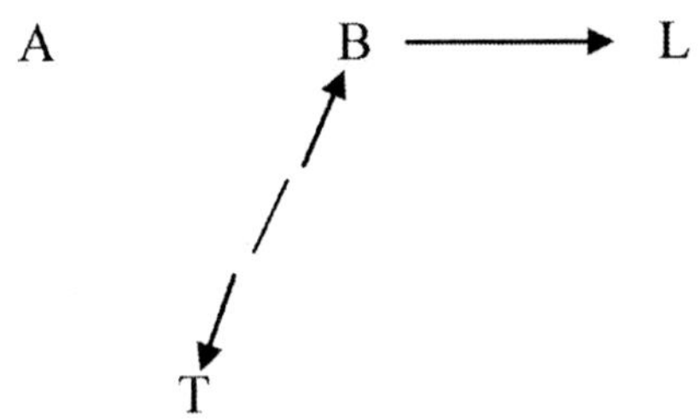

ILLUSTRATION 8.16

This process is the same as scenario 15 except with the other partner.

17. A views light device while neither therapist nor B can see A. Dialogue between therapist and A, therapist and B, as well as A and B (see illustration 8.17).

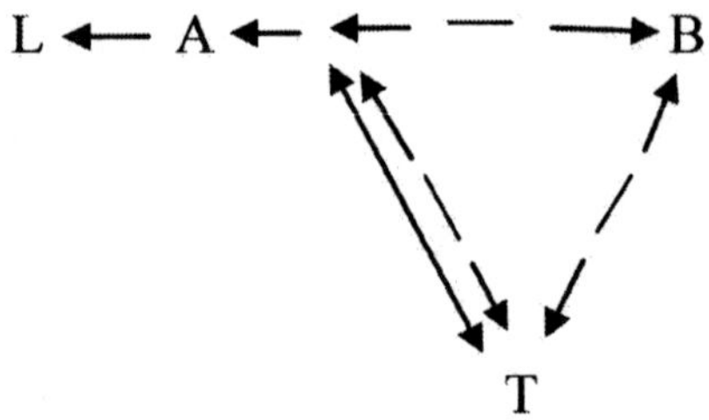

ILLUSTRATION 8.17

This is a variation but similar to scenarios 15 and 16.

18. B views light device while neither therapist nor A can see B. Dialogue is between therapist and B, therapist and A, and A and B (see illustration 8.18).

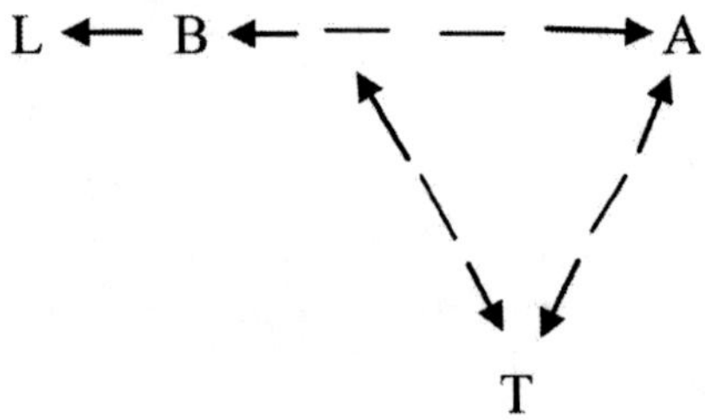

ILLUSTRATION 8.18

This is a variation but similar to scenarios 15, 16, and 17.

19. A uses peripheral goggles and B cannot see A or therapist, and therapist cannot see A (see illustration 8.19).

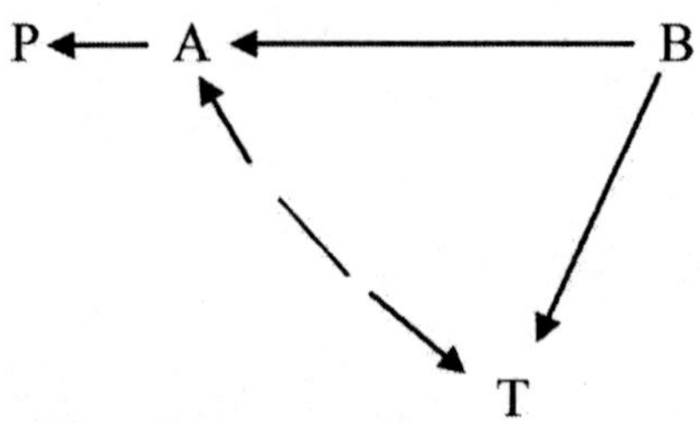

ILLUSTRATION 8.19

This approach can be very valuable when one partner is experiencing intense overwhelming emotion to the extent that the person cannot reasonably participate in verbal interaction. The use of the peripheral goggles can provide rapid control of flooding affect by systematically breaking down overwhelm of multiple intense emotions that have not been soothed by interpersonal process. PES also provides a strategy to access positive internal potentials. Since the PES procedure is relatively rapid, it can be conducted with one or both individuals during the middle of a couple session. Once the person is less overwhelmed, a resumption of guided couple interaction can take place with a significant change in the quality of the interaction. The purpose of this intervention is not to dismiss or block emotional responses but rather to reduce intensity of affect and organize cognitive or physical experience so that emotions can be better regulated during couple therapy.

20. B uses peripheral goggles and A and therapist cannot see B (see illustration 8.20).

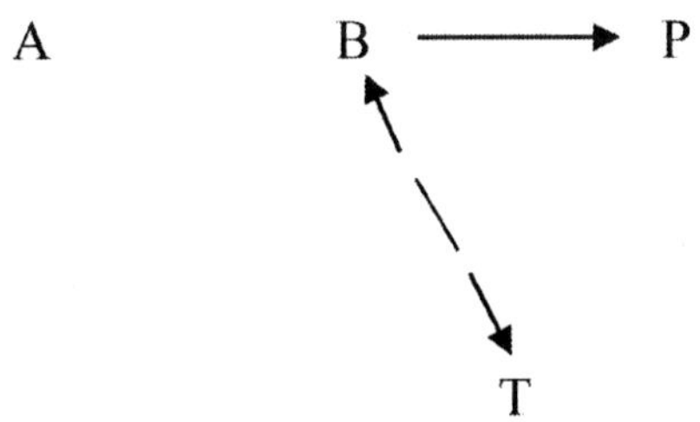

ILLUSTRATION 8.20

This is a variation from scenario 19 that possesses similar capacities.

21. A uses peripheral goggles, and B and therapist cannot see A, but dialogue extends to A, B, and therapist (see illustration 8.21).

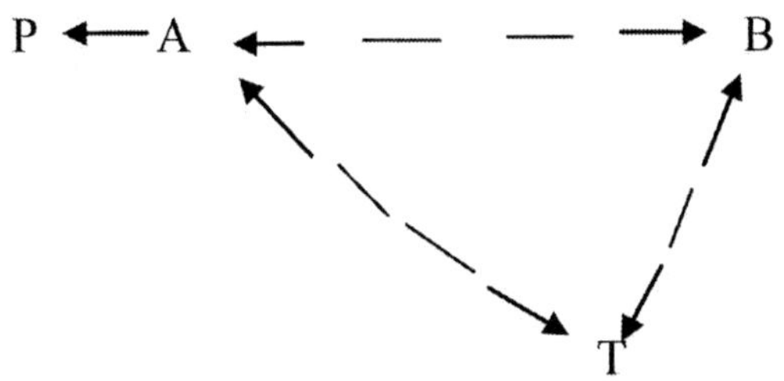

ILLUSTRATION 8.21

This is a variation from scenario 19 that possesses similar purposes.

22. B uses peripheral goggles and A and therapist cannot see B, but dialogue extends to A, B, and therapist (see illustration 8.22).

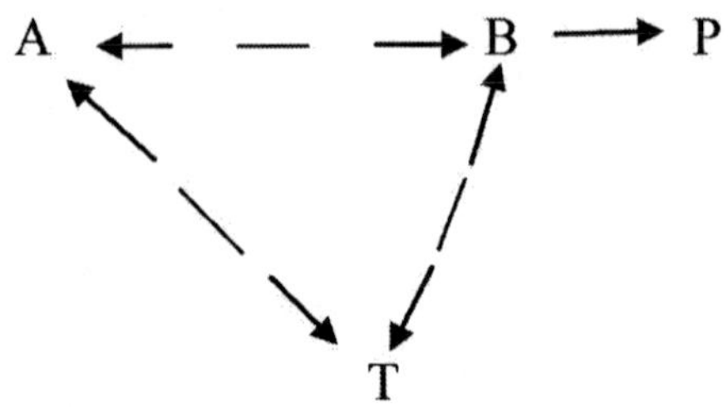

ILLUSTRATION 8.22

This is a variation of scenario 21 that possesses similar purposes.

The variety of formats of client visual ecology during couple sessions coupled with attachment-based interactions provides several potential benefits when managed optimally.

- Clients are responded to in a custom-tailored manner that directly addresses each client's attachment pattern and ultimately improves emotional regulation.
- By optimally managing the direct eye contact of both partners, visual ecology, aversive psychological triggering, and escalation of conflict is substantially reduced.
- By using ETT® tools at key points of impasse, emotional intensity or fixation can be rapidly changed.
- By using SRT, dissociated affect can be retrieved so that emotional exchanges between the partners can achieve a new depth and quality.
- By the combined use of the client's visual ecology and attachment-based interactions, couple therapy can achieve far more rapid outcomes.

FOLLOW-THROUGH HOMEWORK

Clients are encouraged to recall new awareness gained during sessions and to follow through on the practice of new skills and agreements occurring during sessions. Each beneficial negotiated agreement, as well as means for achieving conflict resolution, should be summarized in the form of a take home task and then monitored in future sessions. At the beginning of each subsequent session an evaluation of follow-through on homework tasks is assessed, and if it did not occur, the reasons for this should be explored. Once these reasons are identified, they should be placed on the agenda for couple therapy objectives for the session.

While direct eye contact between both partners should be initially avoided when the partner's eye contact serves as a trigger for escalating negative affect, as the couple relationship improves this may change. As the love object of the other partner, when positive affection is evident direct eye contact enhances the bond. This means that the therapist must be keenly aware of each partner's emotional state in order to manage the visual contact between partners. While the therapist can mange protection from triggers during sessions the couple can continue to trigger each other outside of sessions. If the therapist can inhibit emotional triggering during early sessions long enough to evoke constructive changes about highly sensitive matters, then the triggers themselves become desensitized and effective bonding can be encouraged. Eventually the skills acquired during sessions should translate into skills and rapport that occurs when the partners operate on their own together.

COUPLE THERAPY AS AN ADJUNCT TO INDIVIDUAL THERAPY

Couple therapy can function as an adjunct to individual therapy. Frequently individual progress is so rapid and so transformative with ETT® that one person's changes have an impact on other family members. How other family members react to these changes can stabilize or disrupt these improvements. In order to insure the likelihood of supporting improvements, the other partner may need to be involved in at least a few sessions. The purpose of this involvement is to acquire support of the client and provide assistance in the partner's adjustment to changes within the client. A couple session in this context allows the support partner to ask questions of the therapist and for the therapist to seek any information about the client that might contribute to a better knowledge of the client from the partner's viewpoint.

Several different issues may be present:

- The partner outside of therapy may oppose psychotherapy for a variety of reasons.
- Some people do not believe in therapy and philosophically oppose participation.
- Some people are focused upon the cost of therapy and want therapy to stop in order to reduce the financial strain.
- People may be suspicious of the particular therapist and/or his methods.
- Some partners do not understand that symptoms may temporarily appear to worsen when the therapy is in fact helping, but intense emotions or behaviors may arise during certain phases of the therapy journey.

A conjoint session with a significant other can be used to address the type of issues listed. For example, in one case I had requested that a woman include her spouse in order to help him understand the enormous but confusing changes she was going through. The client did not want him to be included and believed that he would not want to participate. Months later when she agreed to include him in a session, he reported anger at me for not including him. He had been in opposition to the therapy until he found out that I had actually sought to include him at an earlier point. After a discussion he became supportive of her therapy and was included from time to time as needed.

It is important to avoid situations in which the client brings his or her spouse into sessions for the purpose of confronting and criticizing the spouse. While this may have some value at times, it should not be the main reason a spouse is brought into sessions because this will contribute to the spouse eventually not supporting the client's therapy sessions. Since a therapist may not develop the same type of relationship with the spouse as with the primary client, I usually invite the spouse to help me to help the client. I make it known that the spouse is far more important and impactful to the client than I am and could be very important in joining our therapeutic team to reach that client's goals. If the spouse wants the client to acquire "happiness," the spouse usually cooperates. The client is usually asked to inform his/her spouse about therapeutic gains along the way so that the spouse has a reason to be supportive. The degree of disclosure to the spouse varies from person to person and is evaluated according to what is in the best interest of the couple relationship.

Sometimes what began as individual therapy evolves into couple therapy or vice versa. It is important to determine if an individual's issues are derived from pathology in a couple system. It may not be apparent that the couple relationship is the dominant factor in an individual's issues until the couple is seen together. On the other hand, an individual may attribute the source of his or her issues onto the partner. All of these issues are unlikely to be discerned unless couple sessions are conducted. If the primary source of the issues is found to lie within the couple system, the neuro visual ecology model can be used to rapidly improve these systemic issues.

9

From Light to Enlightenment

Counseling that focuses on spiritual issues can be life-changing. While in many cases religious/spiritual topics have little or no bearing on the client's objectives for treatment, when spiritual topics are related, an exploration of these issues is in order to achieve treatment objectives. This exploration often challenges the therapist's sensitivity and understanding beyond the limits of most mental health training.

There are, in fact, diagnostic issues related to religion or spirituality described in the *Diagnostic and Statistical Manual IV R* (*DSM IVR*), which means it is appropriate for counseling and can be acceptable for third party reimbursement. These V code designations can supplement a mental health diagnosis. The two categories listed in the *DSM IVR* are as follows:

- Psycho-religious problems are experiences that a person finds troubling or distressing and that involve the belief and practices of an organized church or religious institution.
- Psycho-spiritual problems are experiences that a person finds troubling or distressing and that involve that person's relationship with a transcendent being or force. These problems are not necessarily related to the beliefs or practices of an organized church or religious institution (American Psychiatric Association, 2000, p. 741).

In 2000, Zinnbauer and Pargament published an article describing four basic perspectives that are exhibited by therapists in regard to religion/spirituality. It is important for each therapist to be aware of which viewpoint he/she possesses. The first is the "rejectionist approach" in which the therapist possesses a position that is opposed to religion, spirituality, or the existence of God. Major leaders in the history of mental health have voiced positions such as those of Sigmund Freud that religion is a product of wish fulfillment or fantasy, or of Albert Ellis, that religious belief indicates irrational thinking or impaired mental functioning. On the other hand, the "exclusivist approach" postulates an opposing position:

- God exists.
- Absolute values exist and are grounded in scripture.
- There is a single route to religious or spiritual reality.
- If the client does not believe in the therapist's world view, the client must be convinced to change.

In many parts of the United States there are people who label themselves as "Christian counselors." This may run the gamut from counselors who use only Biblical scriptures to conduct therapy to those who use conventional counseling approaches but identify themselves as Christians.

The "constructivist" approach does not include the existence of an absolute reality but focuses instead on how each person "constructs" their own reality and meanings. This approach focuses on the quality of the client's constructions. For example, are these construction coherent and do they help the client function and adapt to his or her situation?

Many therapists include many elements of the constructivist approach but may or may deny the existence of ultimate reality. Some elements of the constructivist approach are adopted in this author's perspective in counseling.

As a counselor, I adopt the "pluralist approach," which "recognizes the existence of a religious or spiritual absolute reality but allows for multiple interpretations and paths toward it" (Zinnbauer & Pargament, 2000, p. 165). However, some elements of the "constructivist approach" are incorporated at times. This viewpoint recognizes the ability of individuals to construct their own meanings and realities. Attempts are made to work within the value framework of each client, but it is appropriate to challenge beliefs that are irrational, self-defeating, or linked to the presenting issue. At times religion or spirituality is simply a different venue to express addiction, anxiety, self-hate, paranoia, or other psychological pathology. In these cases, the problem is not really about religion; instead, it is about the personal issues a client brings to religion.

Conducting a religious/spiritual history of the client is advocated when it is appropriate to the issues. This history can provide the therapist with a background and context for the client's current concerns. However, it should be noted that religious topics may provoke a potent reactivation of religious/spiritual experiences simply through the process of the interview. The following is a brief version of a religious/spiritual interview:

Religious History
- What was your father's religious background?
- Was he actively involved in religion?
- How did religion affect him?
- What did he tell you about his religious beliefs?
- What was your mother's religious background?
- Was she actively involved in religion?
- How did religion affect her?
- What did she tell you about her religious beliefs?
- What is your religious background?
- Were you actively involved in it?
- How has it affected you?
- What are your main beliefs regarding religion?

Spiritual History
- What does the work spiritual mean to you?
- Have you had a spiritual experience?
- Describe any experience you have had that you see as spiritual.
- How has the experience affected your view of spirituality?

Present Views
- What do you think of the afterlife?
- What does God mean to you?
- Describe any relationship that you have to a higher self, God, the collective unconscious, or other similar concepts.

ATTACHMENT THEORY AND RELIGION

Viewing religion and/or spirituality within an attachment theory context can provide great value for therapy involving religion or spirituality. Attachment patterns are based on relationships. Therefore, can we have a relationship with religion/spirituality? A national survey showed that people viewed faith as "a relationship with God" in the majority of responses (Gallop & Jones, 1989).

Many religious faith systems provide beliefs that describe a sense of proximity to God (as a caregiver attachment figure). For example, a common attribute of God is that of being omnipresent. In Christianity God is often thought to be available all the time. In Hinduism and Buddhism the "godhead" is considered to be the basic unity of all things, which by definition is available everywhere. This omnipresent feature offers the ultimate in proximity. Prayer, a universal phenomenon in all major religions, can be seen as a form of proximity seeking.

Research confirms that when people are alarmed and/or frightened, they often turn to prayer or church to cope (Argyle & Beit-Hallahmi, 1975). In fact, the general public in the United States is far more likely to seek help through religion or spiritual means when distressed than to seek psychological counseling. Prayer is particularly used when life-threatening health symptoms occur (Duke, 1977; O'Brien, 1982). This turning to religion, prayer, or church in times of distress suggests that people tend to view these sources as a safe haven. This safe haven serves as a secure base, which is a characteristic of attachment behavior.

The threat of separation from God or a church often exists among religious adherents. One of the fears Christians have is a separation from God after death, which can be seen as the essence of what "hell" is. Also, in tragic situations when people feel abandoned by God, emotional distress and anger are likely to be experienced. Therefore, the aforementioned five features of an attachment relationship appear to occur in a relationship with religion. This makes it valuable to conduct therapy about religious issues through an attachment context.

TREATING OBSTACLES TO AUTHENTIC SPIRITUALITY

There are numerous reasons for people not having spiritual/religious experiences. In many cases there is simply a lack of awareness about the possibility of having spiritual experiences. Therefore, a lack of interest in spirituality may result. However, there are at least three situations in which spiritual/religious issues may be particularly relevant to psychotherapy.

- An aspect of spirituality may be relevant to the resolution of a psychological issue.
- A person seeking authentic spiritual experiences has been unsuccessful in attaining them.

- A negative encounter with religion, religious leaders, churches, or other elements of religion has promoted avoidance or distress about anything religious.

In these cases it is often helpful to identify how authentic spiritual experiences are blocked. Therapy can focus upon the resolution of these blockages, and when it occurs during ETT®, spontaneous spiritual experiences often follow. The following list of blockages has been found in ETT® sessions:

- inability to bond with others
- inability to bond with oneself
- inability to recognize authentic spiritual experiences
- traumatic experiences associated with "religion"
- lack of trust in confiding spiritual experiences to others
- lack of validation for authentic spiritual experiences

These issues can become objectives for treatment. As these issues are resolved in ETT®, spontaneous spiritual experiences may occur as a byproduct of the process. Distressing issues are pursued like any other psychological problem; they just happen to be about religious/spiritual topics.

NEURAL BRAIN CIRCUITS FOR PERCEIVING "GOD"

There have been scientific studies conducted to determine which brain mechanisms are responsible, in part, for transcendent experiences. Andrew Newberg has used neuroimaging methods to monitor brain activity while Buddhist monks, Catholic nuns and other people were actually experiencing spiritual events (Newberg, A., 2001). Newberg does not suggest that spiritual experiences are only phenomena of the brain, but instead that brain mechanisms are involved in carrying out these events.

> From early childhood on, God exists in every person's brain as a combination of ideas, images, feelings, sensations, and self/other relationships. Here is a thumbnail sketch of key neural structures and circuits that shape our perception of god:
>
> Occipital-Parietal Circuit — Identifies God as an object that exists in the world. Young children see God as a face because their brains cannot process abstract spiritual concepts.

Parietal-Frontal Circuit	Establishes a relationship between the two objects known as "you" and "God." It places God in space and allows you to experience God's presence. If you decrease activity in your parietal lobe through meditation or intense prayer, the boundaries between you and God dissolve. You feel a sense of unity with the object of contemplation and your spiritual beliefs.
Frontal Lobe	Creates and integrates all of your ideas about God—positive or negative—including the logic you use to evaluate your religious and spiritual beliefs. It predicts your future in relationship to God and attempts to intellectually answer all the "why, what, and where" questions raised by spiritual issues.
Thalamus	Gives emotional meaning to your concepts of God. The thalamus gives you a holistic sense of the world and appears to be the key organ that makes God feel objectively real.
Amygdala	When overly stimulated, the amygdala creates the emotional impression of a frightening, authoritative, and punitive God, and it suppresses the frontal lobes' ability to logically think about God.
Striatum	Inhibits activity in the amygdala, allowing you to feel safe in the presence of God, or of whatever object or concept you are contemplating.
Anterior cingulate	Allows you to experience God as loving and compassionate. It decreases religious anxiety, guilt, fear, and anger by suppressing activity in the amygdala. (Newburg & Waldman, 2009, pp. 43–44).

"Transpersonal" refers to experiences across or beyond the "normal" or conventional boundaries of the self. Transcendent experiences are specific transpersonal events. ETT® clients have reported a variety of different transcendent experiences that may occur alone or simultaneously with other transcendent experiences. Sometimes these experiences may occur in a sequence, one after another. For example, one might experience direct contact with God and then feel euphoric afterward. These experiences may occur during or subsequent to an ETT® session.

SPIRITUAL AWAKENING DURING SESSIONS

In 1986 a man entered a session and his experience inadvertently reasserted the reality of a "Kundalini" awakening. He reported that he suffered through an unrelenting experience over which he had little or no control. He agreed to let me see this. Then he suddenly moved to the floor and his eyes rolled back, leaving only the whites of his eyes visible. His body moved into a spontaneous yoga posture. This posture quickly concluded and was followed by another completely different complex posture, followed by then another and another until he must have assumed at least twenty different postures. It was apparent that these were spontaneous body movements that consumed him. This man had no previous experience in yoga, nor did he have a spiritual practice or significant religious orientation. Before this session I had been aware that spontaneous body movements often occurred during Kundalini awakenings, but I had not observed this behavior in a live demonstration. This event provided experience to suspect the universal nature of the Kundalini phenomenon and prompted further study so that this author could have in place to help people with this if it occurred again.

Subsequent to the 1986 Kundalini session, numerous people reported one type of profound transcendent experience or another after the use of a light-emitting device in therapy. Then when a new, precise, and powerful light device was used in ETT®, different types of spiritual awakenings took place.

THE KUNDALINI EXPERIENCE

These awakenings, when initiated by ETT®, may occur in experiences outside of one's previous religious knowledge or preference. For example, atheists may experience contact with the divine, Christians may have an experience known in Hindu or Buddhist traditions, or Jews may experience the presence of Christ. ETT® clients also describe a difficult process of transformation that culminates in distinct changes in perception of inner light along with spiritual awakening.

With over a hundred books on various aspects of Kundalini, a consumer is often left in a state of confusion about the accuracy, practicality, and/or helpfulness of each description. The vast majority of these books focus on one aspect of Kundalini, conceiving of it as an "energy technique" or a sexual experience, or glorifying it as a single, simple process. While there is more than one way to conceive of it, most of the published books are far from a careful portrayal, and the risk of mismanagement of an authentic Kundalini rising is high. Even groups that purport to practice "Kundalini yoga" may vary dramatically in regard to understanding and practices that involve authentic Kundalini experiences. Evidence suggests that Kundalini processes are a universal phenomenon, occurring cross-culturally and throughout many different religions.

THE HISTORY OF KUNDALINI IN AMERICA

For almost a century Western cultures have been exposed to the experience of Kundalini. In 1932 Carl Jung made the first presentation on Kundalini in America from a psychological perspective. Translations of Sanskrit texts into English began to occur as early as 1935 in Swami Sivananda Saraevati's *Kundalini Yoga.* However, it was Gopi Krishna and Swami Muktananda who first really made the concept of Kundalini popularly known in the United States and Europe. I heard about the Kundalini experience initially through the writings of John White who wrote about Gopi Krishna. Gopi Krishna's autobiography described his arduous journey of a Kundalini rising and the persistent experience of the perception of seeing inner lights. Gopi Krishna's writings are very personal and compelling. He emphasized that Kundalini was the activation of genetic endowment and sought scientific research to validate it (Krishna, 1997). Muktananda, on the other hand, frequently aroused Kundalini by means of his touch. While thousands attended Muktananda's presentations and Siddha Yoga centers were opened all over the world, there were some Kundalini risings that occurred unmanaged, and the experience left people confused and disoriented (Muktananda, 2000).

Several books offer help for recognizing and managing Kundalini symptoms. In 1975 Lee Sannella, MD, published a descriptive study of observations of numerous symptoms occurring during Kundalini risings (1987). In 1980 a definitive text on Kundalini in Layayoga was translated from Sanskrit (Goswami, 1980). This book is one of the most authoritative descriptions of Kundalini. Dr. Bonnie Greenwell wrote one of the most readable overviews of the Kundalini process in 1990 (Greenwell, 1990). Christina and Stanislof wrote a book about Christina's Kundalini experience and spiritual awakening. She initiated the Spiritual Emergency Network in 1990 in order to provide understanding and help for people undergoing Kundalini or other forms of challenging spiritual awakenings (Grof & Grof, 1990). In 1991 Phillip St. Romain wrote the first book on Kundalini within a Christian context (1991). Most recently Joan Shivarprta Harrigan's text *Kundalini Vidya* is probably the clearest description of many aspects of Kundalini with practical emphasis on how to understand and manage Kundalini symptoms (Harrigan, 2005).

Gopi Krishna, whose books popularized Kundalini in America, focused on the direct contact between humans and the divine that occurs in the form of the Kundalini experience. In his description of Kundalini, he clearly departed from conventional Kundalini yoga, conventional aspects of Hinduism, and other religious teaching because he thought religious teachings fail to tell the whole story. Specifically, he thought that the discomfort of both bodily changes and psychological challenges on the way to ultimate long-term spiritual fulfillment are far more uncomfortable than we are told in conventional religious teaching (Krishna, 1977).

While phenomena of light are related to the divine described in virtually every major religion, references to light have become relegated to analogies, metaphors, or symbolic meanings of light in most current religious interpretations. Like Gopi Krishna's experience, ETT® sessions produce the experience of spiritual awakening preceded by, and including, a vivid, distinct experience of the actual perception of light within one's body.

RESEARCH IN BIOLUMINESCENCE

There is scientific study that is designed to detect emanations of light from living organisms including humans. It is in an area of physics called biophoton emission. This research has identified and measured spontaneous emission of ultraweak light emanating from humans (Popp, et al., 1988). While some studies focus on potential medical applications, other studies attempt to understand biophoton emission in conjunction with changes in consciousness. However, findings regarding the variation of states of consciousness and biophoton emission have not yet been consistent or substantial (Nakamura, et al., 2000; Van Wijk & Van Wijk, 2005). While the study of biophoton emission may possess some promise for identifying and measuring transcendent states at some time in the future, it has not yet yielded significant findings that consistently verify these types of states of mind. However, it is interesting to note that researchers are pursuing measurement of bioluminescence in humans.

THE SPIRITUAL EXPERIENCES OF JAKOB BOHME

A search for the earliest evidence of a light-stimulated spiritual awakening led to a German mystic in the Middle Ages who may have had an occurrence similar to those initiated by ETT®. According to some theorists, the evolution of a species takes place in the form of incremental changes, but at some point certain "leaps" in physical change must take place. This same principle tends to occur in the human evolution of thought, philosophy, or knowledge. In the case of spiritual evolution, the ideas of the German shoemaker, Jakob Bohme, have been considered "original thought" or a leap in perspective within the Christian Lutheran perspective of his day. Historical researchers report puzzlement about how Bohme came up with ideas that departed so greatly from what anyone knew about in that time and place (Weeks, 1991). Although local authorities in Gorlitz, Germany, rebuked his ideas as heretical, other people of his time revered these ideas, and scholars have continued to study them for centuries.

In 1600 Bohme had a profound mystical experience initiated by inadvertently looking into a beam of sunlight reflected in a pewter dish. He believed this vision revealed "the spiritual structure of the world," as well as the relationship between God and humans. He asserted that God exists without time and space and regenerates himself throughout eternity (Swainson, 1921). Subsequent to this experience he had other experiences and wrote several books based on these experiences. He departed from the accepted theology of his day in several ways:

- emphasizing the role of God's grace
- referring to the "son" in the holy trinity as "light"
- focusing on the idea that man often must go through severe challenges in order to reach spiritual fulfillment (congruent with today's concepts of personal transformation and "purification")
- describing a form of spiritual evolution. According to Bohme, all original unities undergo differentiation, desire, and conflict in order for God's creation to evolve to a new state of "redeemed harmony."
- believing that as God interacts with a creation that was both part of and different from himself; God could continually reach a new self-awareness
- thinking that free will was God's gift that allows us to seek grace by choice, which allows us to remain individuals
- conceiving that the incarnation of Christ meant the possibility of a new state—the integration of part human and part divine

Bohme's original concepts—all activated by a human relationship with visual light stimulation—altered Christian perspective for centuries and inspired Milton, Blake, Shaupenhaur, and others.

BOHME AND ETT®

Jakob Bohme's experience with a beam of light that evoked consequential spiritual awareness bears a strong resemblance to what people frequently experience during ETT®. Such experiences include the following:

1. Visual brain stimulation
2. Profound transpersonal awareness (direct experience of the divine)
3. Insights, new perspectives that emerge spontaneously
4. Expansion of psycho-spiritual capacities
5. An inner-light experience

It is beyond coincidence that these themes would be evoked in the year 1600 and the year 2010 by a very similar means. Apparently, visual brain stimulation provokes a universal phenomenon, and Bohme was simply the first to recognize and write about it.

RECOGNIZING KUNDALINI SYMPTOMS

Kundalini Shakti is a feminine divine entity whose essence extends beyond the terms for energy like "prana" or "chi." This feminine deity possesses several unique characteristics. In Sanskrit the term "Kundalini" means coiled serpent, which represents the power and motion of the movement of Kundalini (Harrigan, 2005). A perception of inner light, heat, cold, and many other symptoms often occur during her expression. The rising of this universal spiritual energy occurs more easily when one's relieved psychological and physical issues have been resolved. This purification by means of ETT® couples with the development of an intimate subjective relationship with light and promotes a novel means for eliciting Kundalini Shakti.

The Indian Vedic, Layayoga, Puranic, and Tantric traditions appear to provide the most accurate, detailed understanding of the Kundalini process. The Veda system of India involves sacred scriptures. "Veda stands for the parts known as mantra and bramana" (Grimes, 1996, pp. 337–340). "Layayoga" refers to an Indian system of yoga that means "dissolution, absorption, to merge" (Grimes, 1996, p. 175). Purana is an Indian system that includes "eighteen major Purana, or sacred books, containing stories, legends and hymns about the creation of the universe, the incarnation of God, and the instructions of various deities as well as the spiritual legacies of ancient sages and kings" (Grimes, 1996, p. 250).

Tantra is an Indian tradition that refers to rules, rituals, and scriptures. "As religious treaties, they are usually in the form of a dialogue between Siva and Sakti. . . . The goal of Tantra is attaining self-realization through Kundalini awakening and through uniting the two principles" (Grimes, 1996, pp. 314–315).

It is important that these peculiar or disturbing symptoms be recognized as part of a Kundalini spiritual awakening because they can easily be mistaken for medical problems or some form of psychosis. Numerous uncomfortable symptoms occur in this process of transformation. These symptoms may appear like other well-known psychological or medical symptoms but generally are unique or more unusual when seen as a whole than conventionally known symptoms. The process can be seen in context with proper guidance.

The following symptoms have been found in people experiencing a Kundalini awakening. "K" represents symptoms reported by Gopi Krishna; "S" represents symptoms found in a study by psychiatrist Lee Sannella in a U.S. population; and "V" represents symptoms that I have found in ETT® clients. Outside of taking a religious/spiritual history, no attempt was made to bring up or encourage spiritual/religious topics when Kundalini spontaneously arose. Fourteen symptoms occurred in all three reports of Kundalini.

Kundalini Symptoms

Psychological Changes

1. Extreme emotions of intense fear, anxiety, or depression (K,S,V)
2. Detachment (K,S,V)
3. Doubt and disbelief about the reality of the experience (K,S,V)
4. Thoughts speeding up, slowing down, or stopping altogether (S,V)
5. Increase in intelligence (K,V)

Physiological Experiences

6. Tingling, itching, or vibrating skin sensations, sometimes moving up from the feet (K,S,V)
7. Intense heat at times (K,S,V)
8. Extreme coldness at times (K,S,V)
9. Physical pain (K,S,V)
10. Significant digestive problems of a temporary nature (K,V)
11. Amplified sexual drive, primarily in men (K)

12. Fatigue (K,V)
13. Ability to survive with little or no food for long periods of time (K,V)
14. Intense circulatory pulsations (K,V)
15. Changes in body odor (V)
16. Muscle spasms (S,V)
17. Extreme changes in sleep patterns (K,V)

Energy and/or Movement Phenomena

18. Perception of energy emerging, moving from the base of the spine upward to the crown of the skull (K,S,V)
19. Spontaneous body movements including the eyes (S,K,V)
20. Spontaneous postures, often classic hatha yoga postures (S,V)
21. Spontaneous, unusual breathing patterns (S,V)
22. Temporary paralysis; inability to move (S,V)
23. Spontaneous chanting (K,V)

Perception of light

24. Perception of inner white light within the head and/or body (K,S,V)
25. Perception of inner color within the body (K,S,V)
26. Perception of lights or color around certain areas of the body (V)
27. Visions of the divine (V,G,S)

Transpersonal Experiences

28. Perception of internally heard sounds (K,S,V)
29. Perceived expansion of the physical body (K,S,V)
30. Transpersonal experiences of various types (K,S,V)
31. Extreme emotions of ecstasy, peace, and love (K,S,V)
32. Out-of-body experiences (S,V)
33. Single seeing (S)
34. Communication with the divine (V)
35. Spontaneous ability to heal others (V)
36. Spontaneous rapid self-healing (V)
37. Communication with spirit guides (V)
38. Communication with deceased people (V)
39. Omniscient perception of the entire universe (K,V)

ETHICAL CONCERNS

People who have experienced symptoms of a Kundalini awakening without guidance or completion of the event are at risk. Some clients have been observed who reported Kundalini symptoms earlier in their lives due to meditative practices but who resisted the Kundalini. The results of resisting the process vary substantially based on which symptoms were experienced and by what other means these symptoms were managed. If psychological symptoms were addressed by antipsychotic medication or any number of drugs, this remedy could lead to chronic issues of physical, psychological, or spiritual dysfunction. It has been observed to be even worse if people self-medicated with illicit drugs. If the physical symptoms were targeted by medication or surgery, temporary relief might have occurred, but symptom substitution is likely. The degeneration of mental activities due to the inadequate activation of one's natural potential can result in a lack of purpose or direction.

The powerful unleashing of Kundalini by ETT® has brought forth ethical concerns. While on one hand this process activates people to the full expression of their potential, on the other hand the journey itself can often be arduous. It often requires a high number of sessions (biweekly up to one year) to alleviate extreme cases that involve literally hundreds of traumas, severe psychopathology, and attachment deficits of a profoundly compromised nature. The frequent exposure to powerful visual light stimulation during these processes infuses the human system with far more prana in a shorter time than would take place by any other means. Resistance leaves the client at risk of relapse due to entrenched psychological imprints, which can create distressing symptoms during the Kundalini process. Since some of the symptoms can be extremely distressing, clients should make an informed decision about whether to proceed. The Therapist (now better described as guide) guide should educate the client about Kundalini. This education can be particularly challenging when the person's religion or philosophy does not include openness to anything outside of his/her belief system. An objective of this education would be to reduce discomfort and risk while enhancing the activation of one's authentic potential, not to convert anyone to a specific belief.

Kundalini Issues

Several factors are involved that make the Kundalini event different from conventional religious practice and/or methods of healing.

1. Most religions describe ultimate fulfillment but often fail to adequately describe the challenges on the journey in detail. This leaves people in the position of
   - being believers without enough detailed guidance necessary to arrive at the destination of direct experience with the divine
   - lack of recognition of many symptoms that are features of internal spiritual movement
   - lack of knowledge of universal spiritual experiences that are not included within the doctrine of a specific religion
2. Most people seek relief of unpleasant psychological and physical symptoms in the form of pharmaceuticals, illicit drugs, food addictions, alcohol, surgery, and other means to stop discomfort without regard to the value of overcoming meaningful adversity. Since these approaches are designed to stop the discomfort without regard to new learning from the experience, a natural progression toward transformation is often delayed, prevented, or interrupted altogether.
3. While meditation enjoys some degree of popularity, it is so slow by comparison to ETT® that there is a strong tendency for most people to drop out of the practice before ultimate fulfillment arrives. ETT® offers a much faster way to the same spiritual fulfillment, which is fitting for today's psyche in the western culture.
4. ETT® may provide an advancement in managing Kundalini symptoms.

According to Gopi Krishna (ed. by Kieffer, 1988), the following features characterize mystical or transpersonal experiences that occur in the Kundalini awakening (p. 63):

1. vivid sensations of light both within and without
2. a feeling of extreme rapture that is reflected in the whole appearance of the individual
3. often streaming tears at the majestic and sublime nature of the spectacle
4. a sense of intimacy or proximity to an infinite presence or a celestial being
5. contact with an infinite fount of knowledge
6. horripilation (gooseflesh)
7. a sense of unbounded wonder and awe at the surpassing vision
8. intellectual illumination with Jnana—that is, perennial wisdom

Gopi Krishna elaborates further on his description of transcendent experiences, so the aforementioned features are not all-inclusive. He goes to great lengths to differentiate this experience from those that occur during LSD trips, biofeedback, hypnosis, and certain other religious methods (Kieffer, 1988, pp. 58–63). While these other methods may provoke peace or transcendence, Gopi Krishna asserts that they do not infuse prana into the system and thereby fail to promote genetic activation. While there are many people who have proposed some form of human evolution, Gopi Krishna describes the process and symptoms within the individual that have been observed to spontaneously occur in naïve ETT® clients leading to evolutionary experiences.

There are various means attributed to the triggering of transcendent states of consciousness. Keutzer found that nature scenes are the most common trigger for these states (1979). J. Wade reports that sexual experiences are the most common activity that elicits transcendent states (2004, p. xi). However, both of these triggers occur randomly and are unpredictable. M. Persinger demonstrated that magnetic stimulation of the temperoparietal cortex can provoke mystical experiences (2010). Traditionally, meditation or the imparting of "shaktiput" from a guru or another spiritual person provides a way to trigger transcendent states. Only these last two means have been linked with an eventual continuous transcendent state of extreme wellbeing. ETT® is a third means to continually facilitate both transcendent states and eventually long-term states of extreme wellbeing. People who reach these relatively continual states of wellbeing become capable of stimulating transcendent states in others via interpersonal spiritual means as part of extended capabilities. The Kundalini Research Network conducted surveys that identified many of these triggers (Kason, 2008, p. 152). ETT® is the newest means to continually facilitate both transcendent states and long-term states of wellbeing.

ATTACHMENT PSYCHOLOGY AND FACILITATING TRANSCENDENCE

Attachment theory is important in this Kundalini phenomenon. ETT® clients who have gone through these transformations have had attachment disorders derived from their severely dysfunctional families of origin, disorders resulting in some of the most extreme forms of psychological dysfunction. These clients reported issues that were intense, long-term, and consisted of dozens of traumas in their lives. This struggle parallels the portion of Bohme's theory that one must undergo differentiation, desire, and conflict in order to evolve to a new state. By focusing on identifying and changing dysfunctional attachment patterns in ETT® sessions, the correction of how a client relates to others and how he/she regulates emotions can take place. This correction improves inner harmony by internalizing a healthy client-guide external relationship into a new inner relationship with oneself.

Because the reversal of attachment deficiencies plays such a critical role in the process of transformation, it requires a different variation of the role of the mental health professional. The symptoms of the Kundalini expression may be perceived as so severe and/or unusual to the person experiencing them that the need for close contact and support by a guide is far more frequent than the types of guidance provided by conventional weekly counseling sessions. Rapport and trust with the facilitator often becomes more important than in many other therapeutic endeavors because this interpersonal foundation may be the basis upon which deficient attachment patterns are corrected. Since Kundalini symptoms are not well understood by conventional psychology, religion, or medicine, appropriate guidance becomes vital. Ideally, facilitators should have undergone the Kundalini experience personally in order to enhance their guidance, but well-informed guides who can affirm these experiences and educate clients about them can be helpful. The management of Kundalini symptoms involves interpersonal bonding, light stimulation, nutritional guidance, and breathing techniques. Expertise in all four of these modalities is advisable for optimal guidance.

Gopi Krishna believes that spiritual awakening through the Kundalini process is a universal process and one that provides people of different religions a means of making direct contact with the divine. Since there is some degree of individualization in the expression of Kundalini, different cultural terminology, and variant interpretations of similar phenomena, different religious concepts develop around a person's spiritual experience. However, Aldous Huxley and others have advocated the "perennial philosophy" in which it is conceived that people who have mystical experiences may have more in common with fellow mystics in different religions than with people within their own religious orientation (Huxley, 1945). Gopi Krishna suggests that since this universal process exists in people from all faiths, we should endeavor to facilitate harmony among all religious faiths. It would seem that if ETT® were to continue to produce growing numbers of Kundalini awakenings at a faster rate, Gopi Krishna's vision of religious harmony might be realized.

Case Study: Kim

A thirty-nine-year-old married female was referred to me with symptoms of chronic, intense panic attacks. Kim, a mother with two babies, was also the

CEO of her business firm. The panic attacks occurred almost daily and could last as long as seventeen hours. This woman's condition had been resistant to out-patient treatment, psychiatric medications, and years of interpersonal counseling. Her personal history was fraught with numerous traumatic events and a severely dysfunctional family of origin. Traumatic events were resolved in each session, but then another trauma would emerge. This emergence and resolution occurred over fifty times. Nonetheless, through ETT® we were able to reduce the panic symptoms consistently during each session. However, the symptoms sometimes returned within a day or two. Gradually, the change in panic symptoms and numerous traumas finally arrested after biweekly sessions over several months of ETT®. Then something peculiar began to take place.

This client had no religious background and was essentially an atheist. No discussion of religious/spiritual matters had been brought up in sessions with this client. During one ETT® session she had a sudden awareness of self-transcendence that she assumed was the presence of God. She was affirmed. This startling awareness brought her comfort. However, her husband, family, and all of her friends had no religious background or were simply against religion, which made the discovery awkward.

Next, well after all of her original symptoms had abated, a series of anxiety symptoms began to plague her for unknown reasons. At this crucial point she decided to continue therapy even though her original symptoms were gone. Then she began to have transcendent experiences intermittently. She reported a variety of other odd and uncomfortable symptoms that scared her. These experiences were recognized as symptoms of Kundalini awakening. She was affirmed for her experiences and educated about them. Her discomfort worsened. Gradually the transcendent experiences became more profound and frequent. These experiences exhibited a wide variety of forms. Her contact with her perception of the divine had become auditory, visual, and almost constant. At first this dramatic experience was hard for her to accept. Even though Kim had profound spiritual experiences, her reaction to each event was fearful. She experienced a complete perceived loss of control because these events surprised her each time. The novelty of these experiences provoked fear because of her need to make sense of each one. In addition, her spiritual messages often did not align with her wants or desires for activities on each day. Therefore, she required continual support, resolution of fear, and education in order to stabilize her responses to these massive changes.

How do we know that ETT® clients are simply not hallucinating? Whether this entity discovered by ETT® clients is an authentic God or not may be a subject of debate. At the very least, interest should be focused upon whether these interactions are psychologically healthy or not. The following features of the divine have been reported in Kim's case and in other ETT® cases:

- consistent messages of comfort
- consistent affectionate tone that results in the person feeling loved
- revelation of knowledge derived from an omniscient viewpoint beyond that of the client's
- consistent guidance that yields beneficial effects
- rapid, profound physical healing occurring during direct contact with the divine entity
- awareness of the client's past and certain aspects of the client's potential future
- capacity to provide inspiration
- facilitation of spontaneous abilities not previously possessed by the person
- the capacity to direct activities that frequently coordinate with external events without the client's knowledge of these external events (synchronicity)

These characteristics of Kim's perception of God match those of a secure attachment figure. The omniscient characteristics provided information that became verified, which supports the idea of an authentic transcendent experience instead of a psychotic hallucination. The coherent, consistent messages bear a resemblance to depictions of God in more than one religion. Therefore, the entire experience was given validation during the counseling process.

While Kim reported significant improvement in mental functioning, how do we know that her brain improved? Furthermore, is there any measurable evidence to verify her experience of perceiving white light internally? Kim had a SPECT (Single Photon Emission Computed Tomography) brain scan to assess the elimination of panic attacks, which confirmed the extinguishment of panic attacks but still left evidence of minor dysfunction in the prefrontal cortex and thalamus. Then she underwent the Kundalini process for a year and subsequent to the completion of Kundalini another SPECT scan was performed to evaluate her experience during samadhi when she was perceiving God and inner light. This post SPECT scan showed improvement in the prefrontal cortex and complete alleviation of thalamic dysfunction. At the same time, there was a substantial blood flow in the occipital lobe, where visual activity primarily exists. Therefore, the brain scan verified both improved brain function and visual activation that could account for perception of inner light and the experience of wellbeing. This brain scan clearly revealed a highly functioning brain, which would rule out any visions as emanating from dysfunction such as psychosis.

In addition to Kim's encounter with God, she had numerous other transcendent experiences. She reported direct visual/auditory contact with her deceased grandmother, her only secure attachment during childhood. This contact provided daily guidance for several months. During the culminating Kundalini experience of euphoric energy rising, Kim saw and heard a vision of a beautiful woman who was the Kundalini goddess herself. The appearance of the Kundalini goddess is well known in Hindu tradition. (Muktananda, 2000, p. 125). There is a long history of conceptions of God that include both a male and female God and Goddess. Historical religious scholars report the following:

> In Egypt they were known as Isis and Osirus, in Greece as Persephone and Dionysus, in Syria as Aphrodite and Adonis, in Asia Minor as Cybele and Attis, in Mesopotania as Ishtar and Marduk, in Pershia as the Magna Mater and Mithras, and in the area around Judea as Asherah and Baal. (Freke & Grandy, 2001)

All of these direct contacts with deities ended up being of pragmatic value.

There were also substantial physiological changes as a result of this Kundalini experience. Kim had been medically evaluated to possess over twenty-five different allergies for several years. By chance, allergy testing took place after her Kundalini rising and all twenty-five allergies were completely gone. In another case of Kundalini rising a different woman was diagnosed with an aggressive form of cancer called non-Hodgkin's lymphoma and was scheduled for chemotherapy. However, after a partial Kundalini rising, her blood tests showed a remission. Apparently the Kundalini process impacts the physical body in substantial ways that changes medical conditions.

VARIATIONS OF KUNDALINI

A popular idea is that Kundalini rises from the base of the spine to the top of the skull, which results in an enlightened experience. While this is not incorrect, it is grossly oversimplified and does not allow for numerous profound symptoms that tend to occur over a period of time as well as numerous variations of it for each individual. Harrigan classifies three types of Kundalini risings according to the Vedic tradition: (1) no rising, (2) arousal only, and (3) deflected rising. Deflected risings are the most unstable. In deflected risings, as Kundalini rises it encounters various blockages, which result in numerous strong symptoms as a byproduct. The Indian energy system includes channels known as nadis and energy vortices called chakras. There are several levels of risings:

- No rising: no arousal, arousal only.
- Partial rising: rising below the cap of Bana linga nadi (phallus-shaped movement in Sushurma toward the Anahata) and Kurma Nadi.
- Deflective risings: unstable risings that do not reach the pinnacle (Bindu).
- Intermediate rising: this rising occurs up the Sushuma nadi to the Anahata charka and below.
- Full rising: this rising can move via one of seven different routes to the makara point (the experience of Upper Ajna that involves getting beyond the mind).
- Complete rising: this rising moves from the base of the spine to the top of the skull (Bindu).
- Advanced rising: this includes descending from Bindu and/or re-ascending process (Harringan, 2005, pp. 109–112).

Kim had an unstable deflected Kundalini rising that took several months. However, she ultimately had a complete rising and then an advanced rising. Her process was different because she did not come to therapy for a spiritual purpose. She had the distinct advantage of ETT® processes to purify her numerous psychological issues before she had the Kundalini rising. Management of Kundalini symptoms by ETT® provided a powerful means to handle these potent symptoms.

Post Kundalini experiences often need guidance as well. After the most profound experiences in one's life, challenges of adjustment often exist. Some people can literally become amnesic of these profound experiences or discount them as not real. Other people may change their lives so drastically as a result that it compromises their functioning. A search for the purposeful use of newly learned experiences may ensue. The aftershock of these events needs to be assimilated.

The ultimate function of Kundalini awakenings is for one to achieve complete fulfillment. Yvonne Kason, MD, describes this fulfillment in the following:

> According to the Kundalini hypothesis, after many years of proper, healthy stimulation by the Kundalini mechanisms, the brahma randhra region of the brain

may reach a level of stabilized functioning that allows a person to concentrate on external realities and, at the same time, exist in a perennial state of mystical ecstasy. Such a person would live in a state of high consciousness, constantly aware of subtle energies behind the universe and what is sometimes called the "Bramic Splendor": and yet still be able to participate in daily, worldly activities. This state is known in yoga as "gahaja-samadhi," the "sahaja state," or the "turiya state" . . .

The term "sahaja," meaning "co-emergent," describes the co-existence of two states of consciousness, mystical union and normal mental functioning. (Kason, 1994, pp. 134–135)

NEAR-DEATH EXPERIENCE AND KUNDALINI

The term "near-death experience" (NDE) was coined by Raymond Moody, MD, who interviewed hundreds of people who reported these experiences. Therefore, while the features of these experiences may vary from person to person, there are many experiences in common among those who experienced it. Yvonne Kason, MD, describes the numerous parallels between the Kundalini experience and the near death experience and makes a case for the idea that many near-death experiences are Kundalini experiences initiated by near-death phenomena. The following are the characteristics common to both:

Typically, one of the first sensations during an NDE is a feeling of great peace and calm, a certainty that there is nothing to fear, that all is right with the universe. These feelings are typical of those experienced when the kundalini rises to the heart chakra (sometimes called a heart opening). The fact that these symptoms appear first could be explained by the belief that when kundalini awakens, it often rises to the heart chakra first—a so-called partial Kundalini awakening. As the NDE continues, the kundalini rises further up the body. When the kundalini reaches the third eye on sixth chakra, a psychic awakening occurs, with clairaudience (hearing what is being said around your unconscious or dead body) and then an out-of-body experience. In a NDE, this experience of floating above the unconscious or clinically dead physical body and accurately viewing what is happening below almost invariably occurs after the feeling of peace begins. . . .

According to the kundalini model, once the kundalini mechanism is initially activated or awakened, especially if raised to the crown or seventh chakra, it rarely turns off completely. The kundalini returns to the root chakra after the NDE, but the mechanism continues to be active though only slightly. . . .

The kundalini returns to the root chakra after the NDE, but the shusuma remains partly open, up to the chakra kundalini reached, and the mechanism continues to be active, though only slightly. This supports Dr. Melvin Morse's research observations in *Transformed by the Light,* where he documented that only those NDE experiencers who saw the light were spiritually transformed afterwards, with a loss of the fear of death, an increase in spiritual focus, and an increase in psychic experiences.

For those persons experiencing ongoing kundalini activity after an NDE, the level of activity and the intensity of the symptoms tend to increase over time. These kundalini symptoms may eventually become perceptible to the NDE experiencer as ongoing or recurrent inner sounds, intermittent light perceptions, or intermittent rushes of energy up the body or spine. This activity gradually stimulates the brahma randhra brain center, resulting in more frequent psychic experiences, recurrent mystical experiences, or more rarely as an increase or development of "Inspired Creativity" gifts.

It is important to recognize the parallels between Kundalini and near-death experiences because Kundalini guidelines for treatment can be used to assist issues related to near-death experiences. Most of the people I have encountered who have had near-death experiences disclosed that the let down of coming back to life was so great that they really were not motivated to stay alive. They wanted to return to the glorious state encountered during the near-death experience. Clearly, a constructive assimilation has not occurred with this result. The shock of the powerful drama of either a Kundalini experience or a near-death experience often requires proper guidance in order for an adjustment to a new life to take place. In addition, these events of profound new abilities such as precognition, telepathy, or the ability to speak new languages may spontaneously occur. The possession of new extraordinary abilities can be disorienting and lead to entirely new challenges that many people are not prepared for. However, the upside of these experiences is profound if these changes are managed well.

WHY ETT® PRODUCES KUNDALINI

Bonding with light assists in changing attachment deficiencies. Research suggests that attachment patterns are projected onto our perception of the divine. (Kirkpatrick, 2005) For example, people in the general population with avoidant attachment patterns show a statistically significant correlation with the choice of atheism and agnosticism (Kirkpatrick & Shaver, 1992). ETT® utilizes "amplified attunement" to the client by combining both the facilitator's interpersonal responsivity and the wavelengths of light that match each emotional state. Therefore, this type of attunement establishes a favorable attachment linkage to both the facilitator and the light, which enhances perceived relationships. When attachment disorders are corrected, a person's relationship with light also changes from a detached observation to a subjective bonding with the light itself. This subjective bonding with light can represent an increased ability to bond with ourselves, with others, and ultimately may be internalized as a bond with a perceived inner light.

There are many types of yoga, and many are quite different from the well-known hatha yoga commonly thought of as "yoga" in the United States, which is largely composed of postures. The term "laya" is derived from the meaning "be absorbed in." According to Layayoga, the first step toward the ultimate state of samadhi is to control the senses (pratyahara).

According to translations from ancient texts, the central features of the Layayoga path to fulfillment operate according to the following principles:

> Consciousness becomes limited when it is a field of perceptivity, intellection, and volition. This consciousness is nurtured by the penetration into it of the objective substances lying outside of it. When the sense-principles and sense-mind are absorbed in concentration, this consciousness becomes non-being, not by becoming non-conscious but by being transformed into prajnana, that is superconsciousness. When the sense-consciousness becomes inoperative, the picture of the external world vanishes. Therefore, the absorption of sense-mind, sense-consciousness, intellect, and will-mind creates a state of consciousness which is beyond all these. It is now prajnana—superconsciousness which is super-refined and illuminated by divine light. (Goswami, 1980, p. 72)

Sanskrit does not always translate clearly into English. Therefore, let me convert these concepts into how they apply to ETT®. The sensory stimuli of appropriate light and verbal interaction serve as the "objective substances lying outside" of the person's consciousness that penetrate the recipient's consciousness. Optimal interpersonal attunement and visual light stimulation that resonates with a person's state of mind tends to result in a rapid absorption of a person's attention into the sensory experience. This "concentration" results from the optimal match between a person and his/her sensory environment. Absorbed concentration becomes "non-being" and can be transformed into "superconsciousness." In this state the external world appears to vanish. This results in a state of consciousness that transcends intellect, affect, ego (self-perception), and the five senses. This new state of consciousness becomes "super-refined and illuminated by divine light." The ultimate state of union with the divine is called samadhi.

This process, when repeated, can lead to the arousing of Kundalini. According to Goswami:

> The arousing of Kundalini is the process of the spiritualization of consciousness. The aroused Kundalini manifests absorptive power by which all worldly principles are absorbed, and causes spiritual radiation into consciousness. In this way all sensory pictures and thought forms in consciousness are controlled and consciousness is illuminated by the spiritual splendor of Kundalini. Ultimately, consciousness becomes wholly of Kundalini, and then the spiritualized consciousness is absorbed into Kundalini, and Kundalini into Shiwa when supreme yoga is attained. (Goswami, 1980, pp. 87–88)

The ETT® process parallels this description in many ways. In ETT® the visual sense is used. About 80 percent of all sensory intake is visual, and the four other senses can be cross-referenced with the visual sense within the brain's neural pathways. Therefore, all five senses are involved either by direct or indirect initiation. During ETT® sessions concentration and absorption are not often the intent but tend to occur frequently due to certain elements of the process, such as:

- By the use of attachment-based interpersonal interactions, responses are custom-tailored to each client, which tends to result in more rapid experiences of safety, trust, and absorption into the process. This foundation of trust allows clients to surrender to the process and experience spontaneous transpersonal events.
- Continually attuning to the client, the therapist leads to continuous selection of wavelengths of light that, when matched appropriately with the client's emotional state, result in the extended focus of the client's attention.
- Brainwave entrainment by a strobic light source elicits a matching of the rate of oscillation of light with the client's brainwaves. This results in focused attention.

The continual matching of the client's visual ecology by the facilitator elicits focus of attention by changing the visual stimulus to wherever the client's mental attention already exists. Once a person's attention is captured, it can be sustained more easily. This makes it easier and faster to attain a state of focused attention without the long and sometimes difficult process that Layayoga would normally require in order to learn to control mental attention first and then use this attention to focus on the senses secondly. By virtue of attunement via visual stimuli and interpersonal attention, control of focused attention becomes a byproduct of the process, not necessarily the intent. Therefore, instead of the years of meditation often necessary for one to be able to focus and be absorbed into transcendence, a facilitator using light can focus attention and absorption can take place more rapidly.

In several cases people who have had years of meditation experience have had a profound transpersonal experience during their first ETT® session! This suggests that visual light stimulation and meditation have a mutual commonality in that they activate the brain, body, and spiritual awareness in a similar way. With the development of newer RGB light technology used in ETT®, the precise wavelengths of light necessary for the greatest impact on the brain have dramatically escalated the frequency and power of these events. While profound spiritual experiences have long occurred via ETT®, the enhanced, long-term transformation by means of this Kundalini expression become more frequent.

This extraordinary spiritual experience provokes questions regarding the purpose of such a process. Both Bohme and Krishna assert that Kundalini has a definite purpose both for the individual and for the species. Recent genetic research from the Human Genome Project has found that genetic expression is strongly influenced by the interpersonal environment. By optimizing the impact of the client's interpersonal and visual environment, it is possible that this attachment-based approach alters genetic expression.

GENES AND TRANSCENDENCE

Gopi Krishna went so far as to advocate that the human species must possess a genetic endowment for these divine Kundalini experiences. One of the functions of multiple transcendent experiences is to activate genes that extend human capabilities to the extraordinary. He speculated that if proper scientific inquiry took place, we would find verification of this spiritual tendency to extend human capabilities.

Within the last decade, Harvard-trained geneticist Dr. Dean Hamer analyzed the DNA of over a thousand people to discover the "God gene." While Dr. Hamer states that the term "God gene" is "a gross oversimplification of the theory," he proposes that

> we have a genetic predisposition for spiritual belief that is expressed in response to, and shaped by personal experiences and the cultural environment. These genes . . . act by influencing the brain's capacity for various types and forms of consciousness, which becomes the basis for spiritual experiences. (2004, p. 8)

According to Nobel Prize laureate Gerald Edelman, monoamines (such as serotonin and dopamine) link objects and experiences with emotions and values, which allows these transcendent experiences to take place. Dr. Hamer found that the VMAT2 gene functions as the mediator between emotions and values. Although the biological process is more complex than will be explained here, Dr. Hamer found that experiences of self-transcendence are largely related to the key role of the VMAT2 gene's activities. According to Dr. Hamer's research, it appears that Gopi Krishna's assertion about our genetic propensity toward transcendent experiences is correct.

While this genetic predisposition exists, optimal personal experience that leads to experiences of self-transcendence is necessary in order to activate these genes. Both meditation and ETT® lightwork facilitate these processes. Theoretically, ETT® appears to function as the ultimate catalyst to activate these dormant genetic functions. By using a variation of the means described by Jakob Bohme and the meditational experiences described by Gopi Krishna and Goswami, we can provide a catalyst (light stimulation) and a means to manage the journey conducive to optimal spiritual development.

EXTENDED HUMAN CAPABILITIES

Both Jakob Bohme and Gopi Krishna describe a spiritual evolution that indicates substantial change and improvement. Gopi Krishna goes farther by saying that repeated specific transcendent experiences during the process of Kundalini can eventually lead to extended human capabilities. Gopi Krishna is so clear about this spiritual evolution that he advocates scientific inquiry to validate his contention that these experiences expand mental capacities to extraordinary levels (Kieffer, 1988, pp. 39–50).

Abraham Maslow actually conducted research that demonstrated a correlation between people who had frequent transcendent or "peak experiences" and people who activate a greater than usual use of their human potential (Maslow, 1950). Maslow was an atheist and purposely avoided religious terminology in his description of "peak experiences" (Hamer, 2004, p. 20). However, Maslow's description of peak experiences matches the transpersonal experiences described by Gopi Krishna as well as other "spiritual descriptions." Maslow's phrase, "human potential," also equates with Gopi Krishna's description of elevated human capabilities and "genius" abilities.

Michael Murphy also compiled significant evidence that extended human capacities have been developed recently and even proposes what an evolved human might be like (1992). Unusual and advanced psychospiritual abilities have been seen in ETT® clients who have undergone transformation via ETT®. The expression of these advanced capabilities suggests that our genetic endowment is provided to assist in further adaptation of the human species to increase the chances of survival as new challenges are encountered. The following types of transcendent experiences have occurred during or subsequent to an ETT®:

- extraordinary intelligence (transcendent intelligence)
- spiritual dreams and the ability to intervene in one's own dreams as well as other's dreams (transcendent dreaming)
- perception of contact with a higher power (self-transcendence) such as God, guides, angels, the Great Spirit, Brahman, and others
- perception of profound beauty in "ordinary" things (transcendent beauty)
- near-death experiences or contact with deceased people (life-transcendence)
- perceived expansion (space transcendence). For example, great body or expansion to the entire universe
- past life, inter-generational memory, the numinous present, or precognition experiences (time transcendence)
- euphoria, ecstasy (emotional transcendence)
- universal love (transcendent love)
- wisdom (thought transcendence)
- the ability to spontaneously speak other languages without any previous exposure to them (transcendent linguistics abilities)
- profound peace (transcending distress)
- spiritual healing (transcendent healing)
- deep ecology (transcending nature)
- mental telepathy (transcendent communication)
- out-of-body, astral travel (transcendent location)
- extraordinary movement/strength (transcendent body)
- clairaudience or remote viewing (transcendent sensory experiences)

While extended human capabilities may appear to be welcomed abilities, their peculiarity in society offers a new set of challenges. First of all, many people experience shock and denial when they see a vision, access another person's thoughts, or spontaneously heal someone. This shock can cause enormous distress when people have difficulty assimilating the experience into their self-perception. Frequently, their experience is not believed by others, which may result in a sense of alienation from other people. It is important not to underestimate the shock of entering the transpersonal world, even if this has long been a client's desire. The adjustment must be supported. An entirely new set of issues and problems may arise that may be unanticipated. For example, Kim was frequently anxious about the future. Unfortunately, when she developed precognitive abilities, she saw things about her family's future that she did not wish to know. This new skill brought with it new challenges.

A second type of challenge encountered by people who suddenly acquire extended capabilities concerns the response of the ego. New abilities can contribute to ego inflation of people conceiving of themselves as special or superior to other people. Some people may immediately see opportunities to acquire money, power, sex, or excessive control through the use of these skills. Ultimately, the destruction of relationships and the loss of one's authentic sense of self loom as the most damaging potential consequences.

However, the third and most constructive response to the acquisition of extended capabilities might be to enhance self-love, relationships with others, and ultimately society or the human race. Extended capabilities can be seen as by-products of spiritual journeys. Instead of focusing on extended capabilities, one might be guided toward ultimate spiritual fulfillment and these special gifts may simply be used to enhance the journey.

History is replete with stories of bloodshed and war laid at the feet of those prompted by religious conviction, and people who have had divine contact and spoken about it have been crucified, burned at the stake, or beheaded. Obviously, a spiritual awakening can be risky. On the other hand, those who have been spiritually awakened have provided inspiration, hope, and healing for millions of people. Though the risk of misunderstanding exists and must be managed carefully in each person's social context, the payoff is enormous. Spiritual awakening holds the extraordinary potential to guide each of us to ultimate fulfillment.

10

The Boundless Possibilities of ETT®

An encounter with ETT® usually leaves these clients stunned, not only by the fact that they have finally improved, but also by the speed at which this progress has taken place. At the time of this writing, my caseload consists primarily of people who have come to me after experiencing failure with numerous other methods. While I and my trainees have experienced an impressive volume of positive outcomes, these findings have come from hundreds of sessions, not carefully constructed scientific studies. Verification via scientific scrutiny is currently ongoing. The implications for treatment are enormous. A radically new advancement now exists for the treatment of a wide array of disabling conditions.

New approaches emerge frequently, and professionals have become skeptical consumers, especially when some of these new methods have previously proven to be disappointing. In fact, many "alternative" approaches have been outright harmful to some clients. As a result clinicians are often jaded about the prospect of any new method. Therefore, some therapists pursue treatment paths that are traditional and possess a lot of research to support them, assuming that anything new must not work as well. While limiting choices to conventionally accepted methods sounds reasonable, it eliminates the possibility that more potent methods exist. My experience has been that the most scientifically researched methods of psychotherapy tend to be the least effective. Scientifically untested does not equate to inferior. A less scientifically tested method simply refers to a method that has not been selected as a topic for study by the scientific community. Unfortunately, the reasons for not selecting a particular method for study may have nothing to do with that method's effectiveness. Instead, reasons may range from a lack of funding to a researcher's narrow philosophical orientation. Every verified method showed some degree of clinical success initially, before it had scientific verification. The lack of scientific validation did not mean that the method did not work. Nonetheless, exciting research on ETT® is taking place.

ETT® operates via a paradigm that exists outside most professional belief systems about how treatment works. The concept that a person's visual ecology can impact the brain so rapidly and powerfully is difficult for many people to accept. I have conducted numerous live demonstrations in which I demonstrated the use of a person's visual ecology to reduce distress within seconds or physical pain within minutes. Even though these improvements took place directly in front of people, many still did not believe it. Next, they wanted explanations. When provided detailed, scientifically-based explanations, many people still could not accept the reality of the demonstrated outcomes. To some extent it may not matter how much scientific research is accumulated or how thorough and logical the explanations are. If the ideas occur outside of a person's belief system, they may be rejected. Developing ETT® and presenting it to professionals has provided an exercise in observing cognitive dissonance. Openness and belief are largely choices. For therapists whose driving motivation is finding ways to overcome human suffering, this motivation tends to overcome the need for methods that operate within their established beliefs. Nonetheless, many people have seen the evidence of ETT® outcomes, are motivated to resolve human suffering, but simply crave further explanation and verification of ETT®. It is for these professionals that this book has been written.

Most people recognize that we live in a visual environment, but they have never been healed of emotional or physical distress by it. Therefore, I have observed that it is no small leap of faith for people to accept that our visual environment possesses the potency to facilitate powerful change in the manner in which ETT® accomplishes it. Among the factors not taken into account in this skepticism are that (1) the spectral chart used in SRT possesses a maximum degree of color saturation and thus an unusual impact on the brain unlike anything seen in our daily environment, (2) the Chromapulse II utilizes one among hundreds of precise degrees of wavelengths and saturation levels of light at the exact instant an emotion arises, which would almost never happen in our daily environment, (3) peripheral eye stimulation is precisely controlled in ways that is unlikely to be experienced by anyone in the typical visual environment, and (4) the MDEM process matches the exact eye scanpath of the client with a precise visual stimulus in ways that are extremely unlikely to occur in everyday life. All of these techniques also involve optimal interpersonal interaction that is unlikely to occur in many people's social interaction. Taken together, these processes maximize the impact of the visual environment to a level of radical impact that is virtually unknown in day-to-day visual environments. Without relevant direct experience of the power of one's visual ecology, most people lack the foundation of perspective upon which to form an acceptance of ETT®. Therefore, openness to this novel paradigm is challenging. However, appropriate education and marketing about this new paradigm could overcome this obstacle.

GLIMPSES OF NEW POSSIBILITIES

Once the obstacles posed by research verification and openness to belief are overcome by more people in the future, the proliferation of ETT® has the potential to set new standards for healing on a massive scale. We have already seen glimpses of possibilities in single case studies that suggest that we are not even close to identifying the ceiling limit of ETT® for healing human suffering. The following cases illustrate outcomes that suggest further study could uncover even greater potentials than described thus far in this book.

Amy's Case

Amy volunteered to be a recipient of MDEM in front of a group of other professionals at an ETT® workshop. I wanted to demonstrate its use on a physical symptom. Amy said that she had had continuous bouts of urinary tract infections for over twenty years. She would go to her physician, get a diagnosis, and then receive antibiotics. After the medical regimen the infection would go away, but then a week later it would reoccur. The same cycle of symptoms and treatment had taken place again and again.

I proceeded to process this condition in the same manner I used with physical pain conditions (chapter 5). First, the emotional distress occurring in response to the condition would be processed to conclusion, and then the physical symptom itself would be targeted. Amy described frustration and hopelessness about this infection cycle. After her eye scanpath related to these emotions was identified, MDEM was used to quickly eliminate emotional distress. Then I targeted the physical symptom itself with MDEM. Within a couple of minutes the physical symptoms were eradicated. However, we would not know for sure if it had worked until she urinated, in order to discern whether the burning sensation had stopped. An hour later she reported that all urinary tract infection symptoms were completely gone. One month later Amy emailed the whole class to let us know that all symptoms were still abated. This is remarkable when we take into account that these symptoms had never before ceased for more than a week. Then four months later Amy reported that all symptoms were still gone. These symptoms have never returned.

I recognized that this was not a controlled scientific study and careful measurements of the mechanisms of change were not conducted. On the other hand, it had occurred after all conventional medical approaches had failed. While I recognize that this was just a single case on the one hand, on the other hand it might represent an entirely new breakthrough for alleviating this condition. Just imagine the implications for this possibility.

Urinary tract infections have been found to be caused by a bacterial infection, and antibiotics are the standard treatment. However, the manner in which ETT® worked involved no medication, or other means that would fit the bacterial paradigm. The MDEM procedure is believed to precisely access the neural network in the brain, which extends to the targeted body part responsible for a set of specific symptoms, and then eliminates the symptoms via the identified neural network. In this case where did the destructive bacteria go? Apparently, we must think outside of the prevailing cause and treatment paradigm in order to explain this occurrence. Possibly the rapid shift in the stress component helped impact a specific neural network that signaled biochemical changes within seconds. This may have allowed the bacteria to either die, exit the system, or somehow transform into innocuous forms. It suggests that we have accessed endogenous factors that possess the capacity to rectify dysfunction in the human body by means outside of the current medical model.

If these ideas are proven to be accurate, it might be possible to replicate a similar process for other bacterial infections. We do know that scientific research has verified the use of blue light at 470 nm to eradicate MRSA upon contact. Therefore, the light to bacteria concept has been established. However, external light via the eyes through the brain circuits to the body's internal biochemistry resulting in the cessation of a bacterial infection within minutes has not been previously known. This new route, if scientifically verified, could present an entirely new paradigm for healing that could be conducted in minutes to achieve long-term results.

Jason's Case

Jason was a fifty-five-year-old man diagnosed with amyotrophic lateral sclerosis or ALS (also known as Lou Gehrig's disease). This condition is incurable by current medical practices. ALS is a deteriorating condition in which the patient gradually loses function of the physical body while the mind remains largely intact.

When I first saw Jason, he was severely depressed because of the hopeless diagnosis of ALS. He was losing bodily functions, and he could barely walk. However, his main complaint was that he could not raise his arm enough to comb his hair. Jason was referred to me by a colleague in Philadelphia when I was there for a few days. I had never worked with someone with ALS before. I first utilized the spectral chart to assess and process Jason's despair. His response was slow because his emotional awareness was limited at first. However, as we proceeded, his distress became resolved better and better. One emotion would be relieved and then another one would arise. At one key point Jason said he felt repulsed by his condition. I had him view the border between green and yellow to process this. A dramatic shift from despair to hope arose from this within minutes. This emotional change also affected his physical body. It was obvious that he could now move his physical body better, including raising his arm to comb his hair.

Subsequent to this session Jason reported being able to jog three miles the next day. His hope was temporarily elevated and he could comb his hair. Unfortunately, Jason was unable to continue treatment with me. Therefore, we do not know how much farther his healing may have gone. However, this dramatic improvement in a single session might tell us that ETT®, and especially the SRT process, possesses possibilities for healing ALS. More trials would be necessary in order to know for sure.

Jack's Case

Jack was a twenty-three-year-old single male diagnosed with *ankelosing spondilities*. This condition involves chronic pain and the gradual fusing of the spine until ultimately no flexibility exists. It is thought to be a degenerative condition. Jack had seen numerous conventional physicians as well as alternative doctors to no avail. Jack saw me for five days of sessions for one week.

I elected to pursue the relief of Jack's physical pain according to the principles described in chapter 5. In each session his emotional distress improved and his physical pain diminished. By the fifth session Jack was pain free and had a flexible range of motion for the first time in years. I heard from Jack's mother weeks later. She reported that Jack continued to be pain-free. Since I never saw X-rays or other medical measurements, I do not know how or if his physical body was changed, but I do know that all the symptoms were relieved. In fact, a year later I received another report that Jack continued to be pain-free. Since this was the only case of *ankelosing spondilities* in which ETT® was applied, we do not know if ETT® can cure *ankelosing spondilities* for everyone, but it did achieve resolution in this case. Therefore, it would seem wise to pursue more cases of this type with ETT® to explore the potential.

In several cases, as we focused on the stress component of various forms of cancer, clients experienced a radical improvement. In many cases we were able to neutralize the symptoms that were side effects of chemotherapy and radiation within a session or two. To fail to pursue exploration into the aforementioned possibilities for healing might be seen as irresponsible.

If we were to peer into the future based solely on the procedures described in this book and outcomes described in the case studies reported herein, let us imagine the implications. Let us assume that more scientific research was conducted on the use of ETT® in which several different conditions had verified resolution (that we have already seen hundreds of times in clinical settings). Let us also assume that the obstacles of cognitive dissonance and limited belief systems were overcome by education and marketing. Imagine that fifty percent of psychotherapists, psychiatrists, and physicians were trained in ETT® and its use proliferated all over the United States. Let me reiterate that these ETT® accomplishments have already been achieved as described throughout this book. We are simply projecting the number of trained ETT® therapists and their clients onto a larger scale of implementation.

THE FUTURE OF DEPRESSION TREATMENT

Imagine a future in which major depression is routinely resolved in just a few sessions as described in the book *Emotional Transformation Therapy: An Interactive Ecological Psychotherapy*. Sexual dysfunction, weight gain, and all the other side effects of medication would no longer be an issue if a drug free method could consistently eliminate depression. Instead of just masking depressive symptoms and fostering a dependency on a substance outside of ourselves, we might actually cure depression rapidly by harnessing our own inner resources. Most importantly, the misery of living with depression for millions of people could end.

Grief due to the death of a loved one involves several emotions, with sadness typically being the greatest. Bereavement is a universal phenomenon, one that many people claim they will never get over. There are numerous books and theories about the process of grief. Traumatic grief in which an abrupt death occurs is generally considered to be a long and painful type of grief. Among the types of losses, the death of one's child is considered one of the most challenging, with the likelihood of long-term devastation. In many cases ETT® has accomplished complete alleviation of traumatic grief of the loss of a child in a single session. Even I had cognitive dissonance initially when this took place. These were sometimes done in live demonstrations with many witnesses, but it has happened in numerous private sessions. While all traumatic grief resolution does not occur this fast, much of it does with ETT®. This is not to imply that people do not experience the emotions, nor does it mean that people don't go through stages such as those described by Kubler-Ross as phases of grief. However, it does mean that the emotional processing occurs extremely rapidly. In one case a series of six separate deaths were concluded in one session. This entire process of ETT® shakes the core of grief theory and has forced me to re-think grief psychotherapy. I am not aware of anywhere in the psychological literature that this form of rapid grief processing has been described. Nonetheless, what if this means for processing traumatic grief became a common practice in counseling? The impact on mental health and work productivity could transform the universal experience of grief as we know it.

The current epidemic rise in the number of people suffering from bipolar disorder could finally be reduced by teaching people how to regulate their most overwhelming emotional swings. The wild fluctuations of emotions could finally be resolved without drugs. The impact of this improved ability to self-regulate one's emotions would affect the entire constellation of the client's family and friends. Instead of family members and friends begging the person to shut-down his/her emotions by getting back on their medication, self-regulation of emotions could be commonplace.

THE FUTURE OF ANXIETY TREATMENT

What if anxiety disorders were routinely conquered within a short time as described in the book *Emotional Transformation Therapy: An Interactive Ecological Psychotherapy*? So many people are tormented by the continual worry and stress of daily life to the point of overwhelm in generalized anxiety disorder. Imagine a world in which people were consistently calmed down and under control within a few sessions. The quality of life for millions of people could take a substantial shift for the better.

The intense fear associated with phobias like fear of speaking in public, fear of flying in planes, fear of high places, and many others can limit our full experience of life. Instead of being pre-occupied with avoiding things, what would it be like for people with phobias if we could eradicate phobias within a few sessions? If ETT® became the norm in counseling, this outcome could become the expected result.

Panic disorders may be the most intense form of anxiety. If the successful treatment of panic attacks took place on a consistent basis, it would promote a profound sense of security and safety for people who otherwise live in terror. ETT® would provide a drug-free answer that would not just alleviate these horrible symptoms, but wipe out the problem long-term and do it in a relatively short time. Imagine a society in which substantial fear would no longer have a significant presence.

THE FUTURE OF ADDICTION TREATMENT

Addiction to elicit drugs, prescription drugs, and over-the-counter drugs may be the most extensive mental health problem in the world. While there are all types of drug treatments from AA to expensive rehabilitation programs, the sad fact is that most often they simply don't really work. The relapse rate for substance addiction is not good. Many of the treatments are very sound except that they do not possess a non-drug means to eliminate addictive craving on a consistent basis, let alone achieve a rapid, long-term elimination of craving. ETT® has achieved this. Imagine transforming addictive craving, as described in chapters 6 and 7, on a massive scale. Without craving there is really not an addiction. While there are other issues to be addressed in addiction treatment, if addictive craving becomes easily stamped out, we can address the real issues like relationship dysfunction, inability to feel pleasure, and all of the reasons people so badly want to escape through drug use. Imagine lives if addiction could be routinely treated effectively in a short period of time.

The internet has generated numerous benefits, but it has also allowed the pornography industry to grow into a multi-billion dollar enterprise. While pornography may simply be a brief recreational adventure for some people, it has fostered a blossoming of severe sexual addictions for millions of people. Hypersexual craving, spurred to new levels, has become a frequent focus of therapists as more and more people are dominated by sexual addictions. One of the greatest breakthroughs for the use of ETT® has been its use for sexual addiction recovery. In many cases, as described in chapter 6, the addictive craving template is eliminated within a few minutes. This plague has become a relatively easy condition to resolve with ETT®, whereas it is often a treatment enigma otherwise.

REVOLUTIONIZING COUPLE THERAPY

Of all the forms of psychological counseling, couple and relationship therapy may yield the lowest success rate. When marriages collapse, the effect reverberates to the children, the parents, and an entire array of other people. While there have been some advances in couple therapy, the combined use of attachment-based approaches and the client's visual ecology has provided a substantially faster and very powerful means for changing the emotional climate in couple relationships. When this approach is adopted by thousands of therapists, the possibility of lowering the divorce rate, reducing family violence, and promoting strong families would not only promote fulfillment but actually save countless lives. If people could rely on the likelihood of positive, rapid outcomes of couple therapy, a new hope could arise.

RESTORING SLEEP AND RELIEVING PHYSICAL PAIN

A simple good night's sleep is no longer an assumption that people take for granted. More and more, normal sleep does not take place as verified by the number of sleep study clinics popping up all over the United States. With that growth is the escalation of sleep medication use and the addiction tendencies that often come with these pills. Our minds and bodies possess sleep mechanisms in the brain that are largely controlled by light and dark environments. By harnessing control of both emotional distress and the brain's biological clock, ETT® has provided a breakthrough in sleep disorders as described in chapter 4. What if the vast majority of sleep disorders could be routinely resolved on a consistent basis by a local therapist? Imagine how daily functioning and productivity could soar if natural sleep became commonplace again.

The number of people experiencing chronic physical pain continues to grow despite "medical advances." Types of chronic pain like fibromyalgia, regional pain syndrome, and arthritis have become nearly epidemic. While medicine offers medication for chronic pain, it simply reduces the pain. It does not cure it. Surgery may sometimes help pain, but risks new problems. The remarkable resolution of physical pain with ETT® is typically rapid and usually long-term. If this option were used extensively, literally millions of people could become pain-free. The change in the quality of life might shift dramatically when this takes place.

MAKING TRAUMA OBSOLETE

Of all the different applications for ETT®, its use for trauma has been the most extensive. Therefore, trauma therapy via ETT® is the most fully developed use of ETT® and has been tested in practice the most. An entirely new level of speed and long-term outcome has occurred in applying ETT® to trauma. Numerous examples of ETT® used for PTSD are described throughout this book. However, complex, cumulative types of trauma like repeated childhood sexual abuse, cumulative rape experiences, war trauma, and the consequences of repeated violence predominate in my caseload. In these cases, years of therapy, or no resolution at all, is the norm. Imagine a world in which these complicated, severe types of trauma are routinely and rapidly alleviated long-term. Not only are these devastating experiences relieved, but ETT® often transforms them into positive experiences. Imagine a time when almost all trauma can be turned into joy.

EXTENDED HUMAN CAPABILITIES

In addition to discovering ways to resolve severe "incurable" conditions, ETT®® has been used to activate our abilities to extended capabilities. For example, one amateur golfer had never won a tournament before ETT® use. After a couple of months of ETT® he won three tournaments in one month. In another case, a distance runner always seemed to "hit a wall" and could not go past a certain point no matter how much he trained. After one ETT® session focused on this blockage, he reported being able to run on and on way past his previous limitations. Issues that seem likely purely physical issues turn out to be a function of mind-body interaction. A yoga teacher found that by using the peripheral goggles she could extend her body into poses that she could not previously achieve. Even a professional football player found that an ETT® session substantially accelerated recovery from knee surgery. Who knows what other yet untested possibilities' exist with ETT®?

FACILITATING ULTIMATE STATES OF FULFILLMENT

For many people the facilitation of states of extreme wellbeing and spiritual experiences may provide the ultimate outcome of ETT®. In some cases these are temporary states of ecstasy, peace, euphoria, or various spiritual phenomena, but in many others deep, long-term transformations of people into long-term spiritual adepts takes place. As I write this, I currently have five cases of this nature (as described in chapter 9). If this process became frequently conducted, the possibility exists that a fundamental shift in human consciousness might occur in large numbers of people. This possibility offers more than relief of anxiety or depression, but instead a profound sense of purpose and meaning in life.

Ultimate long-term "happiness" and fulfillment itself enters into an entirely new domain in these cases. Imagine the proliferation of this phenomenon.

THE FUTURE EVOLUTION OF ETT®

The development of ETT® applications was not just a single discovery, but instead a twenty-year evolution in which outcomes became quicker and more lasting. The likelihood is that the full potential of ETT® may not yet have reached its highest level of proficiency. Therefore, if we project the growth of ETT®, based upon its previous trajectory, in ten years from 2012 ETT® will use better equipment, more efficient processes, and be applied to a wider range of applications. If these trajectories occur in conjunction with increased numbers of trained ETT® professionals, the possibilities of change in treatment may occur beyond our most creative fantasies.

History has shown that new and better methods usually do make their way into mainstream use. Assuming that ETT® continues to improve and that its proliferation continues, in a decade or two its impact may begin to affect our species as a whole. This projected growth forces us to take a new look at human evolution. The term evolution is plagued with controversy, but the ETT® impact on evolution does not necessarily refer to the type of evolution related to Darwin.

BEYOND DARWINIAN EVOLUTION

Charles Darwin first described his concept of evolution in his book *Origin of Species* in 1879. His basic premise was that survival of the fittest yields a natural selection of features that are passed on to the next generation. However, this concept alone might not have explained evolution if it were not for Gregor Mendel's discovery of genes, the units that make natural selection possible. At this time massive scientific evidence in the forms of fossil evidence, replication evidence, and genetic evidence is used to support the theory of evolution. However, there has been a strong opposition to Darwin's theory by creationists who believed that humans were place on earth, all at once, by God. This dichotomization of the conflict is not the only way to view evolution. In fact, there are at least eight other views that most people are not aware of and some of these predate Darwin by centuries.

In 1600 Jacob Bohme had an experience via light stimulation that initiated the concept of "spiritual evolution" (chapter 9). In 1697 G. W. Leibnitz wrote *The Ultimate Origin of Things*, the first book on spiritual evolution. The German philosopher Immanuel Kant and the French philosopher J. B. Robinet described spiritual evolution in the 1700's. Interestingly, the playwright Goethe wrote *Theory of Colours* and also began to develop a theory of spiritual evolution in 1820. While these theories did not capture the popularity of Darwin's theory of evolution, they co-existed and developed along a separate line of thinking.

Today, Darwinian concepts have mutated into entirely new domains due to new scientific discoveries. Among these divergent tracks are the biological determinists referred to as Human plus (H+). This view involves such methods as cloning, neuropharmacology, nanotechnology, and artificial intelligence. Through these methods, some believe, we should take control of biological evolution and create humans to be what we want them to be. While these methods might help us to avoid certain forms of human imperfection, this concept runs a high risk of making all people alike. Other ethical concerns have created another strong backlash.

The creationists of today now refer to their view as intelligent design. This viewpoint asserts that biological complexity can best be explained by life being the work of an intelligent designer in the form of the Christian version of God. This position opposes Darwinism and Human Plus.

The Human Plus approaches offer one direction of evolution spurred by surgery that implants electrodes into the brain and surgery that changes genes in our bodies to stop unwanted symptoms. By contrast ETT® offers a process that catalyzes our own natural potential to evolve. Evidence, described in chapter 9, suggests that advances in healing and brain function already exist within us as latent potential. However, it is the power of the human bonding process and the activation of visually initiated neural brain circuits that appear to be the catalysts to facilitate a leap in our own individual evolution. Even better, these catalysts feel good as repeated states of extreme wellbeing provide the stepping stones toward not just the reduction of disturbing symptoms but also to a higher levels of brain functioning.

Research within biology itself has now changed our understanding of the genetic components upon which Darwin's theory rests. The Human Genome Project (chapter 5) now makes it clear that environmental influences largely control genetic expression. This field is called epigenetics. Specific interpersonal influences and external light stimulation impact genetic expression. This suggests that ETT® possesses the capacity to alter genetic expression, which is a basis for the possible impact of ETT® on human evolution.

However, a fourth "evolutionary" concept exists outside the arena of the aforementioned conventionally known opposing concepts. Complexity theory suggests that when a dynamic system, such as the human organism, is stressed toward chaos and disequilibrium, at some point it shifts into a more integrated and complex structure (chapter 1). Through this process of self-organization and emergence, something different arises that is more than it was before the shift. Complexity or chaos theory has become an accepted scientific and philosophical theory. The growth of clients experiencing ETT® can be seen within the context.

A totally different viewpoint, one first espoused by the naturalist Kropotkin in 1902, offers a completely opposite concept to survival of the fittest. It basically suggests that the cooperation among species has a greater impact upon survival than competition. Examples are heard animals, flocks of birds, and insects like bees and ants, all of which tend to survive better than other organisms. Of course, this concept would include humans who live in families, villages, or societies. This perspective implies that evolution advances better with collaboration and altruism than with conflict, competition, and war. Since ETT® strategies tend to strengthen people by resolving inner conflict through Peripheral Eye Stimulation (chapter 1) as well as interpersonal conflict (chapter 8), this perspective is congruent with ETT® and suggests that ETT® furthers this principle

A sixth evolutionary concept concerns directionalism. Rather than aimless natural selection, a teleological purpose might be guiding evolution. Particularly when ETT® clients acquire clarity, they often appear to discover a direction for their lives as though the force of evolution is taking them in a specific direction. This is more of a philosophical than scientific concept.

There is a very strong divergence from the simplistic Darwin vs. Intelligent Design conflict when we take into account the facts of quantum physics. Darwinian concepts all rest on a Newtonian form of physics in which time is seen as linear, matter and energy are viewed as separate, and human consciousness is seen as separate from space, time, matter, and energy (chapter 3). However, quantum physics has verified that time is not linear, and, in fact, is a continuous "now," and the future and past may not occur in a linear fashion. Since time is not linear and the past and future exist in the present, evolution cannot move "forward." The concept of evolution is based on linear time flow. If this concept is no longer a scientific reality, it causes us to re-conceptualize Darwinian evolution altogether. However, the quantum physics concept of consciousness interacting with matter, energy, and space suggests new possibilities for a different type of evolution.

Physicist David Bohm has developed an approach to reconcile the seemingly conflicting attributes of quantum reality with daily reality. Bohm conceives of Newtonian physics as the ordinary world of our five senses in the "explicate order," and the universe as an undivided whole of perpetual flux outside of conscious awareness to be the "implicate order" of quantum physics. He suggests that both realities co-exist, and that the implicate order is more primary and the explicate order emerges from it (Bohm, 1980). Therefore, instead of evolution focusing on physical change, it may be viewed as moving from the implicate order to the explicate order. In psychological terms awareness from implicit non-conscious memory into explicit conscious memory is congruent with this evolution of consciousness. Therefore, methods like ETT® that facilitate transformative change could be viewed as assisting evolution from the implicate order into the explicate order of our daily lives.

This viewpoint of evolution leads to yet another concept of evolution. If we can become consciously aware of our potential for evolution, evolution can then become a conscious choice. This empowerment can allow us to advance our species via new process like ETT®. Essentially, when we understand how to improve ourselves toward a greater purpose and fulfillment, we can create human fulfillment.

In order for a new reality to emerge it is helpful to envision it. While obstacles to this vision of hope may delay or shift this vision, it is unlikely to happen anytime soon if we do not allow ourselves to create a vision. When visions such as the possible future of ETT® are based on actual results, their possibility of manifesting are elevated. As we improve our relationship with light itself, the possible human might manifest differently. This book is one step toward a new vision of a different level of healing and hopefully a new vision of humankind.

Appendix A

Neural Pathways of Visual Light Stimulation

Most people are not aware of the fact that the eyes have many more functions than simply seeing. The eyes can be thought of as an extension of the brain. Scientists have performed hundreds of studies to discover the exact pathways that impulses, initiated by light into the eyes, travel throughout the nervous system. These neural circuits have turned out to be far more extensive than most people imagined. In fact, there are three major visual neural pathways through which light- initiated impulses travel. When we take into account all of the areas of the brain and nervous system impacted by these impulses, virtually every significant brain function is affected by light- initiated impulses. Therefore, by altering such factors as (1) wavelength, (2) angle at which light enters the periphery, (3) brightness, (4) psychological activity at the time of visual light stimulation, (5) length of time of exposure, and (6) strobe rate of light emissions, one can potentially direct the impact of impulses to specific brain functions. This ultimately leads to specific outcomes of emotional and somatic regulation.

The first pathway of light-initiated impulses largely controls how visually initiated functions integrate with experiences beyond visual activity. Miesenbock (2008) notes that the photoreceptor cells in our eyes contain rhodopsins, which are like absorbing antennae that instruct ion channels in the cell membrane to open and close when they are illuminated. This mechanism converts light into a flow of ions that produce electrical impulses (p. 56). This pathway integrates vision with auditory functions, movement functions, eye movement, and general orientation in the world. The following chart depicts the exact visual pathway (see illustration A.1).

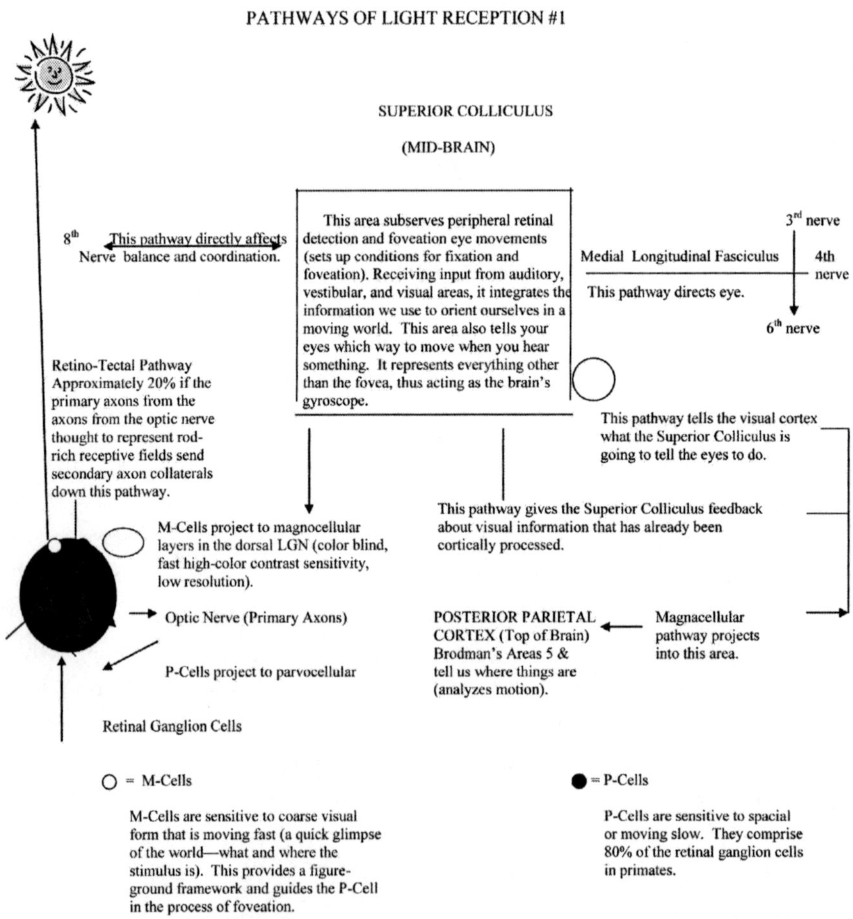

ILLUSTRATION A.1
With permission from Jacob Lieberman, OD, PhD, 1990.

The second light-initiated impulse pathway is far more complex. This pathway impacts integration of all sensory inputs to orient us to movement. The lateral geniculate nucleus (LGN) in the thalamus selects which visual information will be further relayed to the visual cortex for us to see. The visual cortex is the largest sensory area in the brain and further relays information to three major integration centers. The LGN sends impulses to the hypothalamus, which controls our autonomic nervous system, fluid balance, heat regulation, circulation, breathing, activity, sleep, growth and maturation, reproduction, and emotions. Through this pathway light affects both the hypothalamus and the pineal gland, which control virtually all of our glands, hormones, and almost every significant physical function including the immune system. The suprachiasmatic nuclei, known as the "biological clock," controls our entire waking-sleeping rhythms. The following is the second neural circuit of light-initiated impulses (see illustrations A.2, A.3, and A.4).

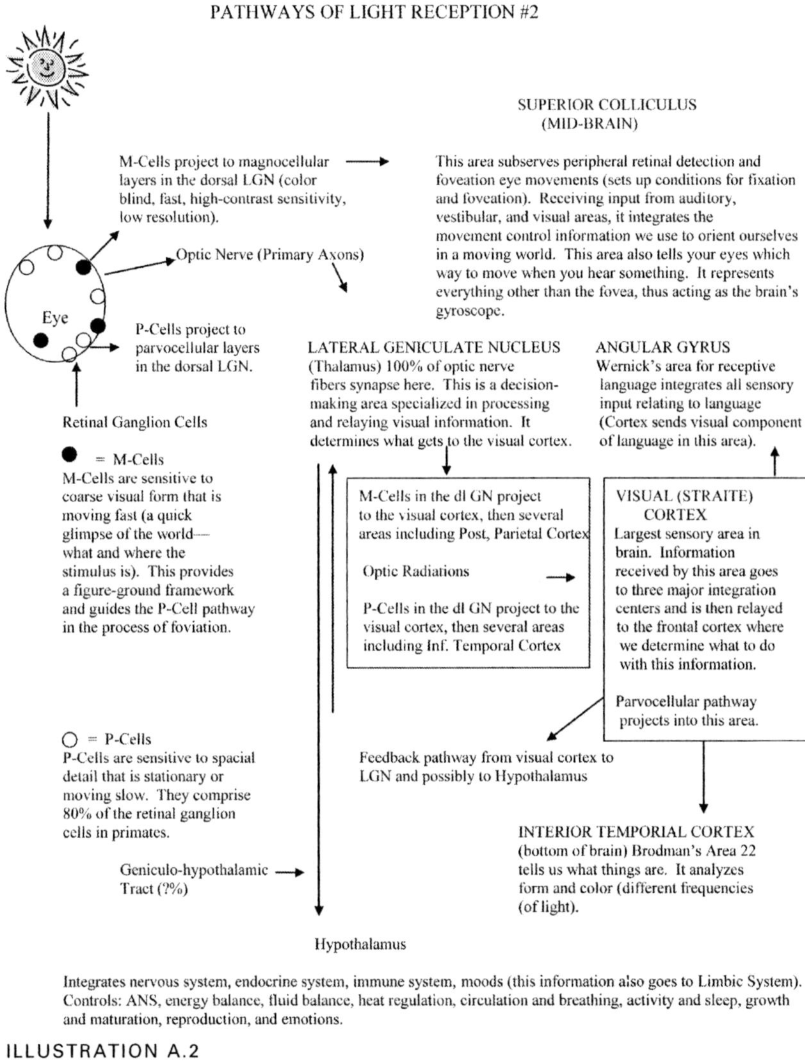

ILLUSTRATION A.2
With permission from Jacob Lieberman, OD, PhD, 1990.

PATHWAYS OF LIGHT RECEPTION #2 continued

Site of the body's biological clock.

Supra-Chiasmatic Nuclei | LATERAL GENICULATE NUCLEUS | Par ventricular Nuclei → Median Forebrain → Inter-Mediolateral Cell Column → Preganglionic Sympathetic Neuron → Superior Cervical Ganglia → Nervi Conari

Hypothalamus
Integrates nervous system, endocrine system, immune system, moods (this information also goes to Limbic System).
Controls:
ANS, energy balance, fluid balance, heat regulation, circulation and breathing, activity and sleep, growth and maturation, reproduction, and emotions.

Anterior Medial Hypothalamus
(Controls Parasympathetic)

PARASYMPATHETIC

Ocular Effects
1. Contracts pupil
2. Widens eye slit
3. Increases lacrymation
4. Upper lid-ptosed, puffy
5. Ocular hypotension
6. Increases accommodation
7. Causes esophoria-reflex
8. Low abduction tendency
9. Activates ocular activity

Posterior Lateral Hypothalamus
Controls Sympathetic)

SYMPATHETIC

Ocular Effects
1. Dilates pupil
2. Protrudes eyeball
3. Lessens lacrymation
4. Upper lid retracted, lagging
5. Ocular hypertension
6. Lessens accommodation
7. Causes exophoria-flex
8. Low adduction tendency
9. Inhibits ocular activity

Neural | Releasing factors

Post. | Ant.
Pituitary

Mam. Gland – Oxytocin
Kidneys – Anti-Dui. Hor.
(Vasopressin)

Prolactin – Breasts
Growth Hor. – Musc./Bones
Thy. Stim. Hor. – Thyroid
Melan. Stim. Hor. - Skin Pigmentation
Follicle Stim. Hor. – Teste
Luteinzing Hor. – Ovaries
ACTH – Adrenal Cortex

PINEAL GLAND
(Body's "Light Meter")
Affects:
1. Reproduction functions
2. Growth
3. Body temperature
4. Blood pressure
5. Motor activity and sleep
6. Tumor growth
7. Brain neurotransmitter metabolism
8. Immune system
9. Modifies functions of:
   Adrenals
   Pancreas
   Pituitary
   Thyroid
   Thymus
10. Possibly affects longevity and aging and development of chronic degenerative diseases.

The pineal gland secretes the hormone melatonin, which influences the functioning of every cell in the body, thus orchestrating the internal physiology of the entire organism in order to synchronize it with external environment.

ILLUSTRATION A.3
With permission from Jacob Lieberman, OD, PhD, 1990.

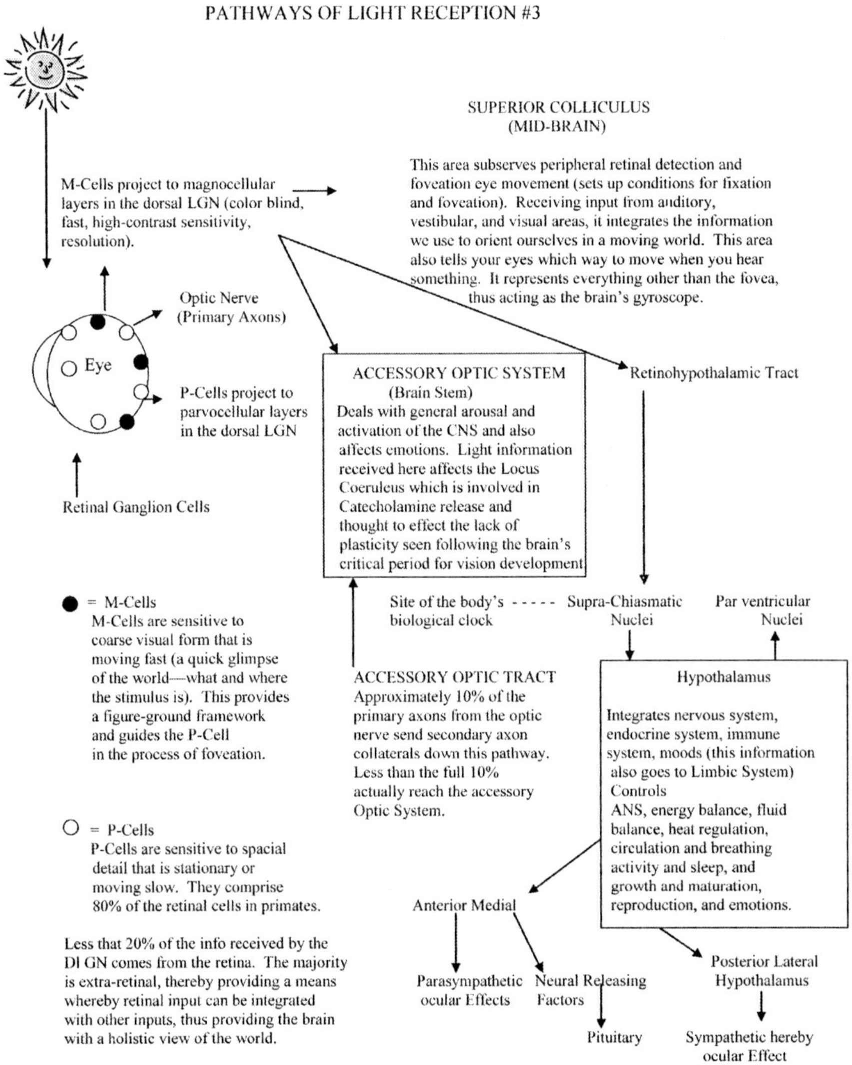

ILLUSTRATION A.4

With permission from Jacob Lieberman, OD, PhD, 1990.

The third pathway of the visual system also accesses some of the previously mentioned brain functions but activates other functions as well. This pathway is unique in that it activates the brain stem as well as general arousal, the central nervous system, and emotions. It provides yet another route for accessing the mid-brain and the hypothalamus.

NEWLY DISCOVERED PHOTIC NEURAL PATHWAYS

For over one hundred years rod and cone cells were considered to be the only photosensitive cells in the eyes that converted external light into neural impulses. In 1991 Russell G. Foster and Ignacio Provencio discovered a different photoreceptor in mice that was shown to mediate circadian rhythms. This stunning discovery was not recognized by the scientific community until a publication in 2000. In 2007 Zaidi, Foster, Brainard, Czersler, and Lockley first identified a non-rod, non-cone photoreceptor in humans. This photosensitive cell was called an intrinsically photosensitive Retinal Ganglion Cell (ipRGC). These cells represent only 1 to 2 percent of retinal ganglion cells. Melanopsin is excited by light that is mainly in the blue portion of the visible spectrum, peaking at 480 NM.

- The melanopsin-expressing ganglion cells send light initiated impulses via the retinohypothalamic tract to the suprachiasmatic nucleus of the hypothalamus.
- The ipRGC send neural stimulation to the olivary pectal nucleus of the mid-brain, which regulates pupillany size and other behavioral responses.
- These cells contribute to the regulation of melatonin.
- Melanopsin-containing ganglion cells are believed to influence the brain by releasing the neurotransmitter glutamate and pituitary adenylate polypeptide (PACAP).
- Melanopsin-containing ganglion cells receive input from rods and cones that modifies their input to visual neural pathways.
- Melanopsin-expressing ganglion cells contribute to both non-image forming brain mechanisms and conscious sight.

These recent discoveries have stimulated ongoing research that may substantially supplement or revise these initial findings. However, it is important to note these other neural pathways because they impact brain functioning and have implications for targeting brain mechanisms responsible for psychological symptoms.

Appendix B

Training and Research in ETT®

TRAINING IN ETT®

Emotional Transformation Therapy International Association (ETTIA) is a 501(C)(6), nonprofit, professional membership organization, developed to train and support mental health clinicians in the practice of Emotional Transformation Therapy® (ETT®). The mission of ETTIA is to promote global awareness of the rapid and permanent resolution of emotional distress that can be achieved through Emotional Transformation Therapy® (ETT®) and to support its member practitioners with quality professional development, therapeutic tools, and access to ETT® research. ETTIA has available to members informative brochures, explaining the variety of areas in which ETT® relieves numerous symptoms of distress. ETTIA offers formal training in ETT® and presents the latest applications and research of ETT® at annual conferences. ETTIA is responsible for maintaining a level of excellence in clinical application of ETT® by offering a variety of options for continuing education training. Members are formally trained in ETT® and are using it clinically or for research purposes as mental health professionals. ETTIA offers members a forum for peer clinical discussion, sharing innovative protocols, and member support by ETTIA-trained and approved supervisors and teachers. ETTIA offers various levels of certification for professionals interested in achieving recognizable levels of excellence in the application of ETT®.

Through ETTIA, clinicians have access to the latest ETT® research and clinical information.

ETTIA can be contacted at: TheETTIA.org

RESEARCH ON ETT®

The Research Board for ETT® International, officially registered as the Institute for Quantum Healing, Inc., is chartered as a non-profit, 501(c)(3) organization created in 2009. Our purpose is to raise funds in order to develop high-quality, evidence-based research on ETT® (Emotional Transformational Therapy®) to establish its efficacy and publish established findings.

We welcome the opportunity to interview potential research partners, and are grateful for donations to make this effort possible. All donations are tax deductible. You may contact us through the ETTIA website (ETTIA.org) under the "Research" link.

Appendix C

What Neurophysiological Mechanisms Account for PES?

The pathway of impulses initiated by light into the eyes takes a slightly different route than light into the central area of the eyes. When light enters the direct center of the pupils it enters the middle of the retina on the back of the eyeball. However, when light enters the periphery it enters the pupil and the impulses travel in the following sequence (Kozlowski, 2005):

1. Stimulation appears on the opposite side of the retina as a diffuse light source.
2. Then, the optic nerve tract (optic chiasm) receives the stimulation and these impulses travel along the lateral part of the optic nerve.
3. Next, this lateral stimulation goes through the medial portion of the optic chiasm to the opposite lateral part of the nerve.
4. Impulses reach the lateral geniculate nucleus on the posterior part of the thalamus.
5. Impulses travel through fibers that branch off and go into the anterior hypothalamus, where the suprachiasmatic nucleus (biological clock) exists and controls day, night, and seasonal cycles.
6. Impulses travel from the optic chiasm to one of the seven layers of the lateral geniculate nucleus. Stimulation from one eye goes to layers 1, 3, 5, and 7, and stimulation from the other eye goes to layers 2, 4, and 6.
7. From the lateral geniculate body, the neurons form the Meyer's loop to area 17 of the visual cortex.

8. Impulses from peripheral stimulation locate in the visual cortex (upside down and backward). The further the stimulation is on the periphery of the eyes, the further forward impulses locate on the visual cortex.
9. Central vision goes to the parietal lobe, which places it into conscious perception. Peripheral vision goes to the frontal eye fields, which relates to the control of eye muscles. Peripheral stimulation also travels to the superior caliculus (reflexive centers).

Stimulation that originates from the periphery of the eyes provides further stimulation at different locations of the visual cortex. Each of these locations has a multitude of different neural connections to numerous parts of the brain such as the following:

- Impulses travel from the visual cortex to the mid-brain to cranial nerves 3, 7, and 9 for parasympathetic control.
- Impulses that travel from the visual cortex to the longitudinal vissicules go to the frontal lobe and pre-frontal cortex, which controls emotional centers.
- Impulses travel from the visual cortex to the limbic system through the cingulate gyrus.

References

Adinoff, B. (2004). Neurobiologic processes in drug reward and addiction. *Harvard Review of Psychiatry, 12*, 305–320.

Aharon, I., Etcoll, N., Ariely, D., Chabris, C. F., O'Connor, E., & Breiter, H. C. (2001). Beautiful faces have variable reward value: FMRI and behavioral evidence. *Neuron, 32*, 537–551.

Ainsworth, M. D. S. (1985). Attachments across the life span. *Bulletin of New York Academy of Medicine, 61*, 792–812.

Ainsworth, M. D. S., Blehar, M. C., Waters, E., & Wall, S. (1978). *Patterns of Attachment: A psychological study of the strange situation.* Hillsdale, NJ: L. Erlbaum.

Alcoholics Anonymous. (1981). *Twelve steps and twelve traditions.* New York: Alcoholics Anonymous World Services.

Allen, J. G. (2002). *Traumatic relationship and serious mental disorders.* West Sussex, England: John Wiley and Sons, Ltd.

American Psychiatric Association, (2000). *Diagnostic and Statistical Manual of Mental Health Disorders IV-TR.* Washington, DC: American Psychiatric Association.

Anderson, H., & Gerhart, D. (eds.) (2007). *Collaborative therapy: Relationships and conversations that make a difference.* New York: Routledge/Taylor and Francis Group.

Argyle, M., & Beit-Hallahmi, B. (1975). *The social psychology of religion.* London: Routledge.

Atkins, D. C., Bortnik, K. E., Hahlweg, K., & Klann, N. (January–March, 2011). The association between marital discord and depression in a community-based sample of couples seeking treatment. *Journal of Couple and Relationship Therapy*, 20–33.

Babcock, J. C., Green, C. E., & Robie, C. (2004). Does batterer's treatment work? A meta-analytic review of domestic violence treatment. *Clinical Psychology Review, 23*, 1023–1053.

Baker, E. (1967). *Man in the trap.* New York: Avon Books.

Barker, R. (1968). *Ecological psychology.* Stanford, CA: Stanford University Press.

Barrick, C. (1994). Psychometric assessment of two new self-rating scales: The Schiraldi depression checkup and the Correa-Barrick depression scale. *Doctoral Dissertation*, University of Maryland.

Barrick, C. B., Taylor, D., & Correa, E. I. (February 2002). Color sensitivity and mood disorders. *Journal of Affective Disorders, 68*, 67–71.

Bartolome, J. V., Bartolome, M. B., Lorber, B. A., Dileo, S. J., & Schanberg, S. M. (1991). Effects of central administration of beta-endorphin on brain and liver DNS synthesis in preweanling rats. *Neuroscience, 40* (1), 289–294.

Blood, A. J., & Zatorre, R. J. (2001). Intensely pleasurable responses to music correlate with activity in brain regions implicated in reward and emotion. *Neuron, 19*, 591–611.

Blum, K., Braverman, E. R., Holden, J. M., Lubar, J. O., Chen, T. J., & Comings, D. E. (2000). Reward deficiency syndrome: a biogenic model for the diagnosis and treatment of impulsive, addictive, and compulsive behaviors. *Journal of Psychoactive Drugs, 32*, Suppl: i–iv, 1–112.

Blum, K., Chen, A. L. C., Chen, T. J. H., Bowirrat, A., Waite, R. L., Kerner, M., Blum, S. H., Downs, B. W., Savarinwether, S., Roades, P., Reinking, J., Braverman, E. R., Braverman, D., Di Nubile, N., & Oscar-Berman, M. (2009). Putative targeting of Dopamine D2 receptor function in Reward Deficiency Syndrome (RDS) by Synaptamine Complex™ Variant (KB220): Clinical trial sowing anti-anxiety effects. *Genetic Therapeutic Molecular Biology, 13*, 214–230.

Bohm, D. (1980). *Wholeness and the implicate order.* New York: Routledge.

Bouhuys, A. L., Meesters, Y., Jansen, J. H. C., & Bloem, G. M. (1994). Relationship between cognitive sensitivity to (symbolic) light in remitted seasonal affective disorder patients and the onset time of a subsequent depressive disorder. *Journal of Affective Disorder, 31*, 39–48.

Bowirrat, A., & Oscar-Berman, M. (January 2005). Relationship between dopaminergic neurotransmitter, alcoholism, and Reward of Deficiency Syndrome. *Am J Med Genet B Neuropsychiatr Genet, 123B* (1), 29–37.

Bowlby, J. (1969). *Attachment and loss. Vol. 1: Attachment.* New York: Basic Books.

Bowlby, J. (1973). *Attachment and loss. Vol. 2: Separation, anxiety and anger.* New York: Basic Books.

Bowlby, J. (1980). *Attachment and loss. Vol. 3: Loss, sadness and depression.* New York: Basic Books.

Brainard, G. C., Hanifin, J. P., Greeson, J. B., Byrne, B., Glickman, G., Gerner, E., & Rollag, M. D. (2001). Action spectrum for melatonin regulation in humans: Evidence for a Novel Circadian Photoreceptor. *Journal of Neuroscience, 21* (16), 6405–6412.

Branan, N. (December–January 2008). A bird in the mirror. *Scientific American Mind, 19* (6), 13.

Braydon, E. (1993). *A source book for helping people with spiritual problems.* Aptos, CA: Lightening Up Press.

Breiter, H. C., Gollub, R. L., Weisskoff, R. M., Kennedy, D. N. M., Makris, N., Berke, J. D., et al. (1997). Acute effects of cocaine on human brain activity and emotion. *Neuron, 19*, 591–611.

Brisch, K. H. (2002). *Treating attachment disorders.* New York: Guilford Press,

Bruce, A. (2005). *Beyond the bleep.* New York: The Disinformation Co.

Calle, E. E., Rodriguez, C., Walker-Thurmond, K., & Thun, M. J. (April 3, 2002). Overweight, obesity, and mortality from cancer in a prospectively studied cohort of U.S. adults. *The New England Journal of Medicine, 348* (17), 1625–1638.

Carnes, P. (1991). *Don't call it love: Recovery from sexual addiction.* New York: Bantum Books.

Carnes, P. (1997). *The betrayal bond: Breaking free of exploitive relationships.* Dearfield Beach, FL: Health Communication.

Carnes, P., & Adams, K. M. (eds.) (2002). *Clinical management of sex addiction.* New York: Brunner-Routledge.

Carnes, P., Delmonico, D. L., & Griffin, E. (2001). *In the shadows of the net: Breaking free of compulsive online sexual behavior*. Center City, MN: Hazeldon.

Carpenter, R. R., & Lloyd, B. T. (2009). Assessing psychological symptom patterns of patients seeking help for hypersexual behavior. *Sexual & Relationship Therapy, 24*, (1), 47–63.

Cohen, E., & Hunter, I. (1978). Severity of depression differentiated by a color selection test. *American Journal of Psychiatry, 135* (5): 611–612.

Cohen, M. X., Young, J., Back, J. M., Kessler, C., & Ranganath, C. (2005). Individual differences in extraversion and dopamine genetics predict neural reward responses. *Brain Res Cogn Brain Res, 25*, 851–861.

Connock, M., Juarez-Garcia, A., & Jowett, S., et al. (2007). Methadone and buprenorphine for the management of opioids dependence: a systematic review and economic evaluation. *Health Technology Assessment (Winchester, England), 11* (9), 1–171, iii–iv.

Cox, R. P., & Howard, M. D. (2007). Utilization of EMDR in the treatment of sexual addiction: A caste study. *Sexual Addiction and Compulsivity, 14*.

de la Fuente-Fernandez, R., Phillips, A. G., Zamburlini, M., Sossi, V., Calne, D. B., Ruth, T. H., et al. (2002). Dopamine release in human ventral striatum and expectation of reward. *Behav Brain Res, 136*, 359–363.

Dearing, B. G., & Singg, S. (1996). Photosensitivity assessment: A study of color preference, depression and temperament. *Subtle Energies and Energy Medicine, 7* (2), 89–110.

DeJongh, A., Broeke, E., & Renssen, M. R. (1998). Treatment of choking phobia by targeting traumatic memories with EMDR: A case study. *Clinical Psychology and Psychotherapy, 5*, 264–269.

DeJongh, A., Broeke, E., & Renssen, M. R. (1999). Treatment of specific phobias with eye movement desensitization and reprocessing (EMDR): Research, protocol, and application. *Journal of Anxiety Disorders, 13*, 69–85.

Deltito, J. A., Moline, M., Pollak, C., Martin, L. Y., & Maremmani, I. (1991). Effects of phototherapy on non-seasonal unipolar bipolar depressive spectrum disorders. *Journal of Affective Disorders*, 23, 231–237.

Dobson, K. S. (1989). A meta-analysis of the efficacy of cognitive therapy for depression. *Journal of Consulting Clinical Psychology, 57*, 414–419.

Drevets, W. C., Gautier, C., Price, J. C., Kupfer, D. J., Kinahan, P. E., Grace, A. A., et al. (2001). Amphetamine-induced dopamine release from human ventral striatum correlates with euphoria. *Biological Psychiatry, 49*, 81–96.

Duke, E. H. (1977). *Meaning of life and acceptance of death in terminally ill patients*. Unpublished doctoral dissertation, Northwestern University–Evanston, IL.

Dunn, R. J. (1979). Cognitive modification with depression-prone psychiatric patients. *Cognitive Therapy and Research, 3*, 307–317.

Eastman, C. I., Young, M. A., Fogg, L. F., Liu, L., & Meaden, P. M. (1998). Bright light treatment for winter depression. *Arch. Gen. Psychiatry, 55*, 883–889.

Eisner, B. (Spring 1995). Notes on the mysterious phenomenon of loading. *Advances: The Journal of Mind-Body Health, 11* (2), 55–57.

Elliott, D. B., Simmons, T., & Lewis, J. M. (2010). *Evaluation of the marital events items on the ACS*. Washington, DC: U.S. Census Bureau.

Ellis, A. (1958). Rational psychotherapy. *The Journal of General Psychology, 59*, 35–49.

Epstein, N. B., & Volk, L. A. (1981). Research of the results of psychotherapy: A summary of evidence. *American Journal of Psychiatry, 138* (3), 1027–1034.

Faw, T. T., & Nunnally, J. C. (1967). The effects of eye movements on complexity, novelty, and affective tone. *Perception and Psychophysics, 2*, 263–267.

Feldman, D., & Whiting, J. B. (2009). Abuse, control, and batterer intervention programs: Implications for marriage and family therapists. Unpublished manuscript.

Fields, J. K. (September–October 2009). The psychology of pain. *Scientific American Mind*, 43–49.

Flores, P. J. (2004). *Addiction as an attachment disorder*. New York: Jason Aronson.

Fosha, D. (2000). *The transforming power of affect*. New York: Basic Books.

Freke, T., & Grandy P. (2001). *Jesus and the Lost Goddess*. New York: Harmony Books.

Gallup, G., Jr., & Jones, S. (1989). *One hundred questions and answers: Religion in America*. Princeton, NJ: Princeton Religious Research Center.

Gentz, W. H. (ed.) (1986). *The dictionary of the Bible and religion*. Nashville: Abingdon. 749.

Gibson, J. J. (1986). *The ecological approach to visual perception*. New York: Psychology Press.

Glicksohn, J. (1986). Photic driving and altered states of consciousness: An exploratory study. *Imagination, Cognition, and Personality Journal, 6*, 167–182.

Gondoff, E. W. (1995). Gains and process in state batterer programs and standards. *Family Violence and Sexual Assault Bulletin, 11*, 27–28.

Goswami, S. S. (1980). *Layayoga*. London: Rutledge.

Gould, E., Beylin, A., Tanapat, P., Reeves, A., & Shors, T. J. (1999). Learning enhances adult neurogenesis in the hippocampal formation. *Nature Neuroscience, 2* (3), 260–265.

Grimes, J. (1996). *A concise dictionary of Indian philosophy*. Albany, NY: State University of New York Press.

Grof, C., & Grof, S. (1990). *The stormy search for self*. New York: Jeremy P. Tarcher.

Gruber, A. J., Pope, H. G., Hudson, J. I., & Yurgelun-Todd, D. (2003). Attributes of long-term heavy cannabis users: A case-control study. *Psychological Med, 33* (8), 1415–1422.

Hall, C. S. (1954). *A primer of Freudian psychology*. New York: New American Library.

Hall, C., & Nordby, V. A. (1973). *A primer of Jungian psychology*. New York: New American Library (Mentor Books).

Hall, R. E., & Marr, J. B. (1975). Influence of electrical stimulation of posterior orbital cortex upon plasma cortisol levels in unanethetized sub-human primates. *Brain Research, 93*, 367–371.

Hamer, D. (2004). *The God gene*. New York: Doubleday.

Harrigan, J. S. (2005). *Kundalini vidya: The science of transformation*. Knoxville, TN: Patanjali Kundalini Yoga Care.

Hashibe, M., Moregenstern, H., Cui, Y., Tashkin, D. P., Zhang, Z. F., Cozen, W., Mack, T. M., & Greenland, S. (2006). Marijuana use and the risk of lung cancer and upper aerodigestive tract cancers; results of a population-based case-control study. *Epidemiol Biomarkers Prev., 15* (10), 1829–1834.

Hauser, K. F., McLaughlin, P. J., & Zagon, I. S. (1989). Endogenous opioid systems and the regulation of dendritic growth and spine information. *J. Comp. Neurol., 281*, 13–22.

Hay, L. (1982). *Heal your body*. Carson, CA: Hay House.

Heft, J. (2001). *Ecological psychology in context: James Gibson, Roger Barker, and the legacy of William James's redical empriciasm*. Mahwah, NJ: Erlbaum.

Herman, J., Stancliff, S., & Langrod, J. (2000). Methadone Maintenance Treatment (MMT): A review of historical and clinical issues. *Mt. Sinai J. Med. 67* (5–6), 347–364.

Heyman, S. E. (1995). What can neuroscience teach us about addiction? Presented at: *The Addictions: Contemporary Treatment Issues*. March 3–4. Harvard Medical School.

Hirskowitz, M. (2009). Therapy for excessive sleepiness. In Teofilo L. Lee-Chiong (ed.), *Sleep medicine essentials*. Hoboken, NJ: Wiley-Blackwell.

Holman, T. B., & Busby, D. M. (January–March 2011). Family-of-origin, differentiation of self or partner, and adult romantic relationship quality. *Journal of Couple and Relationship Therapy*, 3–19.

Hoy, C. J., Vennelle, M., Klingshott, R. N., Engleman, H. M., & Douglas, N. J. (1999). Can intensive support improve continuous positive airway pressure use in patients with the sleep/hypopnea syndrome? *American Journal of Respiratory Critical Care Medicine, 159*, 1096–1100.

Hugdahl, K., Franzon, M., Anderson, B., & Waldebo, G. (1983). Heart rate responses (HRR) to lateralized visual stimuli. *Pavlovian Journal Biological Sciences, 18*, 186–198.

Hughes, J., & Kosterlitz, J. W. (1977). Opiod peptides. *British Medicine Bulletin, 33* (2), 157–161.

Huxley, A. (1945). *The perennial philosophy*. New York: Perennial Library.

Irons, R. R., & Schneider, J. P. (1996). *Addictive psychiatry*. Miller, N. S. (ed.). New York: Haworth Press, 2–21.

Jarry, J. L., & Paivio, S. C. (2006). Emotion-focused therapy for anger. In E. L. Feindler (ed.), *Anger-related disorders: A practitioner's guide to comparative treatments*. New York: Springer, 203–230.

Jenkins, A. (1990). *Invitations to responsibility: The therapeutic engagement of men who are violent and abusive*. Adelaide, Australia: Dubvich Center Publications.

Johnson, M. P. (2008). *A typology of domestic violence: Intimate terrorism, violent resistance, and situational couple violence*. Lebanon, NH: Northeastern University Press.

Johnson, S. M. (2004). *The practice of emotionally focused couple therapy* (2nd ed). New York: Brunner-Routledge.

Jones, E. (1963). *The life and work of Sigmund Freud*. Lionel Trilling, ed. New York: Doubleday.

Jory, B. (2004). The intimate justice scale: An instrument to screen for psychological abuse and physical violence in clinical practice. *Journal of Marital and Family Therapy, 30* (1), 29–44.

Jung, C. G. (1961). *Memories, dreams, and reflections*. New York: Random House (Vintage Books).

Kason, Y. (1994). *A farther shore*. Toronto, Canada: Harper-Collins.

Kasper, S., Ruhrmann, S., & Schuchardt, H. M. (1994). The effects of light therapy in treatment indications other than seasonal affective disorder/S.A.D. In: M. F. Holick, & E. G. Jung, eds., *Biologic effects of light*, Berlin: Walter de Gruyter, 206–218.

Kaufmann, D. (2001). *The fungus link: An introduction to fungal disease*. Rockwall, TX: Media Trition.

Kelley, C. (1970). *Education in feeling and purpose*. Santa Monica, CA: Interscience Workshop.

Keutzer, C. (1979). Transpersonal experience: A comparison of population. *Character Potential: A Record of Research, 9* (1).

Khantzian, E. J. (1982). Psychopathology, psychodynamics, and alcoholism. In E. M. Pattison, & S. E. Kaufman, eds., *Encyclopedic Handbook of Alcoholism*. New York: Gardner Press.

Kieffer, G. (ed.) (1988). *Kundalini for the new age: Selected writings of Gopi Krishna*. New York: Bantam Books.

Kiesler, D. J., Schmidt, J. A., & Wagner, C. C. (1997). A circumplex inventory of impact messages: An operational bridge between emotion and interpersonal behavior. In R. Plutchik and J. R. Conte (eds.), *Circumplex models of personality and emotions*. Washington, DC: American Psychological Association, 221–244.

Kirkpatrick, L. A. (2005). *Attachment, evolution and the psychology of religion*. New York: The Guilford Press.

Kirkpatrick, L. A., & Shaver, P. R. (1992). An attachment-theoretical approach to romantic love and religious belief. *Personality and Social Psychology Bulletin, 18*, 266–275.

Knudson-Martin, C., & Mahoney, A. R. (2009). *Couples, gender, and power: Creating change in intimate relationships*. New York: Springer.

Koide, R., Ueda, T. N., Dawson, W. W., Hope, G. M., Ellis, A., Somuelson, D., Ueda, R., Iwabuchi, S., Fukuda, S., Matsuishi, M., Yasuhara, H., Ozawa, T., & Armstrong, D. (2001). Retinal hazard from blue light emitting diode. *Nihon Ganka Gakkai Zasshi, 105* (10), 687–695.

Kripke, D. F., Risch, S. C., & Janowsky, D. S. (1983). Bright white light alleviates depression. *Psychiatry Res., 10*, 105–112.

Kripke, D. F. (1998). Light treatment for non-seasonal depression: Speed, efficacy, and combined treatment. *Journal of Affective Disorders, 49*, 109–117.

Kripke, D. F., Mullancy, D. J., Klauber, M. R., Risch, S. C., & Gillin, J. C. (1992). Controlled trial of bright light for non-seasonal major depressive disorders. *Biol. Psychiatry, 3*, 119–134.

Krishna, G. (1997). *Kundalini: The evolutionary energy in man*. Boston: Shambala.

Landgraf, R., Gerstberger, R., Montkowski, A., Probst, J. A., Wotjak, C. T., Holsboer, F., & Engelmann, M. (1995). V1 vasopressin receptor antisense oligodeoxynucleotide into septum reduces vasopressin binding, social discrimination abilities, and anxiety-related behavior in rats. *The Journal of Neuroscience, 15* (6), 4250–4258.

Lam, R. W. (1998). Seasonal affective disorder: diagnosis and management. *Primary Care Psychiatry, 4*, 63–74.

Lam, R. W., & Levitt, A. J. (eds.), (1999). *Canadian consensus guidelines for the treatment of Seasonal Affective Disorder*. Vancouver: Clinical and Academic Publishing.

Lanius, R. A. (2011). How understanding the neurobiology of Complex PTSD can inform clinical practice. *International Society for Traumatic Stress Studies 27th Annual Meeting*, Baltimore, MD.

Lee, C. C. K., Klopp, R. G., Weindruch, R., & Prolla, T. A. (1999). Gene expression profile of aging and its retardation by caloric restriction. *Science, 27* (285), 1390–1393.

Lee, M. C., Zambreanu, L., Menon, D. K., & Tracey, I. (2008). Identifying brain activity specifically related to the maintenance and perceptual consequence of central sensitization in humans. *Journal of Neuroscience, 28* (45), 11642–11649.

Lee, M. Y., Sebold, J., & Uken, A. (eds.), (2007). *Solution-focused treatment with domestic violence offenders*. New York: Kaworth Press.

Leonhardt, G., Wirz-Justice, A., Krauchi, K., Graw, P., Wunder, D., & Haug, H. J. (1994). Long-term follow-up of depression in seasonal affective disorder. *Comparative Psychiatry, 35*, 457–464.

Lesser, I. M. (December 1981). A review of the alexithymia concept. *Psychomatic Medicine*, Vol. *43* (6), 531–542.

Levine, Peter A., (1997). *Waking the tiger-healing trauma*. Berkley, CA: North Atlantic Books.

Lewis, K. E., Seale, L., Bartle, I. E., Watkins, A. J., & Ebden P. (2004). Early predictors of CPAP use for the treatment of sleep apnea. *Sleep, 27*, 134–138.

Liberman, J. (1991). *Light medicine of the future*. Santé Fe, NM: Bear and Company.

Linehan, M. M. (1993). *Cognitive behavioral treatment of borderline personality disorder*. New York: Guilford Press.

Lipton, B. (2005). *The biology of belief*. Santa Rosa, CA: Mountain of Love/Elite Books.

Lowen, A. (1975). *Bioenergetics*. New York: Penguin Books.

MacDonald, J. (1998). *Externalism and authoritative self knowledge*. Wright-Smith-MacDonald, 124–154.

Madrid, G. A., Mac Murray, J., Lee, J. W., Anderson, B. A., & Comings, D. E. (2001). Stress as a mediating factor in the association between the DRD2 Taql polymorphism and alcoholism. *Alcohol, 23* (2), 117–122.

Mahoney, M. (1974). *Cognition and behavior modification*. Cambridge, MA: Ballinger.

Main, J., & Cassidy, J. (1988). Categories of response to reunion with the parent at age 6: Predicted from attachment classifications and stable over one-month period. *Developmental Psychology, 24*, 415–426.

Marcus, S. V., Marquis, P., & Sakai, C. (1997). Controlled study of treatment of PTSD using EMDR in an HMO setting. *Psychotherapy, 34* (4), 307–315.

Martensen, H. L. (1885). *Jacob Boehme: His life and teaching, or studies in theosophy*. Trans. T. Rhys Evans. London: Hodder and Stoughton.

Martin, S. D., Martin, D., Rai, S. S., Richardson, M. A., Royall, R., & Eng, C. (2001). Brain blood flow changes in depressed patients treated with interpersonal psychotherapy or venlafaxine hydrochloride. *Archives of General Psychiatry*, 641–648.

Maslow, A. (1950). Self-actualizing people: A study of psychological health. *Personality Symposia #1 on Values*. New York: Grume and Stratton, 11–34.

Maslow, A. (1968). *Toward a psychology of being*. New York: Van Nostrand.

Maslow, A. (1971). *The farther reaches of human nature*. New York: Viking Press.

McCarty, R. (2003). The energetic heart: Bioelectromagnetic interactions within and between people. Boulder Creek, CA: Institute of Heart Math.

McKenzie, C. D., & Wright, L. S. (1996). *Delayed posttraumatic stress disorders from infancy*. London: Harwood Academic Press, 27.

Melzak, R., & Wall, P. D. (1965). Pain mechanisms: A new theory. *Science, 150*, 971.

Milner, J., & Singleton, T. (2008). Domestic violence: Solution-focused practice with men and women who are violent. *Journal of Family Therapy, 30* (1), 29–53.

Mittleman, M. A., Lewis, R. A., Maclure, M., Sherwood, J. B., & Muller, J. E. (2001). Triggering myocardial infarction by marijuana. *Circulation, 103* (23), 2805–2809.

Moore, T., Zammit, S., Lingford-Hughes, A., Barnes, T. R., Jones, P. Burke, M., & Lewis, G. (2007). Cannabis use and risk of psychotic or affective mental health outcomes: a systematic review. *Lancet, 370* (9584), 319–328.

Montagu, J. D. (1967). The relationship between the intensity of repetitive photic stimulation and the cerebral response. *Electroencephalography and Clinical Neurophysiology, 23*, 152–161.

Muktananda, S. (2000). *Play of consciousness*. South Fallsburg, NY: SYDA Foundation.

Murphy, M. (1992). *The future of the body.* Los Angeles: Jeremy P. Tarcher.

Nakamura, H., Kokubo, H., Parkhomtehouk, D. V., Chen, W., Tamaka, M., & Fukuda, N. (2000). Biophoton and temperature changes of human hand during Qigong. *J. Int Soc Life Inf Sci, 18,* 418–422.

National Institute on Drug Abuse (November 2010). Monitoring the future national survey results on drug use, 1975–2010. Volume II: College students and adults ages 19–50. Department of Health and Human Services.

Nevens, G. W. (1998). Transdisciplinary evaluation of chronic pain: The health psychology perspective. In K. Anchor & T. Felicetti (eds.), *Disability analysis in practice: Framework for an interdisciplinary science.* Dubuque, IO: Kendall/Hunt, 39–71.

Newburg, A., & D'Aquili, E. (2001). *Why God won't go away.* New York: Ballantine Books.

Newberg, A., & Walden, M. R. (2009). *How God changes your brain.* New York: Ballantine Books.

O'Brien, M. E. (1982). Religious faith and adjustment to long-term hemodialysis. *Journal of Religion and Health, 21,* 68–80.

Ogden, P., Minton, K., & Pain, C. (2006). *Trauma and the body.* New York: W.W. Norton.

Oka, M., & Whiting, J. B. (January–March 2011). Contemporary MFT theories and intimate partner violence: A review of systemic treatments. *Couples and Relationship Therapy, 10* (1), 34–52.

Okuno, T., Saito, H., & Ojima (2002). Visual light of short wavelength (blue light) may cause a photochemical injury to the retina, called photo retinitis or blue light hazard. *Journal of Developmental Ophthalmology, 35,* 104–112.

O'Leary, K. D., Vivian, D., & Malone, J. (1992). Assessment of physical aggression against women in marriage: The need for multimodal assessment. *Behavioral Assessment, 14* (1), 5–15.

Oren, D. A., & Rosenthal, N. E. (1992). Seasonal affective disorders. In Paykel E. S., ed., *Handbook of affective disorders* (2nd ed).

O'Rourke, D. A., Wurtman, J. J., Brzezinski, A., Nader, T. A., & Chew, B. (1987). Serotonin implicated in etiology of seasonal affective disorder. *Psychopharmacology Bulletin, 23,* 358–359.

Persinger, M. A. (2010). The electromatic induction of mystical and altered states within the laboratory. *Journal of Consciousness Exploration and Research, 1*(7), 808–830.

Pert, C. B. (1977). *Molecules of emotion: Why you feel the way you feel.* New York: Scribner.

Phillips St. Romain (1991). *Kundalini energy and christian spirituality: A pathway to growth and healing.* Crossroads Publ.

Pilkonis, P. A., Leber, W. R., Docherty, J. P., Fiester, S. J., & Parloff, M. B. (1989). National institute of mental health treatment of depression collaborative research program: General effectiveness of treatments. *Archives of General Psychiatry, 46,* 971–982.

Pincus, H. A., Davis, W. W., & McQueen, L. E. (1999). Subthreshold mental disorders. *British Journal of Psychiatry, 174,* 288–296.

Plutchik, R. (2000). *Emotions in the practice of psychotherapy.* Washington, DC: American Psychological Association.

Popp, F. A., Gurwitsch, A. A., Inaba, H., Slawinsky, J., Cilento, G., Popp, F. A., Li, K. H., Mei, W. P., Galle, M., Neurohr, R., Van Wijk, R., Schamhart, D. H. J., Chiverot, W. B., & Magi, W. (1988). Biophoton emission. *Experienta, 44,* 543–600.

Porreca, F., & Price, T. (September–October 2009). When pain lingers on. *Scientific American Mind,* 34.

Powles, W. E. (1992). *Human development and homeostasis.* Madison, CT: International Universities Press.

Puham, M. A., Suarez, A., Lo Cascio, C., Zahn, A., Heitz, M., & Braendli (2005). Didgeridoo playing as alternative treatment for obstructive sleep apnoea syndrome: Randomised controlled trial. *BMJ* 2006;332;226-270; originally published online December 23, 2005; doi: 10.1136/bmj.38705.470590.55.

Purves, D., Augustine, G. J., Fitzpatrick, D., Katz, L. C., La Mantia, A. A., & McNamara, J. O. (eds.) (1997). *Neuro science.* Sunderland, MA: Sinaur Associates.

Putnam, J. (1975). The meaning of meaning. *Mind, Language and Reality.* Cambridge, MA.

Rao, M. L., Muller-Oerlinghausen, B., Mackert, A., Strebel, B., Stieglitz, R. D., & Volz, H. P. (1990). The influence of phototherapy on serotonin and melatonin in non-seasonal depression. *Pharmacopsychiatry, 23,* 155–158.

Rao, M. L., Muller-Oerlinghausen, B., Mackert, A., Strebel, B., Stieglitz, R. D., & Volz, H. P. (1992). Blood serotonin, serum melatonin and light therapy in healthy subjects and in patients with non-seasonal depression. *Acta Psychiatr Scand, 86,* 127–132.

Raunsaville, B. J., Weissman, M. N., & Prusoff, B. A. (1981). Psychotherapy with depressed outpatients: Patient and process variables as predictors of outcome. *British Journal of Psychiatry, 138,* 67–74.

Reich, W. (1973). *The function of the orgasm.* New York: Touchstone.

Reishtein, J. L., Pack, A. I., Maislin, G., Dinges, D. F., Bloxham, T. J., George, C. F., et al. (2006). Sleepiness and relationships in obstructive sleep apnea. *Issues in Mental Health Nursing, 27,* 319–330.

Robinson, D. (1991). Sexual addiction and adaptive response to post-traumatic stress disorder in an African American community. *Sexual Addiction and Compulsivity, 6* (1), 11–12.

Rogers, C. (1989). *On becoming a person: A therapist's view of psychotherapy.* New York: Houghton Mifflin.

Rosenberg, E. L. (1998). Levels of analysis and the organization of affect. *Review of General Psychology, 2,* 247–270.

Rosenthal, N. W. (1993). *Winter Blues.* New York: The Guilford Press.

Rosenthal, N. E., Genhart, M. J., Sack, D. A., Skiverer, R. G., and Wehr, T. A. (1987). Seasonal affective disorder and its relevance for the understanding and treatment of bulimia. In J. I. Hudson, & H.G. Pope, eds., *The Psychobiology of Bulimia.* Washington, DC: American Psychiatric Press, 205–228.

Rosenthal, N. E., Sack, D. A., Gillin, J. C., Levy, A. J., Goodwin, F. K., Davenport, Y., Mueller, P. S., Newsom, D. A., & Wher, T. A. (1984). Seasonal affective disorder: A description of the syndrome and preliminary findings with light therapy. *Archives of General Psychiatry, 41,* 72–80.

Rossi, E. (1986). *The psychobiology of mind-body healing.* New York: W.W. Norton, 36–45.

Rossi, E. (2002). *The psychobiology of gene expression.* NY: W. W. Norton and Company.

Rothbaum, B. O. (1997). A controlled study of eye movement desensitization and reprocessing for posttraumatic stress disordered sexual assault victims. *Bulletin of the Menninger Clinic, 61,* 317–334.

Saal, D., Dong, Y., Bonci, A., & Malenka, R. C. (2003). Drugs of abuse and stressor trigger a common synaptic adaptation in dopamine neurons. *Neuron, 37,* 577–582.

Saal, D., Dong, Y., Bonci, A., & Malenka, R. C. (2003). *Neuron, 37*, 557–582.

Sannella, L. (1987). *The Kundalini experience: Transcendence or psychosis?* Lower Lake, CA: Integral Publishing.

Scaer, R. C. (2001). *The body bears the burden*. New York: The Haworth Medical Press.

Schactel, E. G. (1943). On color and affect: Contributions to an understanding of Rorschach's test. *Psychiatry, 6*, 393–409.

Schaepfer, T. E., Cohen, M. X., Frick, C., Kosel, M., Brodesser, D., Axmacher, N., Joe, A.Y., Kreft, M., Lenartz, D., & Sturn, V. (2007). Deep brain stimulation to reward circuitry alleviates anhedonia in refractory major depression. *Neuropsychopharmacology*, 1–10.

Scheck, M. M., Schaeffer, J. A., & Gillette, C. S. (1998). Brief psychological intervention with traumatized young women: The efficacy of eye movement desensitization and reprocessing. *Journal of Traumatic Stress, 11*, 25–44.

Schiffer, F. (1977). Affect changes observed with right versus left lateral visual field stimulation in psychotherapy patients: Possible physiological, psychological, and therapeutic implications. *Comp. Psychiatry, 38*, 289–295.

Schiffer, F., Anderson, C. M., Renshaw, P. F., Maas, L. C., Teicher, M. H. (1998). Baseline asymmetry in right temporal lobe blood flow by FMRI correlates with EEG and affect responses to lateral visual field stimulation. *American Psychiatric Association New Res. Program Abstract*, 175.

Schiffer, F., Anderson, C. M., Teicher, M. H. (1997). EEG evidence of hemispheric activation with contralateral visual field stimulation. *American Psychiatric Association New Res. Program Abstract*, 218.

Schore, A. N. (1994). Affect regulation and the origin of the self: The neurobiology of emotional development. Hilldale, NY: Erlbaum.

Schore, A. N. (2003). *Affect dysregulation disorders of the self*. New York: W.W. Norton.

Sealy, J. (1999). Dual and triple diagnosis: Addictions, mental illness, and HIV infection guidelines for outpatient therapist. *Sexual Addiction and Compulsivity, 6* (3), 1995–219.

Senay, E. C. (1998). *Substance abuse disorders in clinical practice*. New York: Norton.

Sexual Compulsives Anonymous. (2009). SCA Sexual Compulsives Anonymous: The Twenty Questions. www.sca-recovery.org/20questions.htm.

Shaban, H., & Richer, C. (2002). A2E and blue light in the retina: the paradigm of age-related macular degeneration. *Biol. Chem., 383* (3–4), 537–545.

Shapiro, F. (2001). *Eye Movement Desensitization and Reprocessing (EMDR)*. New York Guildford Press.

Siegel, D. J. (2007). *The mindful brain reflection and attunement in the cultivation of well-being*. New York: W. W. Norton.

Sinha, R. (2001). How does stress increase risk of drug abuse and relapse? *Psychopharmacology, 158* (4), 343–359.

Skinner, B. F. (1953). *Beyond freedom and dignity*. New York: Macmillan.

Sohal, R. S., & Weindruch, R. (1996). Oxidative stress, caloric restriction, and aging. *Science, 273*, 59–63.

St. Romain, P. (1991). *Kundalini energy and Christian spirituality*. New York: Crossroads Publishing Co.

Steinberg, M., & Schnall, M. (2001). *Stranger in the mirror*. New York: Harper Collins.

Steinmetz, J. L., Lewinsohn, P. M., & Antonuccio, D. O. (1983). Prediction of individual outcome in a group intervention for depression. *Journal of Consulting and Clinical Psychology, 51* (3), 331–337.

Stern, D. A. (2004). *The present moment in psychotherapy and everyday life.* New York.

Stewart, K. T., Gaddy, J. R., Byrne, B., Miller, S., & Brainard, G. C. (1991). Effects of green or white light for treatment of seasonal depression. *Psychiatry Res., 39,* 261–270.

Swainson, W. P. (1921). *Jakob Bohme: The teutonic philosopher.* London: William Rider and Son.

Takigawa, M. (1988). Rhythmic light therapy for depression and data processing analysis effects by directed coherence. *Act Nerv. Super* (Praha), *30,* 177–180.

Taylor, H. R., West, S., Munoz, B., Rosenthal, F. S., Bressler, S. B., & Bressler, N. M. (1992). The long-term effects of visible light on the eye. *Arch. Ophthalmol., 110* (1), 99–104.

Thomas, C. P., Reif, S., Haq, S., Wallack, S. S., Hoyt, A., & Ritter, G. A. (August 2008). Use of Buprenorphine for addiction treatment: Perspectives of addiction specialists and general psychiatrists. *Psychiatric Services, 59* (8), 909–916.

Tiller, W. A., Dibble, W. E., & Kohane, M. J. (2001). *Conscious acts of creating: The emergence of a new physics.* Walnut Creek, CA: Pavior Publishing.

Todd, G. A. (1973). Perceptual factors in color-affect arousal. *Journal oj Personality Assessment, 37,* 225–234.

Tuunainen, A., Kripke, D. F., & Endo, T. (2004). Light therapy for non-seasonal depression (Cochrane Review). *The Cochrane Library, 2.* Chichester, UK: John Wiley and Sons.

Vaillant, G. E. (1983). Natural history of male alcoholism v: Is alcoholism the cart or the horse to socioptathy? *British Journal of Addiction, 78,* 317–325.

Van Wijk, R., & Van Wijk, E. P. A. (2005). Introduction to human biophoton emission. *Forsch Komplementarmed Klass Naturheilkd, 12,* 77–83.

Vazquez, S. R. (Fall 2004). The new light psychotherapy for Seasonal Affective Disorder (SAD). *The Annals of American Psychotherapy.*

Vazquez, S. R. (Winter 2004). The New Power Therapy: Emotional Transformation Therapy®. *Counseling Australia, 4* (2), 55–60.

Vazquez, S. R. (Summer 2005). The new paradigm for PTSD treatment: Emotional Transformation Therapy®. *Annals, Journal of the American Psychotherapy Association.*

Vazquez, S. R. (February 2007). Peripheral light stimulation for rapid emotional, somatic and transpersonal regulation. *Subtle Energies & Energy Medicine, ISSSEEM Magazine, 16* (3), 225–249.

Vogel, W., Broverman, D. M., Klaiber, E., & Kun, K. J. (1969). EEG response to photic stimulation as a function of cognitive style. *Electroencyphalography and Clinical Neurophysiology, 27,* 186–190.

Waddell, J., & Shors, T. J. (2008). Neurogenesis learning and associative strength. *European Journal of Neuroscience, 27,* 3020–3028.

Wade, J. (1996). *Changes of mind: A holonomic theory of the evolution of consciousness.* Albany: State University of New York Press.

Wade, J. (2004). *Transcendent sex.* New York: Paraview Pocket Books.

Washton, A. M. (1989). Cocaine may trigger sexual compulsivity. *U.S. Journal Drug and Alcohol Dependency, 13* (6), 8.

Weeks, A. (1991). *Bohme: An intellectual biography of the seventeenth-century philosopher and mystic.* New York: State University of New York Press.

Weindruch, R., & Sohal, R. S. (1997). Caloric intake and aging. *N. Engl. J. Med., 337* (14), 986–994.

Weiss, G., & Male S. (2009). How to fight addiction. *Parade Magazine.* New York: Parade Publications.

White, M. (2007). *Maps of narrative practice.* New York: W. W. Norton.

Wittling, W., & Roschmann, R. (1993). Emotion-related hemisphere asymmetry: subjective emotional responses to laterally presented films. *Cortex, 29*, 431–448.

Young, J. E., Klosko, J. S., & Weishaar, M., (2003). *Schema therapy: A practitioner's guide.* New York: Guilford Publications.

Young, J. (1994). *The Diagnostic and Statistical Manual of Mental Disorders,* 4th ed. (a). Washington, DC: American Psychiatric Association.

Zinnbauer, B. J., Pargament, K. I., (2000). Working with the sacred: Four approaches to religious and spiritual issues in counseling. *Journal of Counseling & Development,* 78, 162–171. doi: 10.1002/j.1556-6676.2000.tb02574.x.

Index

About the Author

Steven R. Vazquez, PhD, is the founder of the innovative Emotional Transformation Therapy® approach to psychotherapy. He is a licensed professional counselor and licensed marriage and family therapist in the state of Texas. Dr. Vazquez has taught his approach in nine different countries and all over the United States. His work has been cited in several books and he has published numerous articles in peer-reviewed professional journals. Dr. Vazquez holds a doctorate in counseling psychology. He has been in private practice for over thirty-three years.